Abraham Joshua Heschel and Elie Wiesel

You Are My Witnesses

MAURICE FRIEDMAN

Abraham Joshua Heschel
&
Elie Wiesel

You Are My Witnesses

NEW YORK

FARRAR·STRAUS·GIROUX

Copyright © 1987 by Maurice Friedman
All rights reserved
First printing, 1987
Printed in the United States of America
Published simultaneously in Canada by Collins Publishers, Toronto
Designed by Constance Ftera

Library of Congress Cataloging-in-Publication Data
Friedman, Maurice S.
Abraham Joshua Heschel & Elie Wiesel, you are my witnesses.
Bibliography: p.
1. Judaism—20th century. 2. Hasidism.
3. Heschel, Abraham Joshua, 1907–1972.
4. Wiesel, Elie, 1928–   —Criticism and interpretation.
5. Friedman, Maurice S. 6. Holocaust (Jewish theology)
I. Title.
BM565.F68   1987   296'.092'2   86-31992

CONTENTS

Biblical Covenant, Hasidic Fervor, and American Judaism

The title of this book is a deliberate double entendre. "You are my witnesses, says the Lord," reads Isaiah 49:10, and in the Sayings of the Fathers in the Talmud this is interpreted, "And if you are not my witnesses, then I, as it were, am not the Lord." I see both Abraham Joshua Heschel and Elie Wiesel as witnesses in our day for the God of the biblical covenant that Moses proclaimed and the biblical prophets continued to proclaim. But they are also *my* witnesses, since I have stood in a unique personal relationship with them both. My indebtedness to Martin Buber is well known. What is less well known is that I have in addition developed my own thought and life stance in a not unimportant part from my dialogue with Abraham Heschel and Elie Wiesel as thinkers and as persons and friends. My relationship with Heschel continued for almost thirty years before his death in 1972, and I have been close to Wiesel from 1965 to the present.

Abraham Joshua Heschel was a poetic philosopher of religion and of Judaism, with a broad knowledge of the whole of Judaism, and with a worldwide impact on Jewish and Christian thought. Elie Wiesel is a philosophical poet, a survivor of the Holocaust and, more than any other single person, the spokesman for the Holocaust and for the meaning of Jewish life and thought in a post-Holocaust approach that is also existential, mystical, and

Hasidic. Although I have read all the relevant commentaries in the literature that has accumulated on each of them, my primary concern is my own interpretation of their writings and my dialogue with the voice that speaks to me from their writings.

Why have I selected just Heschel and Wiesel out of the whole range of contemporary Jewish thinkers other than Buber that are available to me—Hermann Cohen, Franz Rosenzweig, Lev Shestov, Mordecai Kaplan, or even, to mention only the most prominent of a number of my own contemporaries, Emil Fackenheim? First, it is not the aim of this book to offer a critique of contemporary Jewish thought and still less a comprehensive survey of it. I appreciate Shestov, whom Bernard Martin rightly includes in his book *Four Jewish Existentialists*, and I often refer to Shestov's *Athens and Jerusalem* in my courses on Jewish thought, particularly for its keen insight into the way in which Western philosophy has enthroned the "ensemble of coherences" above God. I offer something of a witness to Franz Rosenzweig in Chapter 14 of my book *Martin Buber's Life and Work: The Early Years*, and in Chapters 3 to 5 of its sequel, *The Middle Years*,[1] and I include extensive passages from Rosenzweig in Part V of my book *The Worlds of Existentialism: A Critical Reader*.[2] Hermann Cohen I have read, but he has had even less impact on me personally than Shestov.

Of Mordecai Kaplan I have published a longish critique in an early essay on contemporary Jewish thought[3] and an abridged version of that same essay in "Peter Pan's Shadow: Tradition and Modernity" in my book *The Human Way: A Dialogical Approach to Religion and Human Experience*.[4] If I do not count Kaplan among those who witness for me and for whom I witness, it is not for lack of appreciation of his immense significance for American Judaism as a way forward from the thin hypostatized God and universalist abstractions of classical Reform Judaism to a rich concern with all the elements of Jewish civilization. It is rather that I find his "modernism" dated, his faith in "the power not ourselves that makes for righteousness" too evolutionary, liberal, and progressivistic for an age that must confront the reality of the Holocaust, and his pragmatic "as if" approach to religion not at all helpful to those who are confronted with the problem of how, in this post-modern age, we can make a genuine religious commitment which is not just another form of aiming at ourselves. As Abraham Heschel has said, "God is of no importance unless He is of supreme importance." To make God into another name for natural processes, or a convenient underpinning for moral values or for Jewish togetherness (in order to be a people— I paraphrase Kaplan—we must act *as if* God had given us Jews the covenant), invites a pragmatic inversion, a faith "as if" that I cannot believe one can really live. William James wrote an essay, "The Will to Believe," which serves as a conclusion to his famous and still important book *Varieties of Religious Experience*. "Religion is real because it has real effects," William James said. Yet none of the saints and mystics whom he portrays in *Varieties* ever believed "as if" or in order to experience these "real effects." Each brought him- or herself wholeheartedly and spontaneously to the meeting with what they experienced as ultimate and regarded the effects on themselves as only the by-product, never the goal.

Emil Fackenheim will someday find the interpreter who will do justice to his remarkable combination of philosophical precision and theological acumen. He is certainly the nearest thing we have to a systematic Jewish religious philosopher and theologian in the contemporary scene. (I am here counting Rosenzweig as belonging to an earlier era, if still a highly important and fruitful one for us.) But it is not given to me to witness for him. Though I have known him for a long time, even longer than I have known Wiesel, I have not immersed myself in his works and lived with them year after year in the way that I deem essential for someone for whom I am to witness.

I have long wanted to write a short book on Heschel and more and more to make a special witness to Wiesel, not despite but precisely because these two men have lived a fuller Jewish life than I have been able to do. This does not mean that they must take my place and be religious for me, as I sometimes fear the congregant wants of the rabbi. (See my chapter "The Paradox of Religious Leadership" in *The Human Way*.) It means rather that my own relationship to Judaism is purer and truer through my dialogue with them and the challenge that they place upon my life and thought.

I can only witness to witnesses with whom I have myself stood in dialogue. I do, of course, try to be faithful to their thought. Yet I do not come to that thought as some hypothetical neutral observer but as the very person that I am. This is no apology for subjectivity. I take no liberties with their thought: I do not read it selectively for what supports my arguments or distort things to fit my purposes. I present the whole range of their writings and, insofar as I am able, do justice to all the leading motifs of their thought. Yet the form that I give to that presentation, the insights that I bring to it, and the applications of their thought that I suggest are all shaped by my own wrestling with the nameless angel who offers the contemporary Jews, as well as Jacob, the blessing of a new name—if we persevere until dawn. For this reason I wish to give the reader some hint in this chapter of where I am coming from religiously and Jewishly, particularly in connection with that tension between religious form and religious spirit to which I devote two chapters in *The Human Way*.

In them I tell how I grew up in a Reform Temple in Tulsa, Oklahoma, in which the Judaism was so thin that I was not barmitzvahed because they had none there. I also tell of my progression from socialism, pacifism, and mysticism to the concern for Hasidism that arose after I read Martin Buber's *Legend of the Baal Shem* and met Abraham Heschel. I also tell of how Heschel sent me to spend a weekend in the home of a Hasid in the Williamsburg section of Brooklyn during the time in 1950 that I stayed as Heschel's guest at the Jewish Theological Seminary. It is with this latter event that I wish to begin some anecdotes that may illustrate the problematic relation of form and spirit in *contemporary* Judaism.

When I spent Shabbat at the home of a Williamsburg Hasid, I stood from ten till two in the morning in a tiny *shtuebl* packed with over a hundred disciples of the Satmar rebbe, good-naturedly fighting and shoving for the *shirayim*, food that the rebbe gives from his thirteen-course meal. I was deeply impressed, particularly at one point when, after wishing the rebbe would pass me a drumstick and then thinking that, dressed as I was, I was the last person he would thus honor, someone handed me a drumstick and said, "The rebbe sent this for you!" Nevertheless, I took away with me a sense of the childlike devotion of the Hasidim to the rebbe, quite foreign to the individualized consciousness of the modern Western man.

When I next visited Williamsburg to witness the dancing on Simhas Torah (the feast that celebrates the giving of the Torah), I naïvely went into the synagogue of the Klausenberger rebbe with a non-Jewish friend to inquire as to the time of the services. I was confronted by a young man with a bright red beard, who instead of answering my question asked me, "Are you a Jew?" "Yes," I replied. "Do you speak Yiddish?" "No," I said. (My parents used Yiddish to keep things from us children but made no attempt to teach it to us, so that I was left with a vague sense of it as something to be ashamed of, something that marked my parents' foreign origin.) "You are a Jew and you don't speak Yiddish!" the young man with the red beard snorted contemptuously. Then he turned to my friend, whose bow tie and cap marked him as a smart Greenwich Villager, and, pointing to him as a Hasid of the time of the Maccabees might have pointed to a swine that had been brought into the Temple, exclaimed indignantly, "And you brought *him* into the synagogue!" My friend shrank out the door, and I began to wonder whether my years of devotion to Hasidism had been misplaced.

Once in Jerusalem, years later, I attended Sabbath services at the Bratzlaver Seminary in the Mea Shearim and was deeply impressed not only by the joy with which we all danced around the Torah but also by the warmth and the kindly way in which several men invited me to "Shabbos" dinner afterward. Yet the students in this same seminary wanted to burn Conrad's *Heart of Darkness* and other secular books of an old friend of mine who was living at the seminary as a Hasid yet studying at the Hebrew University at the same time. At the time of the death of Martin Buber, these students spoke of him in the language one would use of the death of an animal.

Nothing like that would happen, of course, in the Habad House that is situated near San Diego State University. If they are not particularly hospitable to non-Jews, nonetheless they are open to Jews of any and all degrees of Jewishness. Even so, I cannot go along with their separation of men onto one side and women onto the other, with the rabbi standing in front of the men. Whether or not women are a distraction to the men while praying, I cannot stomach carrying over their eighteenth-century attitude toward women, and for that reason cannot pray with them.

I had a great-uncle who was a rabbi in Waco, Texas. When he was eighty-one years old, just two years before his death, he made a special trip to Tulsa to see what to him was the unbelievable phenomenon of a young American Jew who had developed such an intense interest in the Hasidism in which he was brought up as a child in Russia. He taught me some Hasidic songs and gave me two beautiful volumes of the *siddur*, or prayer book, with the special *kavanot*, or mystical intentions, of *Ha-Ari* (the "lion," Isaac Luria, the founder of the Lurian Kabbalah, which provided Hasidism with its main theoretical framework). My great-uncle could only explain me to himself as an atavism, a throwback to my holy great-grandfather. This did me far too much credit, but it expressed vividly his own astonishment at the coming together of two worlds that seemed to him so utterly remote from each other!

Once when I was giving a lecture for the Esalen Institute in San Francisco, a young man asked me if I knew personally the famous Hasidic singer and composer Shlomo Carlebach. "Yes, I do," I replied. "I thought Hasidim had beards," the young man added. "He does have a beard," I responded. "No, I meant you," he protested. "Oh, me," I exclaimed. "I am a neo-Hasid!" Recently I gave a lecture at a large Reform Jewish temple in Dallas, Texas. At the *Oneg Shabbat* afterward a woman whose son had become a Hasid accosted me. "You speak a lot about Hasidism," she said, "yet you are not really a Hasid." "You mean I don't have a beard and earlocks and a *shtreiml* (a fox-fur hat)," I replied, and then added, "One zaddik says there are three basic attitudes that become the Jew—upright kneeling, silent screaming, and motionless dance. I do that. Can you? Another said, 'The way of man in the world is like a knife's edge. There is an abyss on either side and the way lies in the middle.' I walk on that way. Can you?" I was not, as it might appear, claiming to be a true Hasid. For me, even more than for Buber, it would be an impermissible masquerade were I to don the appearance of the Hasid and attach myself to a rebbe. I was trying to say to her that perhaps there is more to Hasidism than appearance, that Hasidism is a matter of basic attitudes that one lives even more than the specific forms of dress and coiffure which, according to my mother's cousins in Israel, characterized the Polish and the Galician Hasidim but not the Lithuanian where they grew up.

Religious tradition is not attitude and spirit alone. It is a dialectic of spirit and form, and here I have come up against a paradox to which I do not know the answer. After I first met Heschel forty years ago and read Buber's *Legend of the Baal Shem*, I was fired to revive Hasidism in American Judaism. In *Touchstones of Reality* I quote the story that the rabbi of Zans used to tell about himself:

> In my youth when I was fired with the love of God, I thought I would convert the whole world to God. But soon I discovered that it would be quite enough to convert the people who lived in my town, and I tried for a long time, but did not succeed. Then I realized that my program was still much too ambitious, and I concentrated on the persons in my own household. But

I could not convert them either. Finally it dawned on me: I must work upon myself, so that I may give true service to God. But I did not accomplish even this.[5]

Commenting on this, I wrote: "The title of this tale is 'Resignation,' resignation without any admixture of bitterness, despair, disillusionment, defeat. No other tale expresses so precisely my own history!" It would be hard for me to say now why I wrote this. Perhaps it was my failure to become a true Hasid, my failure to learn enough Hebrew to study Hasidic texts in the original, and, in contrast with the dreams of my youth, my utter failure to revive Hasidism in America. Yet apart from the merely personal, I wonder whether this failure is not precisely a part of our way.

The Baal Shem brought a new spirit of openness to the forms of his time without seriously modifying those forms, though the Mitnagdim, or opponents of Hasidism, were so scandalized by the minor modifications that they repeatedly persecuted the Hasidim and even excommunicated them. I cannot imitate the Baal Shem by going back to the forms and customs of the eighteenth century. Neither can I leap over the gap that was caused by my mother's rebellion against her father, who spent all of his time in prayer and study and left my grandmother to raise and support thirteen children, nine of whom died in childhood from poverty and sickness. Yet I can hardly remain faithful to the thin Reform Judaism in which I was raised as a result of my mother's rebellion and the state of the Jewish community in Tulsa, Oklahoma, when I was a child. In the Mea Shearim the very streets and houses resemble those of eighteenth-century Poland, as does the dress. I cannot imitate this, and still less do I desire to imitate the closed spirit which marks so many Hasidic communities today. Yet I understand quite well why the zaddikim warned their Hasidim not to come to America, saying, "No spiritual life is possible in America." The dissipation of structure, form, *and* spirit in the modern Western world makes all too comprehensible Professor Lou Silberman's reply to a criticism that I made of Heschel that the problem is not that one way to God is more available than others but that each is all but unavailable to the contemporary Jew! And the same might be said of contemporary man in general.

One of Martin Buber's and Franz Rosenzweig's truly great disciples is Ernst Simon, Professor Emeritus of Education at the Hebrew University of Jerusalem. Ernst Simon has often said that all Buber's disciples are more observant than Buber himself, yet that because of Buber they have more *kavana*, more wholehearted religious dedication and intention, than they would otherwise. But there are some of Buber's disciples, like myself, who must prove exceptions to Simon's rule. Once I attended a Labor Zionist lecture in New York City that Ernst Simon was giving. After the lecture one of the audience recognized me and asked me if I too was a "Baal Teshuvah," literally, a "master of turning," one who has turned away from Judaism and then has turned back. "If you mean was there once a time when Judaism meant almost nothing to me and now it is a central commitment, yes," I replied. "But if you mean am I observant like Ernst Simon, no." "You are young, you will get there," he answered. "Not necessarily," I countered, "I am an American Jew and I may not go his path." I did not mean by this that there is some other path that all American Jews follow or that it would be impossible for an American Jew to become observant like Ernst Simon. My own "disciple" David Lichtman is far more observant than Simon or anyone else living outside a Hasidic community could ever be. What I mean is that each Jew, and each contemporary human being, must decide for him- or herself what is the right tension between his or her relation to tradition and to the present and to his or her own uniqueness.

For years my simultaneous friendship with both Buber and Heschel placed me under great tension concerning the question of observance of the Jewish law, or Halakhah. While Heschel never demanded of me that I become Orthodox, he made it very clear that fulfilling the law was the way to real participation in

Judaism, "the holy dimension of existence." In 1954 I wrote to
Buber about this problem, and he responded from Heidelberg
that he could not see such a question independent of personal
existence: "For me I know that I try to do what I experience I
am ordered to do; but how can I make this into a general rule
about ritual being right or wrong?" What he then asserted gave
me a deeper insight into what he called "the narrow ridge" and
what I call the uniqueness of our touchstone of reality:

> I open my heart to the Law to such an extent that if I feel
> a commandment being addressed to me I feel myself bound to
> do it as far as I am addressed—for instance, I cannot live on
> Sabbath as on other days, my spiritual and physical attitude is
> changed, but I have no impulse at all to observe the minutiae
> of the Halakhah about what work is allowed and what not. In
> certain moments, some of them rather regular, I pray, alone
> of course, and say what I want to say, sometimes without words
> at all, and sometimes a remembered verse helps me in an ex-
> traordinary situation; but there have been days when I felt
> myself compelled to enter into the prayer of a community, and
> so I did it. This is my way of life, and one may call it religious
> anarchy if he likes. How could I make it into a general rule,
> valid for instance for you! I cannot say anything but: Put
> yourself in relation as you can and when you can, do your best
> to persevere in relation, and do not be afraid.

I was particularly struck by Buber's last remark to me. I had said
nothing about being afraid, yet he sensed the anxiety that lay
beneath my questions as to what was the right course and how
I could find it.

Still less than Buber could offer his way as a model for me am
I putting myself forward as a model for anyone else! Yet neither
can I accept that my situation, which is shared by countless
contemporary human beings, is in itself totally without religious
significance or can be dismissed as the fall from grace of those
who do not have the good fortune to belong to a religious
community secure in the continuity of its traditions and in the
right marriage of spirit and form. Nearly thirty years ago, when

I was a visiting professor at Hebrew Union College, the seminary for Reform rabbis in Cincinnati, I questioned Mordecai Kaplan's assertion during a lecture that "history proves that progress is inevitable." A student who is today a prominent leader in the rabbinate of Reform Judaism asked me, "Are you a caustic critic of Reform Judaism?" "In the first place, I was not talking about Reform Judaism but about Mordecai Kaplan," I replied, "and in the second," I added in jest, "I am far too kind and lovable to be a caustic critic of anything. But in the third, I happen to be the only member of this faculty who is an actual product of Reform Judaism. So if what I have to offer you is thin and colorless, it is because I have no rich tradition against which to rebel." Ten years later, my friend at the Bratzlaver Seminary in the Mea Shearim instructed me to tell the students in the course on Judaism that I was scheduled to teach that fall at Manhattanville College of the Sacred Heart that my own Judaism was not the real kind. "I shall try," I replied, "but the trouble is that I am the person they will have contact with and that is likely to have more of an impact on them than what they read in books."

If I have fallen here into a personal vein not unlike the autobiographical section of *Touchstones of Reality*, it is because I cannot imagine dealing honestly with the dialectic of form and spirit in generalities without taking responsibility for the life stance which, at my relatively advanced age, is likely to be the one that I shall persist in until I die. But I also see a general significance here. Our Dialogue with the Absurd offers us no guarantee of a smooth continuity of religious tradition or, in an age when both religious forms and religious spirit have fallen into question, any sureness of finding the right dialectic between spirit and form. We can speak in general of the traditions and forms of particular religions. No description of Christianity would be complete without mentioning Easter, Good Friday, Christmas, and the Mass, and no description of Judaism would be complete without mentioning the various holidays and Sabbath observances that have characterized religious Jews for millennia. But when it comes to our own task of finding the right tension between religious tradition, our personal uniqueness, and the contradictions and absurdities of the world in which we live, no general description can any longer have any meaning. Rather, there are a thousand particulars that give form in a life and express its basic attitudes, a thousand ways in which one can *be* Torah rather than merely say it. For me, these include Shabbat, Passover, Rosh Hashanah, Yom Kippur, and the other Jewish holidays. Yet if it only included them, then I should be falling short of the task of hallowing the everyday and sanctifying the profane.

Once at Hebrew Union College in Cincinnati during the havdalah service that marks the separation of the Sabbath from the "profane" weekdays that follow, I was very much struck by the fact that it was only after the double-twined Shabbat candle is extinguished in the wine and the darkness of the everyday succeeds the joy of the Sabbath that we sang *Eliyahu Hanovi*, the song of Elijah the prophet, who is seen in Judaism as the precursor of the Messiah. It is not during the sacred and eternal day of the Sabbath but during the profane and unhallowed everyday of the rest of the week that the task of redemption is fulfilled. There is no rung of human life that cannot be the ground of hallowing, no rung where we cannot put off the habitual and discover the wonder of the unique and the claim of the hour! We are constantly creating new religious forms as we respond to the spirit and are permeated by it, and we do so in faithful dialogue and tension with the spirit and form of tradition. "To be a spiritual heir, one must be a pioneer," says Heschel, but he also says elsewhere, "To be worthy of being a pioneer, one must be a spiritual heir"!

PART ONE

Radical Amazement and Prophetic Demand

Abraham Joshua Heschel's
Philosophy of Religion

ONE

My Friendship with
Abraham Joshua Heschel

I first met Abraham Joshua Heschel in 1945, just after he had come from Hebrew Union College, Cincinnati, to the Jewish Theological Seminary in New York, where he was to spend the rest of his life as Professor of Jewish Mysticism and Ethics. To convey the significance of this first meeting and of the friendship of just short of thirty years that grew out of it, I recapitulate here the context in which the meeting took place.

I was twenty-four years old and had already spent three years in Civilian Public Service camps and units for conscientious objectors during the Second World War. When I graduated from Harvard in September of 1942, I was a socialist as well as a pacifist and was on my way to becoming a labor organizer and educator. I came to CPS camp permeated with the spirit of Marx, Keynes, and the New Deal, and thought about social problems in exclusively political-economic-historical terms. My experience sawing down trees in the White Mountains of New Hampshire, fighting forest fires, and throwing rocks off the road in the Sierra Nevadas in California, and working as an attendant in an institute for the feebleminded outside of Philadelphia decisively changed the direction of my life. I learned that we pacifists were not ready to build community even among ourselves, and I was forced to probe deeper layer by layer into cooperatives, small communities, and finally, as I have described in my semiautobiographical book *Touchstones of Reality*, into mysticism.

> Out under the bright stars and clear skies of the Sierra Nev-
> adas . . . I began to realize that I had not yet come to terms
> with the meaning of life for myself. Trying to give my life to
> the service of others before I had found either meaning or
> wholeness in my own life now seemed to me an evasion. . . .
> I came to the strong conviction that I would have to change
> my own character before I could change others.[1]

I gave up my off-time work in labor education, gave away all my books, renounced my girlfriend, and immersed myself in the study and practice of mysticism. I combined reading from Hinduism, Buddhism, Taoism, and Christian devotional texts with three hours a day of meditation and, during a ten-to-twelve-hour workday six days a week, several more hours of "recollection," the attempt to keep the mind centered through the inward repetition of Hindu *mantra*, or song-words. As my experiences of mysticism deepened, spiritual growth—the movement toward what the Hindus call *samadhi*, superconsciousness or enlightenment—became for me the self-evident meaning, path, and goal of life. I became an absolute pacifist and a vegetarian. I was certain that when I left Civilian Public Service I was going to lead the life of a celibate monk, either in a Vedantist monastery or in a semimonastic community of seekers.

When in this frame of mind I visited on furlough my home in Tulsa, Oklahoma, my mother became sufficiently alarmed that she told me two facts of which I had been completely unaware up till that time: that there existed a Jewish mysticism, called Hasidism, and that her own father had been a devout and learned Lubavitcher Hasid in Lithuania and belonged to an outstanding Hasidic family. Although a prize pupil in our Reform temple, I had never even heard the word "Hasidism" before. My mother then asked me if I would go to talk with the young Conservative rabbi in Tulsa. He gave me a letter of introduction to his teacher, Dr. Simon Greenberg, then still rabbi of the Har Zion Congregation in Philadelphia as well as professor at the Jewish Theological Seminary in New York. I went many times to talk with Simon Greenberg in Philadelphia and discussed at length with him my interest in mysticism, religion, and metaphysics.

Although he personally found more meaning in Max Kadushin's *Organic Thinking*, which he loaned me, he also loaned me an early translation of Martin Buber's *Legend of the Baal Shem*. Despite the intellectual and emotional poverty of my Jewish upbringing, I found in this book a mystical tradition which touched on depths of emotions I did not even know I possessed and won my heart for all time to Hasidism. After a number of shattering experiences which I tell about in *Touchstones of Reality*, I rejected the solitary contemplation and search for sainthood of my earlier mysticism and turned to Hasidism as an activist communal mysticism in the world which affirmed joy and fervor rather than repressed them. Largely ignorant of both Hasidism and American Judaism, I nonetheless wanted to give my life to reviving Hasidism in America.

With this in mind I went again to see Simon Greenberg, who sent me to talk to Abraham Heschel. Dr. Heschel could not have been more than thirty-eight at the time, and he did not have the beard which later came to seem inseparable from his image. (When he first grew it, I did not like it, for it made him appear severe in a way I had not known him to be!) I found him a gentle man with penetrating eyes and a calm, almost awesome presence which communicated to me, before I had ever read a word of his writings, what he meant by "radical amazement" and the "awareness of the ineffable." When I answered in the affirmative his question whether I was cold, he turned on the radiator and observed, "Isn't it wonderful that one need only turn a knob and heat will come?" I thought of this later when he told one of his favorite stories—about when the first streetcar came to Warsaw. No one in the excited group who gathered around the conductor could understand how the streetcar could move without a horse. But he explained it all to them: "I turn this wheel," he said, "and it turns a shaft which is connected to the wheels of the streetcar, and so the wheels go round and the streetcar runs." "Oh, we see!" exclaimed everyone, highly satisfied.

Dr. Heschel listened sympathetically to my narration of my path up till then and my hopes for the future. Instead of initiating me into the secrets of Hasidic "yoga," i.e., the specific spiritual disciplines which I could undertake to replace those of Hinduism, Heschel emphasized the fact that Hasidism is a part of Judaism and cannot be understood apart from it. He felt that I could best help Hasidism by becoming either a rabbi of a modern Hasidic congregation—"There are several I know," he said—or a writer or journalist. In either case he thought I should go through the seminary. Since I did not know Hebrew, he said I would have to study it intensively for a couple of years before I could be admitted to the seminary. When I reported our conversation to Dr. Greenberg, he generously offered me money from his temple fund to support me during my first six months of study. But I was troubled by the fact that, raised as I was in the thinnest part of Reform Judaism, I had no feeling for or understanding of Halakhah, or the Jewish law, and could not sincerely accept it. Dr. Heschel felt that after two years of study I would be able to accept enough of the Jewish law to enter the Jewish Theological Seminary. This seemed to me possible but, on the other hand, I reasoned that I could not be confident of being able to accept the law even after two years of study. I decided, therefore, that it would be dishonest if I accepted Rabbi Greenberg's money. I was also troubled at that time, as I would not have been later, by the exclusivism that might result from my associating myself with the seminary and becoming a rabbi. I felt very close to my Gentile friends and felt that if I were to find the truth it should be for them as well as for my Jewish friends. For these reasons, I finally abandoned the idea, hoping instead to forge ahead to the place where I could find a truth that would be helpful to all seekers such as myself. Toward this end I entered graduate school.

Nonetheless, I kept in close touch with Heschel. When I tried to tell him some of the feelings of anger toward my mother that had arisen in me in the course of a group interaction, he was shocked. "If I could find my mother to tie her shoestrings," he exclaimed, "I should be the happiest man on earth!" All of his family and friends and, indeed, the whole of the Polish Jewry in which he had grown up had disappeared almost without a trace. He also chided me for my unhappiness over my short-lived and ill-fated first marriage. "Hasidism teaches joy," he said, "and if you cannot attain joy in six weeks, you must not come back to see me." Later he explained to me that the joy of the Hasidim came precisely through suffering, not through the absence of it.

At this time Dr. Heschel shared with me his beautiful little essay "Prayer," which had a profound impact on me. He also talked to me about what the Sabbath meant to him. "If it were not for the Sabbath," he said, "I do not know how I could manage to live through each week." The sense of real joy that he found in the Sabbath and the *mitzvoth* was my first real introduction to what he himself later called the "holy dimension" of Jewish deeds. It gave content to what otherwise might have seemed entirely foreign to me. At this period, too, I began to come into contact with Heschel's disciples among the rabbinical students at the seminary—Montford Harris, who impressed me as a young mystic in his own right, and Hershel Matt, who, under the influence of Heschel and of Will Herberg, had made the journey from Reconstructionism to an altogether different theology and piety.

Later, when I was studying for my doctorate as a Fellow of the Committee on the History of Culture at the University of Chicago, Heschel regularly sent to see me those of his disciples who lived or studied there—Samuel Dresner and Seymour Siegel in particular. Sam was not so gentle with me on the subject of Halakhah as Heschel was. Though the Jewish law remained a constant question and tension between Heschel and me, he emphatically rejected Sam's assertion of that time that anyone on the other side of the line of the law was not a Jew (i.e., not an authentic Jew). I had continued my interest in Martin Buber without ever attempting to contact him personally, since Heschel had told me he was a busy man whom I ought not trouble. But I assumed that Buber was an observant Jew from the fact that he had a beard. Ironically, it was Sam Dresner who informed me he was not and thereby relieved me of at least a part of my tension on the subject!

Heschel himself came to Chicago several times during those years. It was he who first told me to read Paul Tillich on religious symbolism, which I found greatly helpful, and he encouraged me to continue my study of biblical Hebrew at the Oriental Institute and of modern Hebrew at the College of Jewish Studies in Chicago. Once, I attended a lecture Heschel gave in Yiddish and found that he spoke such a pure Germanic Yiddish that I could make out most of it through my knowledge of German despite my total ignorance of Yiddish. Another time there was a gathering in a home in Northside Chicago with Heschel which I attended along with Everett Gendler, an undergraduate then at the University of Chicago whom I had brought into the chapter of the Jewish Peace Fellowship that I started there. In the years since, he has become one of America's leading peace rabbis.

When I received my Ph.D. from the University of Chicago in 1950, Heschel was as proud as if I had been his own son. He went over my dissertation (a six-hundred-page tome, "Martin Buber: Mystic, Existentialist, Social Prophet—A Study in the Redemption of Evil") and made most helpful suggestions as to how to cut out excess verbiage, tighten, and solidify. At the same time, he told me I should be able to complete the task of revising it for publication in a year. He was quite dismayed when, having come into contact with Martin Buber through my mother, who visited Israel in 1950 and who took him a copy of my dissertation, I spent four years acquiring and integrating vast amounts of new material on the implications of Buber's thought for many fields. It was these four years that led to *Martin Buber: The Life of Dialogue*. Heschel was pleased with the result and said that my book would certainly last for a generation as the decisive study of Buber's thought.

When I came to New York City in 1950, Heschel arranged for me to spend a week at the seminary so that I might read the manuscript of his book *Man Is Not Alone: A Philosophy of Religion*. I was fascinated by the way in which he stapled together his aphoristic sentences to produce a gradually emerging organic whole, and I was charmed by the power and the style of his writing. Though he generously credited my help at the back of the book, I am afraid my responses were somewhat disappointing. Instead of the profound philosophical or religious criticisms that he wanted, I would come up with, "Page 66, line 7, semicolon after 'prayer' "—a compulsive habit which I have never been able to shake off as a result of the only subject I have ever detested teaching: English composition. "Wonderful!" Heschel would exclaim in mock admiration. "Where did you get your knowledge of English grammar?"

Nevertheless, this was an important week for me—of closeness to him, of cementing my friendship with Sam Dresner, and, through Heschel's arranging it, of a Shabbat spent in Williamsburg, Brooklyn, among the Hasidim. This last had a great impact on me. In the altogether radiant and spontaneous way in which my Williamsburg host kissed the mezuzah on the door or said the *brachah* over the bread and wine at the Shabbat meal, I could see where Heschel got his own joy in the Sabbath and the *mitzvoth*. I was particularly impressed by the experience of sitting in the dark for hours at the Klausenberger rebbe's while the Hasidim sang *niggunim* after sundown Saturday. On my return I asked Heschel why, if he envied me my weekend there, as he repeatedly said, he did not go to live in Williamsburg himself. "I cannot," he replied. "When I left my home in Poland, I became a modern Western man. I cannot reverse this."

When I was asked to review Heschel's book *Man Is Not Alone* for *The Journal of Religion*, I spent a whole week reimmersing myself in it and working out the logical links between the seemingly lyrical passages. I discovered how very difficult it is to retain the full richness of his poetic imagery and devotional depth and at the same time follow the interconnections of his philosophy of religion. My intensive study confirmed my feeling that this *is* a highly original and profound philosophy of religion, despite his liberal and Orthodox detractors, whom I later answered in *Congress Weekly* in my first article on Heschel's thought. But I also found out that it was not a fully consistent or systematic philosophy. Heschel's genius lay instead in a type of polar thinking that emphasized now one pole and now another, as the particular subject and situation demanded, so that the whole was held together by the tension of his piety—"the communion of the ineffable within with the ineffable beyond," as he put it.

Thus I found myself following the development of Heschel's philosophy of religion and philosophy of Judaism with each new book and working out for myself the links between them. This led to certain criticisms of Heschel's position. I could not follow to my own satisfaction how he got from his universal philosophy to the specific Jewish way of life. Also, in his attempt to combat the subjectivism and emphasis upon a religion of "needs" of his day, he sometimes seemed to me to go too far in the direction of reducing the "I" to an "it" in the eyes of God or the self to "transcendence in disguise." Occasionally I found myself objecting to some of the metaphysical conceits into which, amid his amazing mastery of English, he sometimes fell—a worm on the island of Atol shaking its fist at the atomic bomb or, in imitation of Shakespeare, "We are such stuff as needs are made of, and our little life is rounded by ends." There was a certain emotional insistence that I encountered from time to time in Heschel's writing with which I was never quite comfortable. For the most part, however, I found Heschel to belong to the great devotional writers of the ages.

In the fall of 1951 the Jewish Theological Seminary was the setting of a celebration of the publication of Heschel's profound and beautiful little book *The Sabbath*. On the way to the celebration I asked Martin Buber, who had recently come to America as the guest of the seminary, if he was going. "I have no time for parties," Buber responded shortly. Heschel sent my then wife, Eugenia, and me to see his publishers, John Farrar and Roger Straus, each of whom talked with one of us and presented each of us with a book. Not long after this, we met Heschel's new wife, Sylvia, a lovely woman who had been a concert pianist but gave this up to marry Heschel. At the seminary people joked, playing upon Heschel's title *Man Is Not Alone*. It was through Sylvia Heschel's teacher that I got my baby grand piano. Not too long after that, Susannah Heschel was born, to the everlasting delight of her parents. I saw her a number of times as a small child and then again as a teenager and as a freshman at Trinity College, where she showed me around when I came there to lecture. Now she has become a lovely young woman herself, finishing her doctorate in Judaica, editing books on Jewish feminism, and appearing regularly at the conventions and conferences of the American Academy of Religion, where I often see her. In June of 1985, I went to see Sylvia Heschel for the first time in years. Lovely as ever, in an apartment full of marvelous Heschel pictures, portraits, and mementos, she played the piano for me and inscribed Heschel's posthumous book *The Circle of the Baal Shem Tov*: "Congratulations on your many important contributions, which Heschel anticipated upon his first meeting with you. In admiration, Sylvia Heschel." I was touched that she remembered those early days of almost forty years ago as vividly as I did.

Of the times we were at the Heschels' home, the most memorable to me was the Seder service where Heschel proved himself a true Hasid by eating a two-inch chunk of horseradish and drinking several glasses of wine! Not long before, he had come to lecture at Sarah Lawrence College, where I was teaching. Looking at the new Reisinger Auditorium, the pride of the college, Heschel remarked, "No one will even notice this in twenty-five years." But then he pointed to the Lawrence mansion at the

top of the hill, which served as the college's administration building, and said, "Now, that will last." While there he met one of
my students who claimed to be a direct descendant of the Baal
Shem. When we went to the Seder he asked about her, and I
said she had been expelled from the college for poor performance
in her studies. That seemed to impress Heschel, who no doubt
wondered whether a progressive women's college like Sarah Lawrence had any standards!

The most frequent setting in which I saw Heschel was the
study that he occupied from the time he came to the seminary
till his death. This study was a world of its own, with an unbelievable clutter of old Hasidic books and manuscripts, Judaica
of every description, mixed with modern books, and a file for
the books Heschel was himself working on. I was impressed when
after many years Heschel got into his study one of those super-
comfortable recliner chairs in which he could sit back and smoke
his invariable cigar or even take short naps. After Heschel's death
I heard that his Japanese disciple was undertaking to put the
study in order. It must have been a Herculean feat.

Occasionally, too, I would walk with Heschel from the seminary to his home on Riverside Drive and stop and have orange
juice on the way, or I would see him at some conference or
lecture. Once we were together in Long Island, where a group
of his disciples met. I gave a little speech myself in which I
remarked that ten years before I had wanted to find community
by devoting myself to Hasidism and I had never been so lonely
in my life. Heschel said that was the first time he had heard me
speak. In the late sixties Heschel and I rode together on the plane
to Chicago, where he was the keynote speaker for the Religious
Education Association convention in which I also took part. I
shared with Heschel an article I had written at the request of
Religion and Mental Health on Jewish social responsibility. "It
has no Jewish scholarly grounding whatsoever," he aptly though
not harshly commented.

When I was Visiting Professor of Religious Philosophy at

Hebrew Union College–Jewish Institute of Religion in Cincinnati in 1956, I picked up something of how totally isolated and out of place Heschel must have felt himself there thirteen years before, when he had just come from London. It is to Hebrew Union College's great credit that it brought Heschel over, perhaps saving his life and certainly laying the groundwork for his momentous career in America. But in those days, in some contrast to what it is now, it was so far removed from the Judaism for which Heschel stood that they could hardly have had a common language. Someone told me of how Heschel came there to speak a few years later, after he had moved to the seminary, and of how totally unsympathetic his audience was. When Heschel left Hebrew Union College for the seminary in 1944, he took with him Samuel Dresner and Richard Rubinstein, both of whom had been students there.

When I was chairman of the American Friends of Ichud (a group for Israeli-Arab rapprochement) in the late 1950s, I tried in vain to get Heschel to join our really very distinguished board. "I will not join a board that has on it Hans Kohn, a well-known anti-Zionist," Heschel commented. Hans Kohn, a great historian, particularly well known for his work on nationalism and himself author of the first Buber biography, which appeared when Buber was fifty, had gone to Palestine as a Zionist of the Buber persuasion, but had become so disillusioned that he left Palestine for America and turned his back on Zionism. I mistakenly thought that Heschel's refusal to join the board meant that he was too concentrated on his studies to be concerned with social action. His activities in the sixties and early seventies proved this to be anything but the case.

I once brought Heschel together with my own former professor from the University of Chicago, the great Whiteheadian philosopher Charles Hartshorne. They found they had much in common both philosophically and spiritually. Another time Heschel showed me an inscription that the sociologist-philosopher Eugen Rosenstock-Huessy wrote in a book he gave him: "From the philosopher of times to the philosopher of time." Rosenstock-Huessy's thought was based on a grammar of past, present, and future, Heschel's, particularly in *The Sabbath*, on time as the ever-present, ever-renewed creative event, the medium which encompassed space and gave the reality of holiness to our world.

After I had led two weekends at the Esalen Institute at Big Sur, I followed up a suggestion made by Michael Murphy, the president of Esalen, and invited Heschel to come to Esalen and do a weekend with me. In my letter to Heschel, I extolled Esalen as one of the few places of real openness and growth in America. My criticisms of some of the dominant atmosphere at Esalen only matured in later years, and I never totally lost the impact of those early weekends there. Heschel's response was both negative and skeptical: "I get two hundred invitations a year. Why should I accept this one?" he asked me, and I could not reply to his satisfaction.

I early learned in my relationship with Heschel that if he could not speak well of a person, he would not speak at all. One of the things I most admired about him, indeed, was that constant spiritual awareness and presence which warded off every trace of malice and envy and kept far from him idle gossip and personal spite.

The only exception I remember to Heschel's reluctance to speak badly of anyone was the great German existentialist philosopher Martin Heidegger, whose Nazi speeches were documented in a book Heschel referred me to and which I drew on heavily in my own book *The Worlds of Existentialism*, Guido Schneeburger's *Nachlese zu Heidegger*. Heschel had talked to some American professor who had visited Heidegger in Germany. Heidegger had withdrawn from his Nazi Party activities and the rectorship of Freiburg University in 1934, but he continued to identify himself for some years with its thought and never, even in his posthumously published interview with *Der Spiegel*, made a real recantation. Heidegger remarked to the American professor that he was sorry so many Jewish professors managed to make their escape to America. Since the alternative to this escape was certain death at the hands of the Nazis, we can only assume that this is what Heidegger had in mind for them as, from his point of view, a more acceptable fate!

Heschel went twice to Rome in connection with the Second Vatican Council and two times had audiences with the Pope. His great concern as to the outcome of the council's statements on the Jews was reflected in letters and other ways that have been well documented but also, as the leading public Quaker Douglas Steere humorously told me, in frequent calls that Heschel would make to Steere from Rome. "Douglas," said Steere, imitating Heschel's accent, "we must do something about this!"

I was so timid about bringing up people with Heschel that I never mentioned a Hasidic cousin of his who involved me and quite a number of leading figures in the Jewish academic world in an ambitious scheme to translate and publish Hasidic teachings in a monumental *Corpus Hassidica*. "Why didn't you ask me about him?" Heschel rejoined when I finally mentioned this debacle after it was all over. In those days, the late sixties and early seventies, Heschel's voice was often heard on social matters—the Russian Jews, Martin Luther King's marches in the South, race relations in Chicago, old age, medicine, and Clergy and Laymen Against the War in Vietnam, which Heschel co-chaired with Robert McAfee Brown. I was never more proud of Heschel than when he wrote a truly prophetic letter to *The New York Times* asking what Amos would say about corruption in the very highest places—prophetic in the real sense of the prophetic demand for justice and in the popular sense of proclaiming the corruption a few months before Watergate broke!

Heschel's own dream for me I never fulfilled—that of acquiring a thorough knowledge of Hebrew and making the contribution to Jewish learning and religious thought that he felt I could make. With great and gentle patience, he often used to call me up on Sunday morning during the many years that I lived in New York (from 1951 to 1964 I taught at Sarah Lawrence College) to ask how I was progressing in my study of Hebrew. If he was not pleased at the report, neither did he give up hope during those years. Thus a pattern was set in our relationship which persisted to the end—one of great affection and friendship on both sides and, on my side, one of near but never full discipleship. My loyalty, gratitude, and admiration for him were always coupled with the tension of holding my own position, in some significant ways at variance with his. This tension was always contained within our friendship, which never knew a real conflict or serious strain.

That I was not able to follow Heschel's guidance in Halakhah, the "way of deeds," was as great a disappointment to him as my failure to follow my own goal of really mastering Hebrew and studying with him midrashic and Hasidic texts. Yet neither of these disappointments ever affected his friendship for me. Even when I moved to Philadelphia as Professor of Religion at Temple University, he periodically called me up and urged me to visit him, which I did on my infrequent visits to New York.

One person of whom Heschel and I frequently spoke was Martin Buber. We shared a deep friendship with Buber—Heschel from his close association with Buber during his years in Germany, myself from a much later period in Buber's life. Once, during Buber's first visit to America in 1951, my wife, Eugenia, dropped in to see Heschel at the Jewish Theological Seminary in New York and came on the two men looking at each other so earnestly across Heschel's desk that she retreated without making her presence known. When Heschel heard Gershom Scholem's criticisms of Buber in a public lecture, he remarked to me, "You know that there is much in Buber's interpretation of Hasidism and Judaism that I cannot accept. But how can Scholem speak against him thus? We have no one like him in world Jewry." Still, I think that a third disappointment in Heschel's relationship with me was that I became Buber's disciple to the extent that I did. Heschel wanted me for a more wholehearted life of Jewish praxis. Yet Heschel once remarked to me that every man has some point of reference, some "touchstone of reality," to use my own phrase, which he consults in his life decisions. For me, he knew, it was Hasidism.

My writings on Heschel's thought have been highly appreciative, but they have also contained criticisms, some of which derived from my immersion in Buber's philosophy of dialogue. Once, when I had put into a review article on Heschel's book *The Prophets* a contrast between Heschel's and Buber's treatment of the prophet Hosea, Heschel asked me as a personal favor to take it out so that he would not be obliged to write a public criticism of Buber—something that he had never done. On the other hand, he took a lively interest in the critical biography of Buber that I was writing and freely offered me whatever recollections and suggestions he could. The years in Nazi Germany were the period of Buber's true greatness, Heschel stressed; for great as his books were, Buber was greater still as a man, especially at the time of his people's most terrible agony. One field is the most that anyone can master, Heschel once commented to me, but Buber mastered two—the Bible and Hasidism. Heschel suggested to me that I should take some of Buber's letters to a handwriting expert to see what his handwriting told about his personality. I never did, but the idea intrigued me. When I criticized Heschel's comments on Buber's I-Thou philosophy at one point, Heschel gave me a pained look as if to say, "Do you think I don't understand Buber?"

In a statement he gave my editor at Dutton, Heschel described my book *Touchstones of Reality* as a "deeply moving account of a personal pilgrimage of a highly sensitive and rich soul . . . an ingathering of a vast amount of wonderful insights." Heschel said to me, in fact, that *Touchstones of Reality*, which combines early autobiography with my dialogue with some of the great religions, should have been entitled "The Pilgrimage of a Soul."

Heschel read and commented on all my books. He also made suggestions concerning the English original and the Hebrew translation of the monograph "Divine Need and Human Wonder: The Philosophy of Abraham Joshua Heschel," which I wrote for the second volume of Brit Ivrit Olamit's three-volume Israeli publication, *Spiritual Contributions of American Jewry*. Heschel told me, rather humorously, that my essay read better in Hebrew translation than in the English original! Despite my occasional criticisms, he seemed very pleased that it would appear. My last contact with him was on the subject of this essay, which I wrote as an act of personal devotion to him.

I was, of course, terribly shocked by the news of Heschel's heart attack three years before his death, and still more by his thin and wan appearance when he returned to New York. He told me in detail of his whole attack, clearly as a warning, and made me promise to lose weight. He had gone to Milwaukee for a lecture, could not find a taxi, and ended up walking many blocks with two heavy suitcases. He awoke at four in the morning with a mild heart attack. In the process of receiving blood transfusions, he contracted hepatitis, so that despite a year's recuperation in Florida he looked twenty to thirty years older than he had before. He told me that when he lay in the Intensive Care Unit in the hospital in New York City and his younger friend and disciple Rabbi Wolfe Kalman visited him, he scribbled on one side of a page in Hebrew, "I who wrote a book entitled *Who Is Man?* now lie here like a beast." A few years ago, Heschel's disciple Rabbi Samuel H. Dresner brought out a beautiful spiritual anthology of Heschel's writing which he entitled *I Asked for Wonder*. The photograph of Heschel that he put on the front of this book seemed to me to show ravages of illness. Although this was not in any way Dr. Dresner's own meaning, I could not help feeling as if the photograph were a reproach saying, "I asked for wonder, and this is what I got!" Perhaps because my own face has not reflected either such serious illness or such profound spiritual suffering, it is hard for me to take in that at the moment of this writing I am only two years younger than Heschel was when he died! Heschel was not perhaps a prophet without honor in his own country, but he lived and died the life of a prophet— God's witness and ours at the same time.

When I told Heschel in our last face-to-face talk that I had decided to give up my position at Temple University for a more limited commitment at San Diego State University, he was genuinely delighted. "The center of America is moving to the West Coast," he said to me, "and in any case, you will have more time to study and to write."

When I first visited Heschel at the seminary, almost thirty years before, he told me how some of his colleagues did not appreciate his concern for Jewish piety, such as his essay "Prayer." By the end of his life Heschel had become a dominant force at the seminary and in American and world Judaism, as well as having a great impact on Catholic and Protestant thought. What particularly pleased me was the fact that, contrary to my earlier impression when I had tried in vain to get him to join the Advisory Board of the American Friends of Ichud, Heschel was not afraid to risk himself through social witness. After the years of intense concentration on study and writing, producing one remarkable book after another about the whole span of Jewish life and thought, Heschel emerged as one of the clearest and strongest voices in social action in America. He was, as we have seen, a co-chairman of Clergy and Laymen Against the War in Vietnam; he was, so far as I know, the first public figure to fight discrimination against Jews in the Soviet Union; he personally visited the Pope in an effort to get a better statement on the Jews from the Second Vatican Council; he spoke tirelessly in behalf of the old, the sick, the poor, the discriminated against; and he marched with Martin Luther King in Selma. He gave me with pride an article transcribing a "Conversation with Martin Luther King" at the Rabbinical Assembly ten days before King was assassinated, in which Heschel introduced King and King spoke of Heschel as "one of the truly great men of our day and age," "a truly great prophet," "relevant at all times."[2]

The easier life which Heschel urged on me he was incapable of leading himself. He looked so full of his old vitality and spirit when I saw him in early November 1972 that I was totally unprepared for the news of his death in late December. *Newsweek*'s sympathetic account of his last week of activity before his death showed me how far Heschel himself was from being able to give up the stimulations of the East Coast. How could he, indeed— at the very height of his influence? My only comfort, a small but real one, was that after Heschel went to Connecticut to greet Philip Berrigan on his release from Danbury Prison, David Lichtman, a young student and friend of mine who had never before met Heschel (and who is now a far more Orthodox Hasid than Heschel himself), drove him back to New York City, and a part of their conversation was devoted to their, very different, relationship to me. Thus I knew myself present in Heschel's mind three days before his death—not without analogy to Heschel's own philosophy that we know ourselves as known by God! I learned of Heschel's death indirectly and without any details. While I was still wondering whom to contact to find out about the funeral, Elie Wiesel called me and told me that he had just come from there. When I next went to visit Elie, he read me that early Yiddish poem of Heschel's that he had read at the funeral— a poem amazingly like the spirit of Elie himself:

GOD FOLLOWS ME EVERYWHERE

God follows me everywhere,
Weaving a web of visions around me
Blinding my sightless spine like a sun.

God follows me like an enveloping forest
And continuously astonishes my lips into awesome silence
Like a child lost in an ancient sanctuary.

God follows me within me like a tremor.
I want to rest. He demands: Come,
See how visions lie scattered aimlessly in the streets.

O wander, deep in my own fantasies, like a secret,
Down a long corridor through the world.
Now and then, high above me, I catch a glimpse of
   the faceless face of God.[3]

Elie's reading of this poem and my writing these reminiscences helped me mourn a dear friend and beloved teacher. Thirteen years later I was much moved to learn of Wiesel's last meeting with Heschel, particularly as I was just finishing this book witnessing to the two of them. Heschel called Wiesel and asked him to come see him. Wiesel was in the middle of a conference, but there was something in Heschel's voice that made him leave everything and take a taxi to the seminary. "I came into his study and greeted him, but he did not speak. He cried, he fell on my shoulder. He did not say a word, he simply cried."[4]

The Scion of Hasidism

Abraham Joshua Heschel was born in Warsaw, Poland, in 1907. His birth as well as his later interests grounded him deeply in the world of the Hasidim, the popular communal Jewish mystics of Eastern Europe. He was descended on his father's side from Dov Baer, the maggid of Mezeritch, the successor to the Baal Shem Tov, and from his own namesake Avraham Yehoshua Heschel of Apt, the Apter rebbe. On his mother's side he was descended from the great Hasidic rabbi Levi Yitzhak of Berditchev. Heschel's disciple Samuel H. Dresner gives us a glimpse of Heschel's Hasidic childhood in his introduction to Heschel's posthumous book *The Circle of the Baal Shem Tov*:

> From Heschel's childhood on, there were Hasidic leaders who looked to him as one with unique promise for renewing Hasidic life. . . . Descended from Hasidic nobility on both his father's and his mother's side, young Heschel's talents were early recognized and, though he was only a child of ten at the time of his father's death, the Hasidim began to bring him *k'vitlakh* and wished him to become their Rebbe. "We thought," said the Rebbe of Kopitchnitz, a cousin and brother-in-law, "that he would be the Levi Yitzhak of our generation." A byword after his departure was that "had Heschel become a Rebbe, all the other Rebbeim would have lost their Hasidim." . . . But the awareness of the worlds "outside" was stirring and

22

the young Heschel did not accede to the Hasidim's wishes. His interest in secular studies began at about the age of fifteen or sixteen. His decision to leave Warsaw for Vilna and, later, Berlin to gain a secular education was received with concern. . . . He claimed that he was no longer a Hasid. He had, indeed, abandoned their style of dress and of restricted social contacts for the larger world, both Jewish and German.[1]

Heschel left Poland at twenty to study philosophy at the University of Berlin, from which he received his Ph.D. in 1937. He also studied Semitics and was an instructor in Talmud at the famous Hochschule für die Wissenschaft des Judentums. In 1937 he was chosen by Martin Buber as his successor at the Central Organization for Jewish Adult Education and as the director of the Freie Jüdische Lehrhaus at Frankfurt.

Studying philosophy at the University of Berlin, Heschel became increasingly aware of the gulf that separated his views from those of his professors and fellow students. They spoke of God from the point of view of man, whereas to Heschel the Torah was a vision of man from the point of view of God. They were concerned with how to be good. Heschel was concerned with how to be holy. Prisoners of a Greek-German way of thinking, they were fettered in categories presupposing metaphysical assumptions which could never be proved. Discovering that values sweet to taste proved sour in analysis, Heschel went through moments of profound bitterness and loneliness. Then, walking alone through the streets of Berlin, Heschel became aware one evening that the sun had gone down and that he had not said the evening prayer. Although his heart was heavy and his soul was sad, he rediscovered that evening his task—"to restore the world to the kingship of the Lord."[2]

Expelled by the Nazis in 1938, Heschel taught for eight months in Warsaw at the Institute for Jewish Studies. Then he was fortunate enough to get to London, where he established the Institute for Jewish Learning. He was brought to America by the Hebrew Union College, and from 1940 to 1945 he was Associate

Professor of Philosophy and Rabbinics in Cincinnati, Ohio. In 1945 he moved to New York to become Professor of Jewish Ethics and Mysticism at the Jewish Theological Seminary, where he remained except for a year as the Harry Emerson Fosdick Visiting Professor for Union Theological Seminary, New York City.

Heschel's early books, apart from a collection of Yiddish poetry, were principally on medieval Jewish philosophy: *Maimonides. Eine Biographie* (1937), *Don Jizchak Abravanel* (1937), and *The Quest for Certainty in Saadia's Philosophy* (1944). Heschel also wrote several studies on Ibn Gabirol's metaphysics. Heschel's concern with Hasidism resulted over the years in a number of monographs in Yiddish and Hebrew, and two books—*A Passion for Truth* (a comparison of the Baal Shem Tov, Kierkegaard, and Rabbi Mendel of Kotzk) and a large book on the Kotzker rebbe, which is so far only in Yiddish. Heschel was a pioneer in studies of the early history of Hasidism—the circle of the Baal Shem Tov.

Heschel saw Hasidism neither as a sect nor as a doctrine, but as a dynamic approach to reality that succeeded in liquifying a frozen system of values and ideas. The Hasid studied the Talmud to experience its soul and to envision worlds. Hasidism set life aflame: it brought warmth, light, enthusiasm. Stressing truthfulness and wholeheartedness, Hasidism placed the aphorism and the parable at the center of Hasidic thinking and transformed doctrines into attitudes and facts.[3]

All this was embodied as never before or since in the founder of Hasidism—Israel ben Eliezer (1700–60), who came to be known as the Baal Shem Tov, the good master of the name of God, or, shortened, the Besht. The unbelievable impact that the Besht had in such a short time is explained by Heschel through the fact that, while many Jews talked about God, it was the Besht who brought God to the people.

He who really wants to be uplifted by communion with a great person whom he can love without reservation, who can enrich his thought and imagination without end, that person can meditate about the life . . . of the Besht. There has been no one like him during the last thousand years.[4]

Heschel was given a Guggenheim to write a biography of the Baal Shem, and he did, in fact, leave behind a plan for such a book, plus many notes. The book itself he did not write. The measure of this loss is suggested by Heschel's disciple Samuel H. Dresner:

> Descendant of a Hasidic dynasty and heir of the living tra-
> dition at its most vital source, master of the philosophical and
> historical-critical method of the West as well as possessing
> unusual creative gifts, Heschel was perhaps the one scholar
> who might have given us the definitive work on Hasidism.[5]

What Heschel did leave behind were essays on four of the zad-dikim who formed the circle around the Baal Shem. In a great labor of love spanning ten years, with careful faithfulness and exhaustive scholarly notes, Rabbi Dresner has preserved these for us in Heschel's posthumous book *The Circle of the Baal Shem Tov.* In his introduction, "Heschel as a Hasidic Scholar," Dresner brings together much material that gives us insight into Heschel's deep grounding in and devotion to Hasidism. Heschel stated that this great movement is essentially an oral one that cannot be preserved in written form, a living movement that is not contained fully in any of its books. "To be a Hasid is to be in love with God and with what God has created." If you have never been in love in this way, you will not understand the history of Hasidism and may consider it a madness. Asserting that Judaism is today in need of repair, Heschel labeled the great Hasidim "the repairmen of the Holy of Holies." In the Hasidic movement the spirit was alive in the word as a voice, not a mere idea. Its words have the power to repair, to revive, to create, if one learns how to be perceptive to the voice within them. Its words still ring with the passion and enthusiasm of those who spoke them. "The problem is how to hear the voice through the words." In many Hasidic books God's presence is felt on every page.[6]

Heschel's Hasidic understanding went far beyond books, of course. Due to his early upbringing, he possessed a remarkable sensitivity to the core of Hasidic authenticity as it was transmitted from generation to generation. As a result, Heschel stressed that Hasidism can never be understood on the basis of literary sources alone without drawing upon the oral tradition which preserves its authentic living source. Translated often unsuccessfully from Yiddish into Hebrew, Hasidic literature can never in itself make up for listening to the living tongue of the masters and standing close to Hasidic personages. This Heschel could do as none of those who followed him could hope to emulate. In his childhood and youth Heschel lived in the presence of quite a number of extraordinary persons he could revere, and their presence continued to live in him as an adult. Above all, he retained the capacity to be surprised at life that he saw as the supreme Hasidic imperative. Shlomo Beillis, from the circle of Yiddish poets to which Heschel belonged when he studied at the gymnasium in Vilna, describes how Heschel would surprise him by bringing along his dark hat when they took walks through the forest and, upon entering the woods, would put it on. "When I inquired for the reason, he replied in his soft voice: 'I don't know if you will understand. To me a forest is a holy place, and a Jew does not enter a holy place without covering his head!' "[7]

If Heschel's treatment of Hasidism may be faulted, Dresner comments, "it is in his tendency toward Hasidic apologetics and his preference to stay clear of the ignoble and dark features which are inevitable in a world which included millions."[8] In his emphasis upon the oral as opposed to the written, Heschel is close to Martin Buber. Heschel was also close to Buber in his recognition that there were *two* streams that came forth from Hasidism, and not one, as both Gershom Scholem and his disciple Rivka Schatz-Uffenheimer maintain—that of the hallowing of the everyday which began with the Baal Shem and that of the gnostic nullifying of the particular in favor of the transcendent that began with the Baal Shem's successor, Dov Baer, the maggid of Mezeritch. This contrast emerges with great clarity in Heschel's essay on the Baal Shem's friend R. Pinhas of Koretz (or Korzec). In this essay, writes Dresner, Heschel "delineated the ideological conflict which occurred early in the history of the movement, in which each side claimed that it possesses the true meaning of the Besht's legacy":

> The maggid of Miedzyrzecz [Mezeritch] had stressed the centrality of Kabbalah and established *devekut* as the highest goal. For him, the awareness that all is God would lead man to understand that this world is but so many veils which must be cast aside to enter into the divine embrace. His language is strongly Lurianic, with spiritual ascent beyond time and place the all-consuming goal. For R. Pinhas, on the other hand, the stress is elsewhere. This world is no illusion. It is the place, and now is the time, where man must labor diligently and unremittingly to perfect himself. To escape the world is to violate the Psalmist's admonition that one must first "turn from evil" and only then "do good." . . . R. Pinhas emphasized moral virtue and simple faith.[9]

The maggid introduced the methods of the Lurian Kabbalah into the teaching of the Besht—*kavanot* and *yihudim* (special mystical intentions and exercises), *devekut* (cleaving to God), and *hitlahavut* (burning enthusiasm, or ecstasy). His disciple Shneur Zalman taught that the essence of all things was intellectual contemplation on the greatness of God. R. Pinhas, in contrast, criticized those who wanted to learn the secrets of the Torah and to achieve lofty rungs of insight. He preferred unquestioning simplicity, honesty, and humility to *yihudim* and *kavanot*. "The battle between these two forms of Hasidim—the one, scholarly, speculative, and aristocratic; the other, that of the Ukrainian tzaddikim, poetic, moralistic, and popular—continued for generations." The maggid of Mezeritch and many of his followers, such as Levi Yitzhak of Berditchev, believed that true prayer demanded *hitlahavut* and that *hitlahavut* demanded various kinds of special preparation. R. Pinhas did not hold with special preparations for prayer nor with praying with excessive vigor and in a loud voice. To him, worship and worshipper were part of one whole and prayer not within the domain of man. He saw every word that one speaks, even one's lying down to sleep, as part of the preparation for prayer.[10]

On the door of the house of the head of the Jewish court of Korzec (Koretz) were inscribed the words: "To speak with the rav about worldly matters is only permissible if they are pressing, but one is free to speak to him about spiritual matters at any time, for the road is long and the provisions scanty." This is where R. Pinhas settled. Under the influence of the Besht, R. Pinhas abandoned the way of self-mortification that he had followed from his youth. Whereas earlier Hasidim would keep away from the permissible for fear of any transgression, the Besht taught that one should not be fanatical in performing any *mitzvah* (command of God); for the *Yetzer Hara*, the Evil Urge, seeks to bring us to despondency by terrifying us over not fulfilling our obligations.

The Besht extended special honor to R. Pinhas, and he was likened by those intimate with him to the Besht himself. "In the years of my youth," the Besht once said to R. Pinhas, "I used to feel that when I lifted my hands worlds would tremble. But now I feel nothing." "I feel that when I raise my hands worlds do tremble," replied R. Pinhas. One of R. Pinhas's disciples claimed that he had seen more wonders from R. Pinhas than were reported of the Besht, and another observed that had the generation been worthy, R. Pinhas would have been Messiah. "R. Pinhas was tormented over the suffering of his people and the misery of exile," Heschel wrote. "Though convinced that it was in his power to hasten the Messiah and with him the redemption, he was determined not to 'force the end.' "[11]

Another zaddik from the Besht's circle to whom Heschel devoted an essay was Rabbi Nahman of Kosow. R. Nahman seems to have been a problematic figure, more of a foil to the Baal Shem than a complement, as R. Pinhas was. He traveled and taught people to pray. "Wherever R. Nahman has traveled," said the Besht, "people know what prayer is, and wherever R. Nahman has not traveled they do not know what prayer is." To R. Nahman it was crucial that prayers be said aloud; for "by means of the organs of physical speech, vessels are formed through which divine grace can flow to the physical world."

R. Nahman was particularly concerned with the Evil Urge. The Mussarists, the moralists of the day, held that good and evil are two separate kingdoms. In the school of the Besht, in contrast, good and evil were seen as standing opposite but also within one another. The Evil Impulse suggests ulterior motives for doing a good deed, thus confusing *mitzvah* and sin. More than all the wise men of past generations, the Hasidim who belonged to the school of the Besht were aware of the danger of self-interest tainting the wholehearted service of God, though they also recognized, in the words of R. Nahman, that with every assault of the Evil Impulse, some ultimate good emerges. R. Nahman saw the zaddik as struggling all his life with the Evil Impulse which entices him to sin. So great was R. Nahman's fear of falling into transgression that he longed for death as a saving refuge from the sin and pain of the world.[12] In this he stood in great contrast to the Besht himself:

> While the Besht faced the world with love, with joy, and with compassion, R. Nahman approached it with tension, bitterness, and revulsion. The Besht's demeanor was pleasantness. R. Nahman used to be harsh and authoritative with his disciples, as if he had come to pronounce judgment. The Besht was patient, sought to understand the way of each man, loved peace, and preached it; R. Nahman was short-tempered, waging a constant war for the conquest of men's hearts. . . .
>
> The Besht spoke gently and asked from the people only what they were able to accept, while R. Nahman was all aflame, raging and demanding that they stake their lives uncompromisingly. . . .

> The Baal Shem, who beheld the bright side of the world, was saddened at the humiliation of man and his despair, and taught the way of compassion.[13]

Heschel gives the final word to the Baal Shem. The moral teachers of the eighteenth century were extremely sensitive to problems relating to sexual desire, Heschel observes, introducing all manner of restrictions against this urge and regarding even a minor infraction as a horrendous sin that would delay redemption and bring calamity to the world. Because there was no final mastery over the sexual desire, their apprehension resulted in deep feelings of guilt, self-condemnation, and depression.

> The Besht taught that one should not measure life with too short a rod, that every experience offers man the opportunity to perform countless commandments, and that this should be his primary concern.[14]

THREE

A Passion for Truth

Heschel's reputation as one of the world's foremost Jewish religious thinkers began with his slim volume *The Earth Is the Lord's: The Inner Life of the Jew in East Europe* (1950), succeeded by *Man Is Not Alone: A Philosophy of Religion* (1950); *The Sabbath: Its Meaning for Modern Man* (1951); *Man's Quest for God: Studies in Prayer and Symbolism* (1954); *God in Search of Man: A Philosophy of Judaism* (1955); *Torah Min Shamayin* (in Hebrew, 1962–1971)—a three-volume work on approaches to revelation in the Talmud; *The Prophets* (1962); *Who Is Man?* (1965); *The Insecurity of Freedom: Essays on Human Existence* (1966); and *Israel: An Echo of Eternity* (1968). All the books written in English have been published in paperback, and most of them have been translated into a number of languages. Today Heschel is recognized the world over as one of the most distinguished Jewish thinkers of this century.

Much in my thirty years of personal friendship and dialogue with Abraham Heschel was clarified when I read his posthumous book *A Passion for Truth* and particularly its introduction, "Why I Had to Write This Book," which also served as the introduction for his much larger Yiddish book *Kotzker—A Struggle in Integrity*.[1] This introduction showed Heschel as living his whole life in the tension between the positive life affirmation of Israel ben

Eliezer (1700–60), the Baal Shem Tov, who was the founder of Hasidism, and a zaddik, or Hasidic rebbe, of the sixth generation of zaddikim, Rabbi Menahem Mendel of Kotzk (1787–1859). Heschel's childhood was spent in the atmosphere of Mezbizh, which preserved the memory not only of its last great rebbe, his namesake, the Apter rav, but also of the Baal Shem. The parables of the Baal Shem which Heschel thus learned made the Besht a "model too sublime to follow, yet too overwhelming to ignore"; whereas the Kotzker rebbe, about whom he learned in his ninth year, haunted and often stunted him, urging him to confront perplexities which he might otherwise have passed unnoticed. Thus his soul was at home with the Baal Shem but driven by Kotzker, torn between the joy of the one and the anxiety of the other.

No one understands Heschel who imagines his writings to be a mere outpouring of devotional piety. If his heart was in Mezbizh, his mind was in Kotzk. If he kept the link with the centuries of Jewish faith through the "mines of Meaning" inherited from the Baal Shem, he also kept the link with the modern world through the "immense mountains of absurdity" placed in his way by the model of Kotzk. "The one taught me song, the other— silence." If the former imparted to him compassion and mercy and made his dark hours luminous, the latter eased wretchedness and desolation by forewarnings and premonitions of Auschwitz (Elie Wiesel points out in *Souls on Fire* that the Kotzker rebbe went into his twenty years of self-enforced seclusion just one hundred years before the outbreak of the Second World War). "The Baal Shem dwelled in my life like a lamp, while the Kotzker struck like lightning." The Kotzker debunked cherished attitudes and warned of the peril of forfeiting authenticity, even while the Baal Shem helped Heschel refine his sense of immediate mystery and gave him the gift of elasticity in adapting to contradictory conditions.

> The Baal Shem gave me wings, the Kotzker encircled me with chains. I never had the courage to break the chains, and entered into joys with my shortcomings in mind. I owe intox-

ication to the Baal Shem, to the Kotzker the blessings of humiliation.[2]

These contrasts are continued in the body of *A Passion for Truth* itself, and as such they establish the link between one of the most remarkable religious lives of this century and the philosophy of religion which that life produced. The Baal Shem emphasized love, joy, and compassion for this world, all of which Heschel shared, but the Kotzker demanded constant tension, which Heschel also shared. "The passionate indignation of the Prophets came back to life in the Kotzker." In Abraham Heschel the Baal Shem's realization that "the world is full of enormous lights and mysteries which man shuts from himself with one small hand" led directly to an equally passionate prophetic indignation based not upon the Kotzker's harshness but upon sympathy with God's own indignation at the treatment of the wretched and the poor!

At the beginning of my book *The Hidden Human Image*, I tell of the Hasidim who once told stories of the Baal Shem and lamented, "Alas, where could we find such a man today?" Exclaimed their rebbe, "Fools, he is present in every generation, only then he was manifest, now he is hidden." This tale points, I suggest, to "the unmanifest, hidden, imageless yet present, authentic man of today." It is exactly in this spirit that Heschel wrote *A Passion for Truth* and celebrated in it, at first subtly then ever more powerfully, the Kotzker's insistence *and his own* that Truth lies buried, stifled in the grave, yet still remains alive.

> Truth is homeless in our world. We suffocate for lack of honesty. As a result, man dies while yet alive. Who can speak of resurrection when life itself has become death? Coarse and swaggering, men make insolent speeches and engage in presumptuous dealings. But they are dead, while Truth, though buried in the grave, is alive.

Heschel did not share in the Kotzker's enmity to this-worldliness. The distinction between the righteous and the wicked is that "the wicked are trapped by material things that bring them pleasure," whereas "the righteous are enhanced by the mystery of the Divine inherent in things. Their wonder sustains their lives." This wonder became for Heschel the root of all knowledge and of all meaningful living. In this he remained the disciple of the Baal Shem, who emphasized God's nearness and saw his distance as a game that a father plays with his child. Mendel was profoundly opposed to the Baal Shem's conception of the world infused with the Divine; for, like the prophet, he saw the heart as deceitful above all things and desperately corrupt (Jeremiah 17:9). God dwells in the world, said Mendel, only where man lets Him in. In Heschel wonder and prophetic indignation, the apprehension of the divine in everything and the lamentation at how man shuts out the divine by his insensitiveness, were two sides of the same coin.

For Heschel, as for the Kotzker and his own master the Holy Jew, Truth was not a doctrine or a metaphysic but integrity of personal existence. What the Baal Shem and the Kotzker treated as an either/or, Heschel somehow combined: for the former love and compassion were higher than truth; for the latter a man's love and goodness were shame if he himself was false. Heschel demanded compassion and truth together. Both have for him a single source: the awareness of the ineffable. Yet the tension remains—in *A Passion for Truth* and in Heschel himself.

In the section of the book in which he compares and contrasts the Kotzker rebbe with his near-contemporary, the great Danish theologian Søren Kierkegaard, Heschel quotes a passage from the latter's journals in which he confessed that the key to his own being is that he is destined to be one of those two or three persons in every generation who discover with terrible anguish something by which the rest profit. This is a confession Heschel might have made himself. And it is one he claims, too, for the Kotzker, who "came closer to the meaning of religious expectation than many other thinkers who veiled the inner condition of man and the urgency for his total transformation by focusing on compliance and obedience."

Heschel ends with the astounding, and to me almost unbelievable, conclusion that despite the awe the Kotzker's thoughts
evoke, "he cannot serve as a model. For it is surely not the will
of God that man lead a tortured life." It is true that Heschel
followed the Baal Shem in emphasizing joy, but that joy was in
no way incompatible for him with the terrible anguish of being
one of the very few to be embarrassed by the man of his day! I
would not, indeed, say of Heschel what he said of Kierkegaard
and the Kotzker, namely, that both may have been afflicted with
mental illness and that some of their thinking may have been
conditioned by it. Yet Heschel's embarrassment at the low state
to which man has fallen in our day enabled him equally with
them "to see through the falsehood of society and to come upon
the burial place where Truth is entombed."

The personal illness of the nineteenth century has been succeeded by the massive social illness of the twentieth, and it is for
this reason that Heschel can recognize, as few others, the special
relevance of both Kierkegaard and the Kotzker "today in expos-
ing dishonesty as the disease underlying the political and social
life of the modern world," a retrospective judgment illuminated
by the Nazi Holocaust and the dreaded nuclear age! Otherwise,
how could we explain the pathos with which Heschel recounts
the withdrawal of the Kotzker rebbe during the last twenty years
of his life:

> His voice remained enveloped in darkness, like a wind howl-
> ing in the night. Yet some people will feel smitten some day,
> for those who ran away did not let him finish what he had to
> say . . . the Kotzker did not fail. He may have thought he had
> little impact, but the struggle he waged goes on; his words
> once again act as a battle cry.

It is in the *contrasts* that Heschel makes between Kierkegaard
and the Kotzker that we can see how closely Heschel identifies
himself with the latter. The Kotzker's "agony reached a limit in
dismay, not in despair. He was baffled, not shattered. His misery
defied explanation, yet it was not beyond hope or cure." No more

exact description could be made of Heschel himself. The Kotzker stressed contrast and opposition as well as analogy and cooperation between God and man. "He insisted upon the importance of both human enterprise and divine assistance, human initiative and divine grace." This biblically Jewish emphasis upon the primordial dialogue between God and man issues, in the Kotzker and in Heschel, into Job's protest against God's injustice, "the awareness that God was ultimately responsible for the hideousness of human mendacity." What concerned the Kotzker was the paradox of divine responsibility, *the myth of the buried Truth*, rather than that of fallen man, as with Kierkegaard. In the midst of this Jobian anguish Heschel inserts his own witness to the "mysterious waiting which every human being senses at moments: something is being asked of me." This, too, is a fundamentally dialogical witness: "Meaning is found in understanding the demand and in responding to it." Levi Yitzhak of Berditchev does not pray that God show him the secret of His divine ways but that He show him ever more clearly what this event which is happening to him demands of him, "what you Lord of the world are asking me by way of it."

It is not surprising, in the light of all this, that Heschel devotes a whole section of *A Passion for Truth* to "The Kotzker and Job" and that he adds in a footnote on the title page of that section: "This chapter is not an exposition of the Kotzker's view but, rather, an essay on a major problem of faith which is guided by his sayings." "The dialogical leads inevitably to Job's question to God," Martin Buber has written, and Heschel's dialogical philosophy of religion equally leads him to the protest against the injustice of the world. The Kotzker demanded that man confront the heavens and storm them, and Heschel adds his voice to this complaint:

> In the Jew of our time, distress at God's predicament may be a more powerful witness than tacit acceptance of evil as inevitable. The outcry of anguish certainly adds more to His glory than callousness or even flattery of the God of pathos.

In utter contrast to Kierkegaard, the Kotzker and Heschel insist that man should never capitulate, not even to the Lord. Both were repelled by submission and blind obedience. "A man must be a rebel in his very existence. . . . Even in defeat, continued courage was essential." Some forms of suffering must be accepted with love and borne in silence. To other agonies one must say no. In *The Hidden Human Image* and in this present book, I point to Elie Wiesel as a "Job of Auschwitz" who carries on in our day the trust and contending of the modern Job. Nothing sounds more exactly like Wiesel than this saying of the Kotzker, which Heschel also makes his own: "Three ways are open to a man who is in sorrow. He who stands on a normal rung weeps, he who stands higher is silent, but he who stands on the topmost rung converts his sorrow into song."

For all this, there is an affirmation in Heschel that goes beyond the Kotzker, beyond Elie Wiesel, and beyond even the meaning which I point to in *To Deny Our Nothingness* in my metaphor the "Dialogue with the Absurd." Heschel finds a meaning beyond absurdity and above reason:

> The complete failure of all consolation, the love of life despite its absurdity, holds out the certainty of a meaning that transcends our understanding. We encounter meaning beyond absurdity in living as a response to an expectation. Expectation of meaning is an a priori condition of our existence.

At this point the Baal Shem gains the upper hand over the Kotzker: "Our very existence exposes us to the challenge of wonder and radical amazement at the universe despite the absurdities we encounter. . . . We are not the final arbiter of meaning. What looks absurd within the limit of time may be luminous within the scope of eternity." *This* is the dominant note that is found in most of Heschel's philosophy of religion, and the Kotzker remains like an underground current to surface passionately at times in a passage on the prophets or on the paradox of "Who is man?"

But Heschel does not leave this contradiction, or paradox, totally unresolved. Rather, he recognizes, again in true dialogical fashion, that the growing awareness of history's tragic predicament gives birth to an intuition that man is co-responsible with God, that God needs man, that the problem of the justification of God cannot be separated from that of the justification of man. God does not need those who praise Him when in a state of euphoria but those who are in love with Him even when in distress. God needs man to believe in Him in spite of Him, to continue being a witness despite God's hiding Himself. God needs those who can turn a curse into a blessing, agony into a song, who can go through hell and continue to trust in God's goodness. Faith is the beginning of compassion for God. "It is when bursting with God's sighs that we are touched by the awareness that *beyond all absurdity* there is meaning, Truth, and love."

It is precisely this position that leads Heschel in his conclusion, "The Kotzker Today," to a position significantly at variance with the Kotzker: "The Divine and the human are not by nature conceived to be at odds or in constant tension. Man is capable of acting in accord with God; he is able to be His Partner in redemption, to imitate Him in acts of love and compassion." Yet the final emphasis of the book belongs to the Kotzker—the recognition that it took generations of lies to produce the Holocaust, that Truth is alive, dwelling somewhere, never weary, and all of mankind is needed to liberate it.

> In a world that contains so much sham, the Kotzker continues to stand before us as a soul aflame with passion for God, determined to let nothing stand between him and his Maker. In the nineteenth century he was a towering figure, in solitary misery as in grandeur. Yet his spirit, his accent are those of the post-Auschwitz era.

In the twentieth century Heschel, too, was a towering figure, in anguish and in joy, and his accents are equally those of the Bible, the Talmud, the Hasidim, the Job of Auschwitz, and the terrified inheritors of the nuclear age!

FOUR

The Awareness of the Ineffable

DEVOTIONAL PHILOSOPHY

There are few works on religion by modern American writers that can compare with Heschel's writings in depth of religious insight, intensity of concern, or beauty of style. His religious thinking is of a genuinely existential nature, deriving from and referring back to actual religious life—"that which is immediately given with the pious man." "In the realm of the spirit," writes Heschel, "only he who is a pioneer is able to be an heir." To be an heir is to make religious tradition alive for oneself and for those around one, and this demands a spiritual creativity that can only arise from the depths of an individual and genuine religious life. The rare quality of Heschel's own religious life—its dedicated intensity, poetic sensitivity, and serious concern—expressed itself again and again in passages in which artistic creativity, religious feeling, and mystical intuition are integrally united.

Heschel's style is evocative of devotional literature or religious poetry—the prose of Thomas Traherne, the poetry of Francis Thompson or of William Blake. "What is intelligible to our mind is but a thin surface of the profoundly undisclosed, a ripple of inveterate silence that remains immune to curiosity and inquisitiveness like distant foliage in the dusk." "The universe is a score of eternal music and we are the cry, we are the voice." "There is so much light in our cage, in our world, it is as if it were suspended amidst the stars. Apathy turns to splendor unawares." "Inspiration passes; having been inspired remains . . . like an island across the restlessness of time, to which we move over the wake of undying wonder." Men of faith "plant sacred thoughts in the uplands of time—the secret gardeners of the Lord in mankind's desolate hopes." In its startling imagery and paradoxical use of words, however, it resembles the styles of John Donne and T. S. Eliot. "Things are bereft of triteness." "They hear the stillness that crowds the world in spite of our noise." "We are rarely aware of the tangent of the beyond at the whirling wheel of experience." "Religion . . . comes to light . . . in moments of discerning the indestructibly sudden within the perishably constant." "Faith is a blush in the presence of God."

Heschel's style is of one piece, however, and it is unique. Although his metaphors and language have an energy of their own which sometimes bursts the bounds of the thought, his unusual precision is not the connotative precision of poetry alone. For all its beauty his style is never truly lyrical. It is always, even at its most startling, in the service of intuitive or discursive thought. As a result, nothing flows freely; everything is carried out with great spiritual tension and devotion and the most careful workmanship. "Wonder is not a state of esthetic enjoyment," Heschel appropriately remarks. "Endless wonder is endless tension, a situation in which we are shocked at the inadequacy of our awe."

HESCHEL AND THE MODERN PERSON

In *Man Is Not Alone*, writes one critic, Heschel "created a climate of religious ecstasy for those already committed." Actually, *Man Is Not Alone* has as much power to speak to the unconvinced as any book that American Jewish thought has produced. The atmosphere of the style does, to be sure, breathe faith rather than skepticism, wonder rather than rational doubt; but its faithfulness in the first instance is to the wonder itself. Thus it becomes a fitting instrument for conveying new meaning to the minds of the "unconvinced" who cannot grasp such new meaning through abstract concepts but only through full-bodied symbols in which the intellectual is integrated with the intuitive and the emotional. To the "convinced" the abstract concept is sometimes adequate, since he or she understands to what it refers, but to the unconvinced and uncommitted such shortcuts are not possible. Heschel appeals to those who "want to taste the whole wheat of the spirit before it is ground by the millstones of reason."

Heschel offers an insight into genuine religious experience that may aid the modern in attaining a real personal relation to his or her religion. Heschel's philosophy of religion does not begin with dogma or the law or with recapitulation of classic proofs of the existence of God, but with that sense of wonder and the ineffable that belongs, in greater or lesser measure, to every person's experience, even though "our normal consciousness is in a sense of stupor, in which our sensibility to the wholly real is reduced." Only then does it move toward that transcendent reality to which each finite thing alludes through its own unique and non-repeatable reality.

Liberals have sometimes been cut off from a serious encounter with Heschel's thought by the labels that have been attached to it—"poetic," "mystical," "irrational." Actually Heschel's thought is more rational than most philosophies of religion in its awareness of the special approach which religion demands for real understanding—the "situational thinking" and "depth theology" which endeavor to rediscover the questions to which religion is an answer. The antagonism to Heschel's thought that one occasionally encounters often seems to be motivated by an uncritical faith in the absoluteness of "reason" as the true basis of religion and an irrational fear of any attitude or way of thinking that might wish to move religion off this secure foundation. Scientists and philosophers do not claim that "logic and the laboratory bring us nearer to . . . the apprehension of ultimate truth," as an eminent Reform rabbi suggests in criticism of Heschel. The scientist regards reason as a tool, not as a metaphysic. He is content if it "works" to solve the problems that he has set or to suggest hypotheses which may lead to new problems. The modern scientist would be the first to agree with Heschel's statement that "what is intelligible to our minds is but a thin surface of the profoundly undisclosed."

"It is not," Heschel has remarked, "the Psalmist, Rabbi Jehudah Halevi . . . or Rabbi Nachman of Bratslav; it is Hegel, Freud, and Dewey who have become our guides in matters of Jewish prayer and God." Study, to be sure, has been honored in Judaism for millennia. Not study for its own sake, however, but study of the revelation of God in the Torah, which presupposes a prior meeting between God and man through which that revelation took place. When Moses received the word of God on Mount Sinai and the people responded, "We will do and we will hear," it was not reason that came into play but a genuine commitment. If we cannot make this same commitment today, let us be honest enough to say so. But let us not pretend to read back into the Jewish tradition a worship of reason which derives not from the Bible or the Talmud but from the intellectual climate of modern Western culture and from the Greek and Renaissance thought in which that culture is rooted.

For all its poetic quality, Heschel's style is always an instrument of his thought. The startling combinations of words bring new insights to light and force us beyond the hackneyed to something of that sense of wonder and awareness of the ineffable which is, to Heschel, the first major step in religious life and thought. His style also helps us retain this awareness; for, as he writes, "Even when our thinking about the ultimate question takes place on a discursive level, our memory must remain moored to our perceptions of the ineffable."

Heschel does not disparage knowledge and reason. He recognizes, as most philosophers do, that they are not ultimate, that they rest on intuitions, attitudes, and assumptions which cannot be subjected to proof. "The tree of knowledge grows on the soil of mystery." Wonder rather than doubt is the root of philosophy, for the sense of the ineffable alone leads us to meaning—meaning which can never be fully expressed but only indicated.

POLARITY

The logical structure of Heschel's writings is not easily perceptible, for his style is poetic and his philosophy mystical and intuitive. The difficulty is further increased by the fact that Heschel's thought is dialectical and even paradoxical in nature. Although his individual insights have value in themselves, none of them can be taken as expressing the whole of his philosophy. As a result, it is difficult to grasp the total import of his thought. "Polarity is an essential trait of all things," he writes. Jewish prayer, for example, is guided by the opposite principles of "order and outburst, regularity and spontaneity, uniformity and individuality, law and freedom, a duty and a prerogative, empathy and self-expression, insight and sensitivity, creed and faith, the word and that which is beyond words." If he states in one passage that our relationship to God "is not as an I to a Thou, but as a We to a Thou," he also refers us by a footnote to another passage in which he says, "It is true that a Jew never worships as an isolated individual but *as a part of the Community of Israel.* Yet it is within the heart of every individual that prayer takes place."

In explicit reference to this issue of polarity, Heschel said to me, "What underlies my thinking is something I proved and demonstrated extensively in the two Hebrew volumes of *Torah min Shamayim.*" In this impressive study of talmudic Judaism, Heschel deals with the two schools of interpretation of Rabbi Akiba and Rabbi Ishmael and shows that the contrast between them is one that carries through the whole of rabbinical Judaism. "Jewish thinking moves along two paths," Heschel said to me, "that of critical reasoning and that of imaginative intuition— Maimonides and Yehuda Halevi, the Baal Shem Tov and Moses

Mendelssohn. I am both," he asserted. "I live these two trends. I am neither a rationalist nor an irrationalist."

THE AWARENESS OF THE INEFFABLE

It is not through logic and reason that we come to know God, writes Heschel, but through the awareness of the ineffable. Insights into the ineffable are "the root of man's creative activities in art, thought and noble living." It is radical amazement at what is, the distinction between what may be uttered and what is unutterable, that most distinguishes man from the animals. We encounter the ineffable as a powerful presence outside us, a spiritual suggestiveness of reality which gives knowledge without certainty. The ineffable is the something more in all things which gives them transcendent significance. It is an allusiveness of all being which teaches us that "to be is to stand for." From the hiddenness of things we come to "the mystery of our own presence" and learn that the self also is not something we own but "something transcendent in disguise." The awareness of the ineffable is not an aesthetic experience in which one may rest. It is a question that God asks of us, and this question and our response is the beginning of religion. Thus through wonder we come to the awareness of God "in which the ineffable in us communes with the ineffable beyond us."

GOD NEEDS MAN

God, to Heschel, is One, and "one" means not just the only God, but unique, incomparable, indivisible. "One" means that God is alone truly real, uniting mercy and law, that He is within us and within all things. "God means: *Togetherness of all beings in holy otherness.*" But this does not mean all is God or that all is one. Heschel's philosophy is not a pantheism but a panentheism in which God and man work together to bring about the unification of God and the world. Evil is divergence and confusion, that which divides man from man and man from God, "while good is *convergence*, togetherness, *union*." God is striving to be one with the world, His transcendent essence is striving to become one with His immanent presence, His Shekinah. But there is here no radical dualism of good and evil, natural and supernatural. In responding to God we find Him near to us. The world is not cut off from God, for His presence lingers, and through this presence we may sanctify all physical life and raise it to the beyond. "It is His otherness, ineffable and immediate as the air we breathe and do not see, which enables us to sense His distant nearness."

We are embraced by God's inner life. We know only our relation with God, and we discover this relation when we perceive ourselves as perceived by Him and respond to His demand. God is characterized above all by His compassionate concern for every individual man and for every thing. The essence of religion, particularly the Jewish religion, according to Heschel, is reciprocal relationship in which God binds Himself as well as man, and man has rights as well as God. Not only does God need man, but it is His need of us and our need to be needed which gives meaning to our lives. Opening ourselves to God we share in His concern for all things. The existence of man is tridimensional: Our regard for ourselves is coupled with a regard for others because of the holy dimension which embraces both. We are not bound to self-interest alone; for our awareness of the ineffable shows the absurdity of making the ego an end. Neither the flesh nor self-regard is evil, but only absence of concern for others, and we attain concern for others through responding to the divine demand on us for mercy, justice, and love. "True love of man is clandestine love of God."

FAITH, PIETY, PRAYER, AND DEEDS

Faith, to Heschel, is keeping our responsiveness alive "in a passionate care for the marvel that is everywhere." This faith expresses itself in the dedicated intention which we bring to every moment and to every action, no matter how trivial it may seem. Faith is faithfulness to the encounter with God, the faithfulness of tradition handed down through generations and the faithfulness of the individual who inherits that tradition through his own spiritual pioneering. Creed and dogma are of value only if they claim not to formulate but to allude. When the human side of religion—its creeds, rituals, and institutions—"becomes the goal, injustice becomes a way." "A minimum of creed and a maximum of faith is the ideal synthesis." Man stands before God not for the duration of a ritual but for life, and God is concerned for the whole of our life, our joys and griefs, our physical, mental, and spiritual needs. Religious consciousness is characterized by the consciousness of *ultimate commitment* and the consciousness of *ultimate reciprocity*. This consciousness is, in Heschel's opinion, best embodied in Judaism, the essence of which is the partnership of man and God in unifying God and the world. Through this partnership all needs are spiritual opportunities. The self and passion, accordingly, are not to be denied or simply affirmed but turned to the service of God. Only if we ally our religious aspirations with our strongest passions will we have a force capable of freeing us from our exclusive concern with the ego. "Life passes on in proximity to the sacred, and it is this proximity that endows existence with ultimate significance. . . . Perhaps the essential message of Judaism is that in doing the finite we may perceive the infinite."

Piety, to Heschel, is "a perpetual inner attitude of the whole man," "the orientation of human inwardness toward the holy." It is not a subjective feeling but a relation to the divine beyond oneself—a relation of openness, responsiveness, mindfulness, of reciprocal giving, sacrifice for God, and allegiance to God's will, in short, "a life compatible with God's presence." The pious man is equally concerned for great and small because he senses the divine care that is invested in each thing, and yet for this same reason he will not give way to gloom, for he sees a gift of God in all that comes to him. The pious man desires to give back to God, and death to him is a privilege for he can make of it an "ultimate self-dedication to the divine" through which he reciprocates for God's gift of life. For this same reason the pious man is not concerned about personal immortality and personal salvation. The lasting is not the self but what the self stands for. "The greatest problem is not how to continue but how to exalt our existence . . . Eternity is not perpetual future but perpetual presence."

"Prayer," writes Heschel in *Man's Quest for God*, "is an invitation to God to intervene in our lives." It is an event in which man surpasses himself. "Prayer may not save us, but prayer makes us worth saving." God is not a means to our individual and social ends nor is prayer the road to enriching the self either in a material or spiritual sense. "God is of no importance unless He is of supreme importance." This means that God cannot be regarded as an extension of the self or of human civilization. Religion becomes a useful fiction at the point when it no longer sees man in relationship to God but to the symbol of his highest ideals. "In earlier times," writes Heschel, "symbolism was regarded as a form of *religious thinking*; in modern times religion is regarded as a form of *symbolic thinking*." Like the "religious behaviorism" which preserves the externals of religious tradition for their own sake, this "symbolic thinking" preserves the idea of God but empties it of any reality independent of its usefulness to society or to man's personal well-being.

In a liturgical week in Milwaukee three years before his death, Heschel spoke with the same power as he had in his classic essay "Prayer" in *Man's Quest for God*. "I plead for the primacy of prayer in our inner experience," he stated, for "a soul without prayer is a soul without a home." Only in prayer can the soul "gather up its scattered trivialized life," "divest itself of enforced pretensions and camouflage," "simplify complexities," and attain continuity, intimacy, authenticity, earnestness. Entering the home of prayer as suppliant and stranger, it emerges as witness and next of kin. Heschel prayed not for himself but because the Shekinah, the indwelling Glory of God, is in exile through *our* conspiracy to blur all signs of God's presence. "I pray because I refuse to despair, because extreme denials and defiance are refuted in the confrontation of my own presumption and the mystery all around me." "I pray," he concluded in a note remarkably similar to the Hasidic rebbe in Elie Wiesel's novel *Gates of the Forest*, "because I am unable to pray."

The power of prayer is also a judgment on liturgy without prayer which "instead of erecting a sanctuary of time in the realm of the soul . . . attracts masses of people to a sanctuary in the realm of space." This judgment becomes a thundering condemnation when liturgy lends itself to the bolstering of corrupt and evil social order: "Prayer is meaningless unless it is subversive, unless it seeks to overthrow and to ruin the pyramids of callousness, hatred, opportunism, falsehoods." It was not with a sense of hatred and bitterness but of personal shame and anguish for the horrible distortion of liturgy divorced from prayer that Heschel recalled the Roman Catholic Church adjoining the extermination camp in Auschwitz which offered communion to the officers of the camp, "to people who day after day drove thousands of people to be killed in the gas chambers."[1]

Although Heschel's emphasis on the necessity of supplementing faith and piety by the pattern of deeds prescribed in the Torah may seem somewhat surprising in the light of his equal emphasis on suspending all foregone conclusions and presuppositions, it is in full agreement with the Hasidic tradition of fulfilling the law with spiritual intention *(kavana)* rather than setting it aside. Through the law, says Heschel, our whole life can be set in the pattern of commitment, for through it man can remember God at all times and make every part of his life a part of his relationship with God. The only valid symbol, accordingly, is not the one that we possess—the symbol in *space*—but the one that we are— our life in *time*. To turn our deeds, our *mitzvoth*, into living prayer, to sanctify our daily life, enables us to forget the self and "to stand for the divine."

From my first meeting with Heschel in 1945 to my last almost thirty years later, it was clear that the Psalms stood at the center of his devotional life, but also that that life could never be divorced from the concern of the prophets. A striking illustration of this is the fact, which Heschel himself told me, that he decided to write a book on the Psalms after his doctoral dissertation on "Prophecy" but got carried away by his metaphysical studies of Ibn Gabirol and that he afterward returned to his book on the Psalms only to be interrupted this time by the work he did for Martin Buber in the Mittelstelle for Jewish education in Nazi Germany to compensate for the exclusion of Jewish pupils from German school. This latter work also meant a focusing on the Bible, but more in the sense of the prophets than the Psalms.

"To Be Is to Stand For"

TIME, SPACE, AND REALITY

In *The Sabbath* Heschel contrasts the Jewish view that space is contained in time with the more common view that time is contained in space. "It is the world of space which is rolling through the infinite expanse of time." The world of space is constantly perishing while time, through which it moves, is everlasting. The things of space, which ordinarily dominate our vision of the world, conceal the Creator through their deceptive appearance of independence and permanence. Time, on the other hand, reveals the Creator, for through it we intuit the process of creation. "It is the dimension of time wherein man meets God, wherein man becomes aware that every instant is an act of creation, a Beginning, opening up new roads for ultimate realizations. Time is the presence of God in the world of space." We are called upon to sanctify our life in time rather than the symbols of space; for the source of time is eternity. The secret of the world's coming into being is the presence of the giver in the given. "To the spiritual eye space is frozen time, and all things are petrified events."

In *Man's Quest for God* Heschel's emphasis again falls on the dynamic event rather than on the static object. The central religious event is the meeting with God and the actions and way of life that grow out of that meeting. "The uniqueness of the Bible is in disclosing the will of God in plain words, in telling us of the presence of God in history rather than in symbolic signs or mythic events." Judaism does not understand God's will as a set of abstract, universal principles which exist apart from history and which need only be applied by the individual to particular historical situations. God speaks to man in history, and His revelation in history gives us direct knowledge of His will.

This centrality of time informs all of Heschel's writings. In *God in Search of Man* Heschel contrasts the tendency to look on history as unbroken process with the biblical understanding of history as event, hence as a creative breakthrough of presentness, discontinuous and just for that reason ever in need of being remembered and renewed. In *The Prophets* Heschel shows the "divine pathos" as bound to the events of history and the prophets' "sympathy" with that pathos as a response to and judgment of the events of their time. In one of his last books, *Israel: An Echo of Eternity*, Heschel sets the coming to be of the State of Israel and its significance not only for Jews but for the world history within this context of the sacredness of events in time. "Genuine history occurs," he writes, "when the events of the present disclose the meaning of the past and offer an anticipation of the promise of the future." It is exactly as such an event of the present that Heschel sees the founding of the State of Israel in our time—"a vessel for God's action in the world," "the history of a responsibility, and the prehistory of an answer." This does not mean that God penetrates or dominates history, only that some events testify to God's presence and constitute the threads of His promise. History is not the dead past but the ever-renewed present—the burning bush in which each instant vanishes to open the way to the next one; yet history itself is not consumed. Heschel boldly names the people of Israel God's stake in human history—not that politics can properly be theologized but that here and there, in seeming disarray, are events which can be gathered to "comprehend the unity of seemingly disconnected chords." There can be no material sphere forever cut off from a spiritual one but only the endless task of endowing the material with the radiance of the spirit, sanctifying the common, and sensing the marvelousness of the everyday. Reality is not above time and the concrete, but in them. "The agony of our people particularly in this century was dreadfully concrete and redemption of our people and all peoples . . . must also be concrete." The real is not the heavenly and the eternal as opposed to the earthly and temporary but the deeper unity of both.[1]

CEREMONIES AND *MITZVOTH*

In his discussion of tradition and the law in *Man's Quest for God*, Heschel makes a general distinction between "ceremonies"—conventional folkways which are relevant to man—and *mitzvoth*— requirements of the Torah which are ways of God. Ceremonies, like symbols, express *what we think* while the *mitzvoth* express *what God wills*. This distinction seems of special importance as it applies to the motive for religious observance. What is done merely for the sake of keeping alive the tradition or continuing Jewish culture and civilization can hardly be called "religious" in any meaningful sense of the term. But can one apply this distinction with equal clarity to the content of the action itself, so that one can say in each particular case, This is a subjective folkway and that an objective command of God? "Survival of Israel means that we carry on our independent dialogue with the past," writes Heschel. "Our way of life must remain such as would be, to some degree, intelligible to Isaiah and Rabbi Yochanan ben Zakkai, to Maimonides and the Baal Shem." But how can we be sure that our relation to the past is a genuine dialogue—at once really receptive and really independent? By concentrating not on the "how much" of observance but on the how, says Heschel, by realizing that a little with *kavana* is better than much without.

This answer is at once satisfying and puzzling. In its insistence on holding on to both inwardness and the law, it is faithful to biblical and normative Judaism, even while reminding us of the polarity of Heschel's thought. But it does not appear to answer the question of how one distinguishes in particular cases between subjective folkway and objective command. If a little with *kavana* is better than much without, then the subjective-objective distinction that Heschel makes is not the crucial one. The real question becomes whether our way of life is not only part of a genuine dialogue with the past but part of a genuine dialogue with God, within which both subjective motive and objective law find their meaning.

SUBJECTIVITY AND OBJECTIVITY

In trying to avoid the dangers of subjectivism, "pan-psychology," and ego-centeredness, Heschel frequently goes to the opposite extreme of treating meaning and value as "objective" realities outside of man to which man merely responds. To make this point even clearer, he speaks of God as the subject and man as the object. "The structure which most characterizes Heschel's religious thought," writes Edward J. Kaplan, "is his *displacement of subjectivity* from man to God."[2] This "subject-object" terminology appears incompatible with Heschel's dominant theme of a genuinely reciprocal relationship between God and man. His assertion that the "I" is an "it" to God cannot be reconciled with his statement that God is compassionately concerned for the fate and the needs of every individual. If we are, in fact, embraced by the inner life of God, this does not mean that God thinks of us as we think of an object, but rather that God relates to us as persons in the truest sense of the term.

On the other hand, Heschel as often places the center of value in the relation between man and what is outside him as in the "objective" taken by itself. He speaks of values as independent realities "that reflect objective *requiredness*," only later to state that our conception of these values may change but not our sense of being committed to values. In the former statement the value seems to be *there* and we merely respond to it. But in the latter, value lies not in the objective demand taken by itself but in the relationship through which this demand is placed on us. The value *is*, in fact, the relation, as Heschel has shown by defining good as togetherness of man and God, man and man, and man and the world. He sets the human, or subjective, side of religion over against God's side; yet he also tells us that we do not know God in His essence but only what He demands of us, which means our relation with Him.

In *Man Is Not Alone* Heschel seeks at times to show the reality of piety by speaking of its spiritual content as universal and of piety itself as "an objective spiritual way of thinking and living." Yet he also stresses the individual and existential character of piety by saying in the same chapter, "Piety stands entirely within the subjective and originates in human initiative." The contradiction between these two statements cannot be resolved within the framework of the subjective-objective thinking on which Heschel here relies. It can only be resolved by transcending this thinking, as Heschel himself does in still a third statement that he makes in this chapter: "Piety is . . . not only a sense for the reality of the transcendent but for the taking of an adequate attitude toward it; not only a vision, a way to believe, but adjustment, the answer to a call, a mode of life." The reality of piety that is set forth in this last statement is the reality of dialogue— not the nonreciprocal relation of a subject to an object but the reciprocal relation of an "I" to a "Thou."

While Heschel's stress on the objectivity of the life of the spirit is in part a matter of counteremphasis, it also results in part from a tendency to remove all reality from the self to God. We are, says Heschel, a "possession" of God, and our value resides not in ourselves but in what we stand for. Our essence does not possess the right to say "I," for what we call self is a monstrous deceit—something transcendent in disguise. Will, freedom, life, and consciousness are imposed on us. "What is an 'I' to our minds is an 'It' to God." Heschel speaks of the presence of God as within man as well as beyond him. But unless man's self can in some real way be identified with this inner presence, the communion of "the ineffable within" with "the ineffable beyond" cannot be a real meeting of God and man. A genuinely reciprocal relationship demands that man regard himself neither as God's "possession" nor as an "object" of His thought, but as a really free and responsible person—a partner in dialogue.

It was Heschel's feeling that I take his subject-object dichotomy too seriously. "It is not the heart of the matter," he said to me. In his formative years as a student he was, to be sure, confronted by tendencies toward pan-psychologism, relativism, and reduction to the sociological which he felt it important to fight. But he did so not from the standpoint of the older subject-object epistemology but from that of phenomenology. "I use the phenomenological method to analyze my own consciousness and that of those I respect," he said to me. "I use my own consciousness as a standard." In this respect Heschel is close to Edmund Husserl, not that he ever falls into Husserl's danger of solipsism, but in that he tries to understand reality through analyzing the structures of consciousness.

In contrast to Husserl's "transcendental ego," on the other hand, Heschel stresses the exactly opposite perspective—knowing myself as known by the other rather than knowing the other as known by myself. "Without knowing that when I am before God I am nothing," Heschel said to me, "I have no position at all." It is in this sense that Heschel says, "I am an 'It' to God." "Only after Abraham realized he was dust and ashes could he argue with God." This is not the same as the Hasidic master Rabbi Bunam's saying that everyone must have two pockets to use as the occasion demands—in one of which is written, "For my sake the world was created," and in the other, "I am earth and ashes." For Heschel, as for Abraham, the "earth and ashes" definitely came first. "I do not really mean," Heschel explained to me, "that we have no right to say I. But we have the right to say I only when we understand that the I is transcendence in disguise." When we deal with the mystery of self-consciousness, we must recognize that instead of self-consciousness lending meaning to consciousness, as Husserl held, it is itself in need of transcendent meaning. "To say that the I is an 'It' to God does not mean that God regards us as an It. The I is an 'It' in the light of *our* awareness of God." Therefore, Heschel felt that my objection applied to what he said but not to what he *meant*. Heschel felt that the concept of the "subjectivity of God" enabled him to combine two important ideas—the absolute transcendence of God *and* the idea of the "divine pathos," God's sharing in the suffering and history of man.[3]

"TO BE IS TO STAND FOR"

The real essence of what Heschel is saying here, as elsewhere, is that "to be is to stand for." Taken positively, this is a statement which many are willing to accept as a faithful and creative expression of the relation of man to God. God is not a means to our ends, and our value does not reside in ourselves alone. We are the creatures of a Creator who creates the world anew at every moment. We live by His grace, and even our freedom is sustained in that grace. We discover God's presence through the ineffable that we encounter in all things, and in our response to the ineffable we know ourselves as known by God. We find the meaning of our lives not in ourselves, therefore, but in our relation to what transcends us. This also means, I hold, that our "being" is as real as our "standing for," that we are no mere instrument or tool of God. We become ourselves only through relation to what is more than ourselves. But it is only *through* our becoming ourselves, each of us in his or her own unique particularity and his or her own concrete situation, that our lives take on transcendent meaning.

The polarity of Heschel's thought, the mosaic of individual insights, and the tendency to stress now one point of view and now another—all these make the task of the responsible inter-preter and critic a difficult one. The reader of Heschel's works will avoid much misunderstanding if he will look in the first instance not for a system but for central insights and then move outward from these insights to the structure of Heschel's thought. This structure might better be compared to the concentric circles that are produced when a stone is thrown into a pool than to the precise architectonic that one finds in more systematic phi-losophies of religion, such as Franz Rosenzweig's *Star of Re-demption*. For this reason, it is essential that we suspend any *final* conclusions about Heschel's thought until we have seen not only the stone falling into the pool but the outermost concentric rings. We shall then be able to correct our grasp of the central insights through our understanding of Heschel's successive application of these insights to his philosophy of Judaism, his ethics, and his understanding of prophecy.

SIX

Philosophy of Judaism

In *God in Search of Man* Heschel formulates a method of "depth theology" which endeavors to rediscover the questions to which religion is an answer, to employ "situational thinking" rather than concepts, to challenge philosophy and not merely serve as an object for its examination. Speculation is a question *about* God; religion, a question *from* God. Hence the former is impersonal and general; the latter related to the person and what God asks of him. At stake in the problem of God is the problem of man—his spiritual meaning and relevance. The three trails that lead man to God, according to Heschel, are sensing God's presence in the world, in the Bible, and in sacred deeds. The three parts of Heschel's book correspond to these trails: God (in the world), Revelation (Torah), Response (*mitzvoth*, or commandments).

"Indifference to the sublime wonder of living is the root of sin," writes Heschel. Awe precedes faith and is the root of it, for it is "an intuition for the creaturely dignity of all things and their preciousness to God." Revelation, to Heschel, is human and divine at once. "Prophetic words are never detached from the concrete, historic situation." And the revelation is not of God's very self but of His relation to history. Revelation is a dialogue in which the prophet is an active partner, and the Bible is a record

58

of both revelation and response. "More decisive than the origin of the Bible in God is the presence of God in the Bible," which we cannot sense except by our response to it. This also means the life of the people, uniquely committed through the Covenant to becoming a holy people. Man imitates God through walking in His ways of mercy and righteousness, for the only image of God that we can make is our own life as an image of His will. "Life consists of endless opportunities to sanctify the profane, to redeem the power of God from the chain of potentialities."

Agreement of the heart with the spirit, not only the letter of the law, is itself a requirement of the law. Above all, the Torah asks for love—love of God and love of neighbor—and all observance is training in the art of love. Ritual and *mitzvoth* must be carried out with both body and soul: "Thoughts, feelings, ensconced in the inwardness of man, deeds performed in the absence of the soul are incomplete." Outward performance is but an aspect of the totality of a deed. "God asks for the heart," for *kavana*—that inner intention which redirects the whole person to God. But the way to *kavana* is through the deed. The meaning of the order of Jewish living can be comprehended only in participation and response. "All *mitzvoth* are means of evoking in us the awareness of living in the neighborhood of God, of living in the holy dimension." Here is the practical, if not the philosophical, link between Heschel's general philosophy of religion, which stresses the awareness of the ineffable, and his specific philosophy of Judaism.

The Christian dichotomy of faith and works has never been an important problem for Judaism, writes Heschel; for Judaism is concerned with right living in which deed and thought are bound into one. Religion or ethics comes to grief when it emphasizes motive alone and stresses purity of heart to the exclusion of the purpose and substance of the good action. "What man does in his concrete, physical existence is directly relevant to the divine."

Heschel frequently falls into a tendency to identify his categories and symbols of the ineffable with the ineffable itself. "The categories of religious thinking . . . are unique," he writes, and "on a level that is . . . immediate, ineffable, metasymbolic." But "categories of religious thinking" are already, as such, a step beyond the "awareness of something that can be neither conceptualized nor symbolized." "Religious thinking is in perpetual danger of giving primacy to concepts and dogmas and to forfeit the immediacy of insights," Heschel writes. Yet "insights" are not themselves immediate, even if they are derived more directly from the awareness of the ineffable than concepts. The fact that he is referring to a metasymbolic reality leads Heschel, like the modern Vedantists, to regard the images that he uses to point toward that reality as themselves beyond the symbolic. He overlooks the possibility that here, too, may exist that "profound disparity . . . between experience and expression" of which he is so acutely aware in connection with concepts.

This may account in part for what will seem to some readers to be an unprepared transition from the sense of the ineffable to an acceptance of the unique authority of the Bible and the sacredness of Jewish law in which Heschel identifies the voice of God with objective tradition. He does not show sufficient recognition of the tension that may arise in the relationship of the sense of the ineffable to the inherited form. "The claim of Israel must be recognized *before* attempting an interpretation," he writes, ignoring the fact that our acceptance of this claim already necessarily involves an interpretation. He tends, moreover, to divide revelation and observance into an objective form supplied by the tradition and a subjective spiritual content supplied by our inner response. God "gave us the text and we refine and complete it," Heschel writes. "The word is but a clue; the real burden of understanding is upon the mind and soul of the reader." The reasons he gives for accepting the traditional form tend to fall into this same objective-subjective dichotomy: sometimes it is because it is the will of God and sometimes because through the order of Jewish living one can sense the presence of God.

Finally, aside from repeated assertion, Heschel gives no real answer to the question he himself raises of how we know that what is subjectively true—the sense of the ineffable—is trans-subjectively real, that is, genuinely alludes to or derives from the transcendent. "The indication of what transcends all things is given to us with the same immediacy as the things themselves," he writes in a central statement in *Man Is Not Alone*. But in *God in Search of Man* he recognizes that the *assertion* that God is real transcends our preconceptual awareness of the ineffable. In his first attempt to answer this question he speaks of our belief in God's reality as an "ontological presupposition" that questions the self and goes behind self-consciousness. But this ontological presupposition seems to be only another name for the awareness of the ineffable itself. He later states that the "standard by which to test the veracity of religious insights" must be an idea, not an event, "a supreme idea in human thinking, a universal idea," and he offers as this standard the idea of "*oneness* or *love*." However, in the chapter "One God" in *Man Is Not Alone* to which he refers us, Heschel shows that what he really means is no mere conception. He rejects oneness as an abstract, universal idea in favor of an understanding of God as "*togetherness of all beings in holy otherness*." Such "togetherness" can perhaps be verified *in the life* of the person and his relations to others, but it cannot be abstracted into a universal standard or test by which *objectively* to verify one's religious insights. Both the moment of insight which is the power of religious truth, writes Heschel, and the oneness or love which is its content "may be conveyed in one word: *transcendence*." But this would seem to beg the question. How do we know that our insight *is* the product of the impact of transcendence, that its "love" is not a subjective emotion, its "oneness" not an abstract idea? The answer that Heschel offers to this central question he himself raises seems to be either an abstract universality that contradicts his emphasis on events and immediacy or a reassertion that carries no added knowledge value. This in no way invalidates his basic religious insight that transcendent meaning is immediately given to us in our meeting with existence. But it does raise a question as to how fully he has succeeded in converting this insight into a consistent philosophy of religion.

Although Heschel accepted my criticism as a "challenge to bring out more clearly" the link between his general philosophy of religion and his philosophy of Judaism, he held that he had provided such a link in the philosophy of time expounded in his book *The Sabbath*. Nor did he think it necessary to offer more than a link. "Once I say to you I preserve my sense of mystery more by putting on *tefillin* every day," he said to me, "I do not need to say, 'Why *tefillin*?'" There must be room for "historical contingencies." There is, indeed, no way to remain in the "universal" and ground *any* particular religious tradition or practice on it. That is, no particular religion can ever be justified in the general. This would be to reduce philosophy of religion to an affair of Platonic ideas above concrete space and time. Perhaps a similar objection applies to my question as to how we know that what is subjectively true is transsubjectively real. Heschel himself said that there is no answer to that question; for "you cannot epistemologically and logically demonstrate the transcendent by immanent means." The important link for Heschel is that the "ineffable beyond" is known *with the same immediacy* as the "ineffable within."

The great contribution of *God in Search of Man*, in my opinion, is that it presents the heart of Judaism in unusually broad, rich, and intensive scope. This book is of profound significance to Christianity, both as an interpretation of biblical categories and as a correction of common misconceptions of traditional Judaism as stressing a legalistic observance of externals. At the same time, it strikes a powerful blow against the "religious behaviorism" of many liberal and Reconstructionist Jews, which maintains the inherited customs and rituals of Judaism merely out of respect for tradition or a desire to perpetuate "Jewish civilization." Most important of all, it offers a positive interpretation and understanding of Judaism capable of evoking the highest devotion. "Bringing to light the lonely splendor of Jewish thinking, conveying the taste of eternity in our daily living is the greatest aid we can render to the man of our time who has fallen so low that he is not even capable of being ashamed of what has happened in his days."

The primary difficulty of the modern Jew, Heschel rightly observes, is not his inability to comprehend the *divine origin* of the law, but his inability to sense the presence of divine meaning in the fulfillment of the law. But the modern Jew's sense of the ineffable does not necessarily lead him to follow Heschel in accepting the prescriptions of the law as an objective order of divine will. The presence of divine meaning in observance of the law comes to us through our very commitment to and participation in that observance, writes Heschel. But if those who are not observant Jews do not *now* feel themselves commanded by God to perform the law, how can they perform it with integrity even on the strength of Heschel's assurance that they *shall* know this to be God's will for them through their observance?

"Heschel does not require the transition from the sense of the ineffable to Torah and *mitzvoth*," writes Professor Lou H. Silberman in reply to my criticism above. "Indeed, . . . these three ways are one; hence each must be made available, for all are ultimately required." To say this is to miss the central problem in Heschel's philosophy: the transition from his general philosophy of religion to his specific philosophy of Judaism. We can certainly agree with Professor Silberman, however, when he adds, "The real problem . . . is not that one is more available, but that each is all but unavailable to the contemporary Jew. Heschel's concern is to make man aware of the possibility of sensing the ineffable in the world, in Torah, in *mitzvoth*."[1]

Heschel sees clearly the dilemma of the modern Jew who "cannot accept the way of static obedience as a shortcut to the mystery of the divine will." Although he does not see this dilemma enough from within to build a bridge to Jewish law for those outside it, his thought is and will increasingly be one of the richest sources for confrontation both with modern religious thought and with the whole range of the Jewish tradition.

SEVEN

Symbolism, Pathos, and Prophecy

RELIGIOUS SYMBOLISM

There is a strong tendency to reduce religion to symbolism in which the "symbol" no longer corresponds to a transcendent reality or derives from a meeting with the divine but is merely an imaginative projection of man's own ideals and aspirations. "In modern times religion is regarded as *a form of symbolic thinking*." This reversal of roles "regards religion as *a fiction*, useful to society or to men's personal well-being . . . the symbol of his highest ideals." No pragmatic "will to believe" can make such "symbols" believable. No psychological or social need to act "as if" these symbols had some reality independent of man can enable us to worship them. "Symbols can be taken seriously," writes Heschel, "only if we are convinced of man's ability to create legitimate symbols, namely, of his ability to capture the invisible in the visible, the absolute in the relative."

The validity of these symbols will also depend, Heschel points out, upon our being in possession of criteria by means of which we can decide which symbols represent and which misrepresent the object we are interested in; which to accept and which to reject.

> In order to prove the validity of symbols in general and in order to judge the adequacy of particular symbols, we must be

in possession of a knowledge of the symbolized object that is independent of all symbols. To justify and to judge symbols we are in need of *non-symbolic* knowledge.[1]

Heschel's insistence that our indirect symbolic knowledge must be constantly referred back to the direct knowing of religious reality is of the utmost importance as a corrective to the tendencies to an idolatry that fixes the divine in the objective, visible symbol, to a relativism that accepts all symbols as equally valid, and to a subjectivism that reduces religion to "mere" symbolism. But is Heschel justified in treating the real symbol as a static, visible object that represents and gives indirect knowledge of an invisible divine object rather than as something that communicates the *relation* between man and the divine?

Heschel himself treats symbols in this active, relational way when he speaks of man as a symbol of God and interprets man's being created in the image of God as man's potentiality of becoming like God through imitating His mercy and love. "What is necessary is not *to have a symbol* but *to be a symbol*," writes Heschel. "In this spirit, all objects and all actions are not symbols in themselves but ways and means of enhancing the living symbolism of man." To Martin Buber, too, the highest manifestation of the symbol is a human life lived in relation to the Absolute. The prophets were symbols in that sense, for God does not merely speak through their mouths, as through the Greek oracle, but the *whole human being* is for Him a mouth.

PROPHECY AND DIVINE PATHOS

Although *The Prophets* is a continuation of Heschel's religious philosophy as it has developed in *Man Is Not Alone* and *God in Search of Man*, its original core was a slim German volume, *Die Prophetie*, Heschel's doctoral dissertation published in Poland in 1936. This earlier work contains the germ of some of Heschel's central ideas—the prophets' sympathy with the divine pathos, man knowing himself as known by God, the emphasis on the relationship between man and God as opposed to the classic Greek description of God's nature and attributes. This original core is expanded in *The Prophets* into a "theology of pathos" which is one of the most significant original contributions to biblical thought in our times.

Apart from the introductions and conclusions, *The Prophets* can be divided into three parts: Chapters 1 through 8, which take up separately Amos, Hosea, Isaiah, Jeremiah, and Habbakuk in their historical settings; Chapters 9 through 18, which develop the theology of pathos; and Chapters 19 through 27, which compare prophecy with other phenomena, such as ecstasy, poetic inspiration, and psychosis, and the prophet with other types, such as priest and king. The first third forms an illuminating background for the middle section, which is the real heart and major contribution of the book, while the last third of the book, aside from the comparison between prophecy and ecstasy, is of restricted interest, mostly being a reply to what other scholars in the field have thought.

The person who immerses himself in the prophets' words is "exposed to a ceaseless shattering of indifference, and one needs a skull of stone to remain callous to such blows." This is because the prophets' words are onslaughts that shatter false security rather than general ideas about which one may reflect. Another way of knowing opens up to us in communion with the prophets: our surrender to their impact leads to "moments in which the mind peels off, as it were, its non-knowing" and comprehends by being comprehended. The prophet does not deal, like modern man, with meaninglessness but with deafness to meaning, and the meaning which he speaks is not one of timeless ideas but of the divine understanding of a human situation. Heschel defines prophecy, in fact, as "exegesis of existence from a divine perspective," and he places this exegesis squarely before us as the answer to our own despair: "It is for us to decide whether freedom is self-assertion or response to a demand; whether the ultimate situation is conflict or concern."

The prophet discloses a *divine pathos*, not just a divine judgment. This means, to Heschel, that God is involved with man, bound through a personal relationship to Israel, and that the prophet is a partner and associate rather than a mouthpiece or an instrument of God. This approach leads Heschel to speak of God's inner life—the "dramatic tension in God" between His anger and His compassion—and of God's heart, which the prophet feels. Whereas Martin Buber sees Hosea's marriage to a prostitute as a living symbol of Israel that has betrayed God, Heschel sees it as the education of Hosea himself in the understanding of divine sensibility. The prophet has sympathy at the same time for both God and the people: "Speaking to the people, he is emotionally at one with God; in the presence of God . . . he is emotionally at one with the people." In his treatment of Isaiah, Heschel recognizes, as he does not in his earlier works, that there are times when God seems to deprive man of his sense of wonder and enhances his callousness.

In *The Prophets* Heschel's writing takes on a greater moral force than ever before. "The prophets were the first men in history to regard a nation's reliance upon force as evil," he writes. They discovered that "history is a nightmare" full of a corruption which we dare not accept as God's creation. "Others may be satisfied with improvement, the prophets insist upon redemption." God's demand for justice means not only outward duty but the love of the heart. Knowledge of God does not turn man away from man. It means sharing God's concern for justice, sympathy in action. Injustice is condemned not because the law is broken but because a person is hurt, a person whose anguish may reach the heart of God. The prophets do not discuss ideas or norms, like the moralists. They demand and insist that what ought to be shall be. "In the eyes of the prophets, justice . . . is charged with the omnipotence of God."

Heschel's theology of pathos is formed in conscious contrast to the Stoic doctrine of the divine *apatheia*, as well as to the classical theology which discusses the nature and attributes of God as He is in Himself:

> To the prophets, the attributes of God were drives, chal-
> lenges, commandments, rather than timeless notions detached
> from His Being. They did not offer an exposition of the nature
> of God, but rather an exposition of God's insight into man
> and His concern for man. They disclosed attitudes of God
> rather than ideas about God.[2]

Heschel denies that his concept of the divine pathos is anthropomorphic. Where was there ever a man, he asks, who possessed the patience and loving kindness which the prophets
ascribe to God? Man becomes holy because God is holy. The
prophetic passion is "theomorphic," formed in God's image. To
accept this image of God, we must discard the static idea of
divinity which is the double product of "the ontological notion
of stability and the psychological view of emotions as distur-
bances of the soul." Undergirding the theology of pathos, Heschel thus offers us a philosophy of pathos in which ontology is
"concerned with being as involved in all beings or as the source
of all beings." Such an ontology finds it "impossible to separate
being from action or movement" and thus postulates a dynamic
concept of divine Being. Like Martin Heidegger, Heschel recognizes that we cannot take being for granted, but unlike him
he stresses that being is not *all*. Biblical man begins not with
being but the surprise of being; he realizes the contingency of
being and cannot identify being, even as the source of all beings,
with ultimate reality. Neither can he consider the Being that calls
a reality into being as of the same nature as being itself. On the
contrary, it "transcends mysteriously all conceivable being." "Creation is a mystery; being an abstraction." This contrast between
Creation and "being" illuminates the unbiblical nature of that
Heideggerian ontology that has been taken over by such modern
theologians as Paul Tillich and Rudolf Bultmann.

Heschel has shown the impossibility of separating God's being
from His doing and has pointed to "anthropopathy" as "a genuine insight into God's relatedness to man, rather than a projection of human traits into divinity." Expressions of pathos may
help evoke our sense of God's realness and aliveness if we take

them as allusions rather than descriptions, understatements rather than adequate accounts. It is difficult, nonetheless, for us to understand pathos as a transitive, interpersonal reality rather than an internal, psychological one. This is particularly so because of the opposition Heschel sets up between the apathy of the Stoic God and the pathos of the biblical God. We cannot help but remove pathos into the inner life of God, as Heschel himself does at times. The dialogue between God and man is not within God, of course, and the communication of God's mercy or anger is an essential part of that dialogue. Yet when one talks of God's pathos and the prophet's sympathy with it, it is difficult not to attribute feelings to God in a way very like those of man, even if infinitely greater than his. Thus Heschel cannot altogether escape the problem of anthropomorphism. Nor did he wish to. "Anthropomorphic language may be preferable to abstract language," Heschel said to me, "for when you use abstract language you may have the illusion of adequacy."

The most trenchant application that Heschel makes of his theology of pathos is his treatment of the meaning and mystery of God's wrath. In our culture there are still a great many who, ignorant or not of the multitude of texts which contradict them, persist in setting an "Old Testament God of wrath" in opposition to a "New Testament God of love." Heschel, in contrast, points out that God's anger and His mercy are not opposites but correlatives. God's anger is *suspended* love, mercy withheld or concealed for the sake of love itself in order that compassion may resume. In contradistinction to Rudolph Otto, who sees God's love as "nothing but quenched wrath" and who sees wrath itself as arbitrary and irrational, Heschel insists that the normal and original pathos is love or mercy and that God's anger is a moral judgment preceded and followed by compassion.

> The anger of God must not be treated in isolation, but as an aspect of the divine pathos, as one of the modes of God's responsiveness to man. It is . . . conditioned by God's will; it is aroused by man's sins. It is an instrument rather than a force, transitive rather than spontaneous. It is a secondary emotion,

never the ruling passion, disclosing only a part of God's way
with man.

The Stoic sage is *homo apathetikos*; the prophet, to Heschel, is
homo sympathetikos. Sympathy has a dialogical structure, says Heschel. It is open to the presence of another person and to his
feeling. It is not an end in itself, like ecstasy, but leads to action.
"It is not a goal, but a sense of challenge, a commitment, a state
of tension, consternation, and dismay." In this it is related to
Heschel's "awareness of the ineffable," which becomes religion
only when it is experienced as a question to which our lives must
be the answer. The prophetic sympathy is not spontaneous but
is a response of God's pathos that comes from being attuned to
Him. This attunement is more than a feeling; it is a whole way
of being. "In contrast to ecstasy, with its momentary transports,
sympathy with God is a constant attitude." When the prophet
gives the message of God's anger, he is concerned not only about
the punishment that may descend on the people but about the
disturbance of God which only man's contrition, shame, and
repentance can assuage. Sympathy, used here for the first time
as a religious category, is not to be understood cosmologically
but anthropologically, as man's immediate relation to the divine
pathos. "It is as nonbiblical to separate emotion or passion from
spirit as it is to disparage emotion or passion. . . . Emotion is
inseparable from being filled with the spirit, which is above all
a state of being moved."

Heschel contrasts the union with God experienced in mystic
ecstasy with the prophet's dialogue with God. "The prophet is
responsive, not only receptive"; his personality is not dissolved
but intensely present and fervently involved; he is fully conscious
of the present and the past; he is not ravished by delight but
receives the revelation against his will; he does not have an experience but a task. Prophecy is meeting between God and man
without fusion. The dialogical structure which is never fully clear
when Heschel discusses divine pathos in itself becomes unmis-

takable here. The prophet's "response to what is disclosed to him turns revelation into dialogue"; the prophetic person stands over against the divine person in "a subject-subject relationship." "The prophet encounters real otherness, else there would be no mission; but also retains the fullness of his own person, else there would be no vocation." The prophet encounters not a timeless idea but an act of giving a word and a pathos in time, springing from a divine Presence who "becomes involved and engaged in the encounter with man." God does not reveal Himself, nor does the prophet speak of God as He is in Himself, as ultimate Being. "It is God in relation to humanity, in relation to the world, Who is the theme of his words." Prophecy is "anthropotropic" rather than "theotropic": it directs the prophet to man, not to God, and thus assures the divine concern for man's moral life in the here and now.

For all this emphasis on the dialogical relationship between God and man in prophecy, Heschel never attains decisive clarity on this subject. One reason for this is the ambiguity of the word "pathos," which cannot be altogether divorced from an inner state or feeling. Thus Heschel describes prophetic inspiration as an "event in the life of God" which "happens in God in relation to the prophet." Another reason for this unclarity is Heschel's desire to show man's relationship to God as the opposite of the ordinary subject-object relationship. In clear contradiction to his repeated description of the prophetic relationship as a "subject-subject" one, he speaks in his "Conclusions" of man as "being an object of the divine Subject." "For prophetic apprehension, God is never an 'it,' but is constantly given as a personal spirit, manifesting Himself as subject even in the act of thought addressed to Him." God is encountered "not as universal, general, pure Being, but always . . . in a specific pathos that comes with a demand in a concrete situation." All we know of God is His knowledge of and concern for us: we discover "ourselves as the objects of His thinking."

If Heschel were to use the language of I and Thou, he would

speak, like the Protestant theologian Emil Brunner, of a "Thou-I" relationship in which the initiative is entirely on the side of God. "In view of the gulf which yawns between divine infinitude and the limitations of the human situation," writes Heschel, "a divine-human understanding is ultimately contingent upon an awareness of a divine anticipation and expectation." In his concluding section, "The Dialectic of the Divine-Human Encounter," Heschel describes the "twofold mutual initiative" as one in which "the subject-man becomes object, and the object-God becomes subject." This problem is not merely one of inconsistent terminology. There seems to be a still unworked-through unclarity in the relation between Heschel's divine pathos, in which "the primary factor is our being seen and known by Him," and the dialogical structure of the prophetic relationship which he stresses in *God in Search of Man* and *The Prophets*.

The general effectiveness of *The Prophets* is somewhat weakened by the exhaustive comparison of prophecy with other types of religious experience. Nonetheless, there are many valuable statements about the problem of exegesis in this third section. Most telling is Heschel's critique of those who seek to fit the prophet into a ready-made scheme instead of subordinating themselves "to the object of investigation in order to come upon the unique and singular features which constitute and characterize the personality of the prophet." The mark of authenticity of the prophet, writes Heschel, is that God is not his experience, but he is "an experience of God." With this we are once again thrown back to the problem of knowledge involved in man's being the subject who knows that it is not he but God who is the subject and he is the object! In *God in Search of Man* Heschel says that what is important is not our certainty of the origin of the Bible in God but our awareness of the presence of God in the Bible. In *The Prophets*, however, he says that the validity and distinction of the prophet's message lies in its origin in God. The prophet's "certainty of being inspired by God," writes Heschel, is based on "the source of his experience" in God. Having an *experience* is indeed not central to the prophet, but neither can his "certainty" of the source be objectified into an independent knowledge apart from the relationship with God. Nor does Heschel wish to see this certainty objectified in this way. The unshakable conviction of Jeremiah and Amos that they speak for God might be better understood, in my opinion, in terms of God's call and the prophet's response than in terms of any certainty or even emotional oneness with God that might seem to put man on God's side of the divine-human meeting. Heschel himself said to me that he has pointed to the centrality of the prophet's certainty of being inspired by God not as a dogma but in the sense of Jeremiah's "Of a truth the Lord has sent me," hence as a consciousness of a call.

Existentialism of Dialogue and Social Action

WHO IS MAN?

Heschel's book *Who Is Man?* is a unique aid in understanding his thought. There are many who appreciate the poetic beauty of such works of Abraham Heschel's as *Man Is Not Alone* and *God in Search of Man* but who fail to grasp their profundity as philosophy. The very richness of their imagery makes the task of following the links in the argument a difficult one. Heschel's Stanford University lectures are to be recommended as the clearest and most cogent statement of his philosophy. If they cannot compare with the sustained beauty and profundity of the first hundred pages of *Man Is Not Alone*, they make it easier for the reader to relate his own thought to Heschel's philosophy.

By the title *Who Is Man?* (not *What Is Man?*) Heschel wishes to emphasize that man cannot be understood from the outside, as an object of impartial investigation, but only from within, as a person, as the fruit of self-understanding. Grammatically speaking, Heschel should ask "Who am I?"; yet we may tolerate a grammatical absurdity for the sake of the link that it makes possible between one's understanding of one's own uniqueness and one's understanding of man. A more felicitous way of pointing to this link, as I have suggested in *To Deny Our Nothingness*, is the "image of man." Heschel does, in fact, use the image of man in just this way:

> The decisions, norms, preferences affecting both action and motivation are not simply part of human nature; they are determined by the image of man we are committed to, by the ultimate context to which we seek to relate ourselves.[1]

We are not simply defined as human from without. We become human through making decisions, through discovering the "value involved in human being," through confronting the conflict between existence and expectation that makes our self a problem to ourselves.

HESCHEL AND THE EXISTENTIALISTS

Man has always been a problem to himself, the Book of Job and the Psalms amply testify. But in our age the terrifying seriousness of the human situation has come into focus in a way that would have been unthinkable before Auschwitz. Stripped of our assumptions and illusions, we cannot "think about the human situation without shame, anguish, and disgust." The note of embarrassment at being human which is so often present in Heschel's writings becomes most pronounced in *Who Is Man?* Like a latter-day Pascal, Heschel uncovers behind man's self-satisfaction a poor, needy, vulnerable creature, "always on the verge of misery." "Scratch his skin and you come upon bereavement, affliction, uncertainty, fear, and pain."

The skepticism of contemporary man is not about God but about man. "Today it is the humanity of man that is no longer self-evident." How can a human being achieve certainty of his humanity in the face of the massive defamation of man which has led and may lead again to physical extermination? If we explain man as a thing, we miss the mystery and surprise which constitute his existence as a person. Man "is a being who asks questions concerning himself," and his first question is how to turn his "human being" into "being human," how to become really human. It is not morality in the sense of some external moral act that is the problem but the self itself: our life itself is the task, problem, and challenge. We do not begin with an abstract moral ought but with the love of being alive and the claim that this love places on us. Our task is to respond to the call which addresses us as persons in order to become more than we are.

Like Albert Camus, Heschel sees man as both "solitary" and "solidary." We understand man through understanding our selves, but we do not rest in subjectivity. To be man means to be with other human beings. Human existence is coexistence, sharing, solidarity. "The dignity of human existence is in the power of reciprocity," and this reciprocity extends even to man's most personal concern, his search for meaning. Not only social living but the humanities are rooted in man's care for man. "The degree to which one is sensitive to other people's suffering, to other men's humanity, is the index of one's own humanity." This does not in the least imply that for Heschel the self is purely social. "Life comprises not only arable, productive land, but also mountains of dreams, an underground of sorrow, towers of yearning, which can hardly be utilized to the last for the good of society. . . ."

Heschel's affinity with such existentialists as Martin Heidegger and Paul Tillich makes all the more significant the point where he parts company with them. Unlike Tillich, Heschel does not see the main threat to man as the fear of nonbeing but the fear of *meaningless* being. Unlike Heidegger, he does not stop with the mystery of being but goes beyond it to the mystery of man. "Man is a fountain of immense meaning, not merely a drop in the ocean of being."

Heschel's divergence from such thinkers as Heidegger and Tillich does not mean that he is less existentialist than they. "Ideas, formulas, or doctrines are generalities, impersonal, timeless," writes Heschel, "and as such they remain incongruous with the essential mode of human existence which is concrete, personal, here and now." The infinite meaning to which all things allude is not an *object*, a self-subsistent, timeless idea or value—but a *presence*. To Heschel transcendence is not an article of faith but "what we come upon immediately when standing face to face with reality." An ultimate being that is not related to us and does not care about us can be of no concern to us. This transcendent care Heschel calls "pathos"—the concept that occupies the central place in *The Prophets*.

God's pathos must be met by our response. If man "were simply to 'surrender to being,' as Heidegger calls upon us to do, he would abdicate his power to decide and reduce his living to being." Living, to Heschel, means lending forms to sheer being. Heidegger and Tillich to the contrary, our central fear is not the fear of death but of life "branded with the unerasable shock at absurdity, cruelty, and callousness." The primary problem is how to shape our total existence as a pattern of meaning. "Right living is like a work of art, the product of a vision and of a wrestling with concrete situations."

There is a new note of absurdity in *Who Is Man?* which brings Heschel surprisingly close to Camus. The vocation of man, Heschel suggests, may be "to live in defiance of absurdity, notwithstanding futility and defeat; to attain faith in God even in spite of God." Nonetheless, in contrast to Camus, Heschel holds that the supreme philosophical question is not suicide but martyrdom: what is worth dying for? If Heschel follows Nietzsche in his image of man as a short, critical stage between the animal and the spiritual, he advances the Jewish *kiddush ha-shem*—the readiness to die for the sake of God—in explicit contrast to Nietzsche's *amor fati*, or acceptance of fate. To be ready to die for God's name also means to sanctify God's name in one's living. "We are constantly in the mills of death, but we are also the contemporaries of God." Heschel's ultimate emphasis is not upon absurdity or death but upon our built-in awareness "of being *called* upon . . . to live in a way which is compatible with the grandeur and mystery of living."

This does not mean that Heschel was less concerned with death than the other existentialists. But death to Heschel was an integral part of his existentialism of dialogue, of the partnership between God and man. In a series of reflections on death that Heschel delivered at an international congress on death in 1969, Heschel rejected the focus on the specifics of individual immortality in favor of trust in the relationship with God.

> The meaning of death is in return, regardless of whether it results in a continuation of individual consciousness or in merging into a greater whole.
> We are what we are by what we come from. We achieve what we do by what we hope for.
> Our ultimate hope has no specific content. Our hope is God. We trust that He will not desert those who trust in Him.
>
> It is the experience that those who trust in Him are not abandoned while being in the world that gives strength to the hope of not being abandoned after passing the threshold of death and leaving the world.
>
> Surviving after death, we hope, is surviving as a thought of God.
>
> The religious quest is a quest of the contemporaneity of God. Simultaneity with God is the only element of permanence in the world.
> In speaking of God we have faith and a sense of presence, but no image. In speaking of life after death we have hope and a sense of trust, but no image.[2]

At the same time Heschel insisted that "the love of life calls for resistance to death, resistance to the last, unconditionally." If the life after death is completion, life here and now is opportunity. "It is greater to struggle on earth than to be an angel in heaven." Life as a prelude "is infinitely rich in possibilities of either enhancing or frustrating God's patient, ongoing efforts to redeem the world." "Eternity is not perpetual future but perpetual presence." Hence Heschel's emphasis is not on the "hereafter" but on the "herenow." The deepest wisdom, to Heschel, is to know that we have to conquer in order to succumb, to acquire in order to give away, to triumph in order to be overwhelmed.

> This is the meaning of death: the ultimate self-dedication to the divine. Death so understood will not be distorted by the craving for immortality, for this act of giving away is reciprocity on man's part for God's gift of life. *For the pious man it is a privilege to die.*[3]

THE INSECURITY OF FREEDOM

It is no coincidence, as Franklin Sherman has pointed out, that the resumption of Heschel's work on the prophets and the publication of his 1962 book *The Prophets* "corresponded in time with his own emergence as a spokesman on social issues of the day."[4] If "situational thinking" and "depth theology," as Heschel defines them, are an endeavor to rediscover the questions to which religion is an answer, they must also include the authentication of one's truth in one's concrete existence. The most heartening aspect of Heschel's activity is that he did not confine it to an abstract mysticism, existentialism, or interpretation of Jewish thought but, again and again in the last years of his life, verified his truths by being true to them himself: in the march at Selma, Alabama; in picketing the Soviet legation because of the treatment of Soviet Jews; in co-chairing the national committee of Clergy and Laymen Against the War in Vietnam; in speaking and acting for Israel in the time of its danger; in social protest and concern about medicine, old age, race relations. His book *The Insecurity of Freedom* stands as a great living witness to all these concerns.

One of the most frequently repeated motifs of Heschel's social witness was his condemnation of the central emphasis in American culture on success and power. "More people die of success than of cancer," Heschel dared to tell the members of the American Medical Association. And to a White House Conference on Children and Youth he declared that we are threatened by degradation through power: knowledge as success, values justified solely in terms of expediency, an instrumentalization of the world that leads to the instrumentalization of man. "The evil, the false-hood, the vulgarity of our way of living cry to high heaven," writes Heschel in *The Insecurity of Freedom*. Our age, says Heschel, is the "age of suspicion," and its Golden Rule is "Suspect thy neighbor as thyself." The corruption of values, moreover, means a corruption of the word: "Words have become pretexts in the technique of evading the necessity of honest and genuine expres-sion."

Our culture cannot be redeemed of its vulgarity through teach-ing moral *values*, but only through character education, *cultivation of total sensitivity*. The antecedents to moral commitment are acts and moments within the depth. "You can affect a person only if you reach his inner life, the level where every human being is insecure and feels his incompleteness, the level of awareness that lies beyond articulation." One discovers his soul not through turning inward, however, but through transcending one's self in response to the call of ends that surpass one's interest and needs. This sort of character education is not a mere means to the end of training or success. It is an intrinsic value. In a paper presented at a White House Conference on the Aging, Heschel proposed "senior universities" where the purpose of learning is not a career but learning itself.

Heschel's social witness expressed itself positively in his co-chairmanship of Clergy and Laymen Against the War in Vietnam, of which he was the founder. He was a tireless fighter against the United States' engagement in Indochina. In Heschel's paper to the White House Conference on Children and Youth, his witness for social justice also rang out loud and clear: the protest against this country's squandering of material resources on lux-uries when more than a billion people go to bed hungry every night, his protest against our treatment of the black people of America. In the opening address at the National Conference on Religion and Race in Chicago in 1963, Heschel struck out with all possible force against racism—that unmitigated evil which is man's gravest threat, combining, as it does, the maximum of cruelty and the minimum of thought. "What begins as the inequality of some inevitably ends as inequality of all." Even the wholeness of the religious man is eaten away by the cancer of racism: "Prayer and prejudice cannot dwell in the same heart. Worship without compassion is . . . an abomination." Heschel's constant motif of embarrassment before God now becomes embarrassment before the black man, on whom his very presence inflicts insult. "I, the white man, have become in the eyes of others a symbol of arrogance and pretension, giving offense to other human beings, hurting their pride, even without intending it."

Unlike the New Leftists, Heschel could not combine concern for the plight of the black man with indifference to the fate of the Jews in Soviet Russia. "Discrimination against the political rights of the Negro in America and discrimination against the religious and cultural rights of the Jews in the Soviet Union are indivisible." What is today a widespread movement of protest Heschel began as an almost single-handed fight. It is he who made his younger friend, the novelist Elie Wiesel, aware of the situation of the Russian Jews and prompted him to go to Moscow and to write *The Jews of Silence*. Like Elie Wiesel, Heschel speaks of the moral trauma that haunts the Jews in free countries for failing to do their utmost to save the Jews under Hitler and the nightmare possibility of a new tragic dereliction of duty. Spiritual slavery makes impossible personal wholeness and intellectual creativity for the Russian Jew. What Heschel pleads for is not special privilege but equality—the rights, guaranteed the Russian Jews by the Soviet constitution but systematically refused them in practice, to teach, to hear, to read literature, to communicate with those with a common spiritual heritage. As with the black man in America, "Discrimination against the religious and cultural rights of the Jews in the Soviet Union is a disease that sooner or later will affect the human situation everywhere." It is we, says Heschel, who must speak for the "Jews of silence" for they have no voice. "We must cry in public because they can only cry in secrecy."

We cannot fail to mention the major role Heschel played in the work of Cardinal Bea at the Second Vatican Council to secure a statement on the Jews that would help to end two millennia of built-in Christian anti-Semitism, including a secret personal visit that Heschel paid at that time to the Pope at the latter's request. Later the Pope himself played a significant part in the publication and distribution of Heschel's works in Italy. The letter that Heschel wrote at the time that he saw the Second Vatican Council as falling back into Christian triumphalism bears witness to his passionate concern (as do the calls that Heschel made at the time to Douglas Steere, representative of the Society of Friends at the Second Vatican Council, about which Steere told me):

[Abraham Heschel's mimeographed statement
to the Second Vatican Council]

September 3, 1964

Chapter Four of the Schema on Ecumenism printed and distributed in November, 1963, to the Council Fathers, dealing with the "Attitudes of the Catholics . . . toward the Jews," made special headlines around the world. Except for a few words, troublesome to the Jewish conscience, it represented a momentous declaration and was hailed as an event of historic importance.

Subsequently, this Chapter has been rewritten and the version now distributed to the Council Fathers as publicly reported is not only ineffective, but also profoundly injurious.

The omissions, attenuations and additions are so serious that, if adopted, the new document will be interpreted as a solemn repudiation of the desire which, to quote a distinguished American Archbishop, intended "to right the wrongs of a thousand years."

The new document proclaims that "the Church expects in

unshakable faith and with ardent desire . . . the union of the Jewish people with the Church."

Since this present draft document calls for "reciprocal understanding and appreciation, to be attained by theological study and fraternal discussion," between Jews and Catholics, it must be stated that *spiritual fratricide* is hardly a means for the attainment of "fraternal discussion" or "reciprocal understanding."

A message that regards the Jew as a candidate for conversion and proclaims that the destiny of Judaism is to disappear will be abhorred by the Jews all over the world and is bound to foster reciprocal distrust as well as bitterness and resentment.

Throughout the centuries our people have paid such a high price in suffering and martyrdom for preserving the Covenant and the legacy of holiness, faith and devotion to the sacred Jewish tradition. To this day we labor devotedly to educate our children in the ways of the Torah.

As I have repeatedly stated to leading personalities of the Vatican, I am ready to go to Auschwitz any time, if faced with the alternative of conversion or death.

Jews throughout the world will be dismayed by a call from the Vatican to abandon their faith in a generation which witnessed the massacre of six million Jews and the destruction of thousands of synagogues on a continent where the dominant religion was not Islam, Buddhism or Shintoism.

It is noteworthy that the Vatican document on Mohammedans makes no reference to the expectation of the Church for their conversion to the Christian faith. Is one to deduce from that that Islam offers a more acceptable way to salvation than Judaism?

Our world, which is full of cynicism, frustration and despair, received a flash of inspiration in the ecumenical work of Pope John XXIII. For a few years all men of good will marvelled at the spiritual magnificence which he disclosed, and were touched by his reverence for the humanity of man. At a time of decay of conscience, he tried to revive it and to teach how to respect it. Mutual reverence between Christians and Jews began to fill the hearts. We ardently pray that this great blessing may not vanish.

It is our profound hope that during the course of the forthcoming third session of the Vatican Council, the overwhelming majority of the Council Fathers, who have courageously expressed their desire to eradicate sources of tension between Catholics and Jews, will have an opportunity to vote on a statement which will express this sacred aspiration.

Abraham Joshua Heschel[5]

In a letter to *The New York Times* before the presidential election of 1972, Heschel warned of the corruption that had penetrated to the highest places in our government, and he asked how Amos, Isaiah, and Jeremiah would have responded to our situation. Heschel tried unsuccessfully at that time to convince his co-leaders in Clergy and Laymen Against the War in Vietnam to call for an independent body that might act as the "conscience" for the government. In the light of the events of the months following Heschel's death in December 1972, culminating in Nixon's resignation, these actions appear strikingly prophetic in the popular sense of the term. They were *not* the passing foibles of a great spiritual leader who had fallen victim to the "social fads of the sixties," as Heschel's former student and disciple Professor Jacob Neusner suggested in a memorial issue of the Catholic journal *America* devoted to Heschel. On the contrary, they were the unmistakable carrying over of the indignation and compassion of the biblical prophets to the concrete social existence of our time.

ISRAEL AND THE DIASPORA

It would be surprising indeed if the social-religious witness of *The Insecurity of Freedom* did not extend to the State of Israel and its place in the life and mission of the Jewish people. The two essays there that are specifically concerned with Israel and the Diaspora are significantly amplified by Heschel's book *Israel: An Echo of Eternity*, written after the Six-Day War. In this latter book, Heschel sees the ultimate meaning of the State of Israel in terms of the prophets' vision of all men being redeemed, justice prevailing over power, human understanding being penetrated by the awareness of God. For this reason, although he upholds Israel's right to self-defense against the threat of extermination by its Arab neighbors, Heschel asserts that our aim must be to help bring peace and reconciliation. "Violence postpones problems, it does not solve them." This aim he in no way sees as incompatible with the existence of the State of Israel through which alone the redemption of the Jewish people can be as concrete as the agony that it has suffered in this century. "Our immediate concern must be with justice and compassion in life here and now, with human dignity, welfare, and security."

CONCLUSION

I have dealt with Heschel as a philosopher rather than as a theologian because he does have an original philosophy which, however unsystematic, includes all the aspects of a comprehensive philosophy: an ontology, a theory of knowledge, a theory of values, an ethics, a metaphysics, or a philosophy of religion, and applications in many concrete fields. Heschel is mainly interested in the philosophy of religion and theology, to be sure, but he recognizes that "the primary issue of theology is *pre-theological*; it is the total situation of man and his attitudes toward life and the world." We may speak of Heschel as an existentialist on the basis of his contrast between the evocative, unique, insightful, responsive character of "depth theology" and the universal, abstract, declarative, creedal, and authoritarian nature of theology. Not that Heschel accepts the one and rejects the other. He insists here, as elsewhere, on the necessity of keeping alive the polarity of doctrine and insight, dogma and faith, ritual and response, institution and individual. "We sense the ineffable in one realm; we name and exploit reality in another. To maintain the right balance of mystery and meaning, of stillness and utterance, of reverence and action seems to be the goal of religious existence."

But what is the right balance? Heschel has no hesitation in naming the response from within the person the heart of religious existence. Yet he assumes the only escape from the "catacomb of subjectivism," the only way in which the insights of depth theology can lead from man to man and generation to generation, is their crystallization in the doctrines and principles of theology. Heschel recognizes, to be sure, that "without the spontaneity of the person, response and inner identification, without the sympathy of understanding, the body of tradition crumbles between the fingers." But he does not adequately recognize the gap that remains between the two even when one holds on simultaneously to both the subjective and the objective, nor the possibility of another form of handing down, less explicit and systematic but more integral in its relation to the depth theology which gave rise to it.

Actually Heschel's writing itself points to this other possibility. He has not abstracted his insights into clear-cut formulae but has retained in his very style the traces of the reality to which he points. Poetry and philosophy, wonder and thought conjoined produce a philosophy which does not *define* but *points*, a theology which does not describe but evokes. At the heart of this philosophy lies a trust which informs human deeds rather than replaces them, which gives courage to live in insecurity rather than offers any sure groundwork of faith. "Trust in God *is* God," is God's presence, says Heschel in *Israel: An Echo of Eternity*. "The person in whom I trust is present in my trust. . . . Waiting for Him becomes waiting with Him, sharing in the coming."

This motif of trust, which Heschel himself does not single out as such, runs like a connecting link through all his philosophy and through the "ways of deeds" to which he points. In place of the dichotomy of outer deeds and inner intention, Heschel stresses trust: "We are not obliged to be perfect once for all, but only to rise again and again." "Judaism insists upon the deed and hopes for the intention," writes Heschel in *The Insecurity of Freedom*. More than that, the act, life itself, educates the will. One need not wait for the good motive before doing the good. It comes into being in the very act of doing. But this also means, to Heschel as to the prophets, that it is an act of evil to accept the state of evil as either inevitable or final, whether because of a view of human nature or of the world. The reality of God's love is greater than "the law of love." Where the latter places upon us an impossible demand, God accepts us in all our frailty and weakness. This means an active partnership of man and God, rather than despairing of sinful man and passively relying on the grace of God. "The future of the human species depends upon our degree of reverence for the individual man. And the strength and validity of that reverence depend upon our faith in God's concern for man."

This trust is in no way incompatible with that "theology of dismay" which is what Heschel says is all we can honestly preach. "Our task is not to satisfy complacency but to shatter it." Similarly, the true motivation of prayer is not the sense of being at home in the universe but its opposite: the sense of *not* being at home in the universe. Despite his insistence that we do not approach God as "I," that only God is "I" and we are "It," Heschel's understanding of prayer is, in his own special sense, that of dialogue: "The purpose of prayer is to be brought to God's attention: to be listened to, to be understood by Him." This means that the gate to grace lies in our making our existence *worthy* of being known to God. For God to be present we have to be God's witnesses, and this means, even in prayer, that tension of trust and contending that was present in Abraham, Jacob, and Job, in the Baal Shem Tov and Levi Yitzhak of Berditchev, in Martin Buber, Abraham Joshua Heschel, and Elie Wiesel. We pray the way we live:

> Prayer depends not only upon us but also upon the will and grace of God. Sometimes we stand before a wall. It is very high. We cannot scale it. It is hard to break through it, but even knocking our heads against the wall is full of meaning. Ultimately, there is only one way of gaining certainty of the

realness of any reality, and that is by knocking our heads against the wall. Then we discover there is something real outside the mind.[6]

In a three-way correspondence between Martin Buber, the great Protestant theologian Reinhold Niebuhr, and myself, Buber used this same image to describe his approach to social problems. "I cannot know how much justice is possible in a given situation," Buber wrote, "unless I go on until my head hits the wall and hurts." For Abraham Heschel, as for his and my friend Martin Buber, there is no essential difference between the life of prayer and the life of action. "A religious man," writes Heschel, "is a person who holds God and man in one thought at one time, at all times, who suffers in himself harms done to others, whose greatest passion is compassion, whose greatest strength is love and defiance of despair." Heschel himself was that religious man.

PART TWO

Elie Wiesel:
The Job of Auschwitz

The Holocaust as Touchstone
of Reality

In my book *Touchstones of Reality* I speak of "touchstones of reality" as momentous events that imprint our attitudes and life stances in such a way that we bring them with us into all our future encounters. A touchstone cannot be passively received. It must be won by contending, by wrestling until dawn and not letting the nameless messenger go until he has blessed us by giving us a new name. Walking on our path, we encounter something that lights up for us—an event, a teaching, a breathless view of nature, an hour of unusual calm. Touchstones of reality are like insights, except that they are closer to events. To touch is to go through and beyond subjective experiencing. The very act of touching is already a transcending.

I have often been asked whether there can be negative touchstones of reality. Certainly, and the Holocaust itself is the prime example. Yet our response even to a negative event is not itself necessarily negative, as the work of Elie Wiesel has shown again and again. What is most impressive about Elie Wiesel, indeed, is that he has been able to take this negative touchstone of reality and, without glossing over or denying it in any way, make of it the most positive and meaningful affirmation of life. It is more positive and meaningful by far than that of those "optimists" who imagine that they can affirm human existence by looking away from that which is evil and problematic in it.

In his foreword to Ellen Fine's *Legacy of Night*, Terence Des Pres captures in incomparable words the Holocaust as touchstone of reality and Wiesel's response to that touchstone:

> The Holocaust *happened*. That in itself is the intractable fact we can neither erase nor evade. And the more we think of it, the more it intrudes to occupy our minds, until *l'univers concentrationnaire* becomes a demonic anti-world that undermines our own. After Auschwitz, nothing seems stable or unstained— not the values we live by, not our sense of self-worth, not existence itself. . . . The Holocaust has forced upon us a radical rethinking of everything we are and do. . . .
>
> Every age produces the event which defines it, and in our time the Holocaust is *ours*. It demands that we face the kind of limitless horror our technological and bureaucratic civilization makes possible. . . . The exterminating angel has arisen before us, blocking all light, demanding battle in a night without promise of dawn.[1]

We can find the strength to face this encounter through the voice of the witness, Des Pres suggests; for "the voice of the witness is the source of conscience, and therefore of guidance, in the post-Auschwitz world. Wiesel's writings represent a voice and a vision we can trust. Through him we can learn, as Ellen Fine has said, that to listen to witness is to become a witness." "To read his fiction is to partake of a sorrow that shall perhaps never subside but which gives hope the character of a cause," a cause which is ourselves.[2]

Another sense in which the Holocaust becomes touchstone of reality is through Wiesel's identification of the Jewish and the human condition. "The isolation, dehumanization, and devastation of one-third of the Jewish population during the Nazi regime," writes Fine, "reflect the violence and victimization of twentieth-century man *in extremis*." Still more important, the listener, initiated into the realm of Holocaust darkness, assumes a responsibility to the witness: "One listens, one is anguished, and finally one must change after hearing the tale." The listener's basic values are called into question. "Indeed, his entire life may undergo an upheaval, for he is part of the society that allowed the event to take place."[3]

Following Peter Berger, Michael Berenbaum has suggested that "the death of six million Jews in the Holocaust is the marginal experience *extraordinaire* which has undermined the socially constructed universe of normative Judaism."[4] I would go much further and say that it has undermined the socially constructed universe in general. Even when one speaks, as I have, of Auschwitz and Hiroshima together, we have to realize that we cannot really compare 6 million deaths with 70,000 or 80,000 or even, as in the bombing of Dresden, 120,000. The figure staggers the imagination. People the world over have been moved by *The Diary of Anne Frank* because it enabled them to experience her part of the Holocaust from within. But who can experience from within the death of 6 million? This failure of the imagination was also experienced by the Jews of Europe themselves before they were deported. Even in those rare cases where individuals came back and revealed that the deported were being taken to extermination centers, no one could really imagine something which so destroyed the very cement of social confidence. This destruction went beyond ordinary enmities, beyond anti-Semitism as it had been known, beyond anything conceivable, since society itself implies a certain minimal communication. No one could understand what had never had a precedent in history— that they were going to be turned into cakes of soap, such as I myself have seen on Mount Zion in Jerusalem, with the letters "R.J.F."—"Pure Jewish Fat"—on them. No one could understand, because it had not happened, because actuality does not grow out of potentiality but the other way around, because only when it did happen did it become a very real possibility that can be repeated again and again in human history, despite the solemn pledge of all nations at the United Nations that never again will a genocide be allowed to take place.

Robert McAfee Brown has portrayed the fires of the Holocaust as a gruesome beacon that illuminates *all* the dark corners of our contemporary landscape.

> Little pockets of evil that might otherwise escape attention are exposed when we look at them in the light of the Holocaust. That event of unique magnitude can point us toward other events of lesser magnitude, which we can see more readily and more promptly in its light, and thus be enabled to stamp them out before they get out of control and render us helpless when we confront them, too late.[5]

The whole of Wiesel's works makes use of the Holocaust as touchstone of reality in precisely this sense. The Holocaust, as Wiesel himself has said, was an absurdity without meaning, but just for that reason it is an ontological phenomenon which casts light on all future phenomena.[6] "The human imagination after Auschwitz is simply not the same as it was before," writes Alvin Rosenfeld. Holocaust literature, correspondingly, strives "to express a new order of consciousness, a recognizable shift in being." Holocaust writers accordingly are one-eyed seers, cursed with the knowledge of human perversity and blessed with the knowledge of human strength.[7] "My generation has been robbed of everything, even of our cemeteries," writes Wiesel in *Legends of Our Time*. The world incinerated its own heart at Auschwitz. "At Auschwitz, not only man died, but also the idea of man."[8]

In 1961 Wiesel protested against those who were silent on the question of how the Holocaust could happen for fear of reopening "old wounds": "If we do not question the camps, then we will not question extermination by the H-Bomb." "In the beginning is Auschwitz," Wiesel stated in 1966. It is the unavoidable starting point. "For me, as a Jew of this generation, the Holocaust is the yardstick," Wiesel said in 1968. "I measure the value of an idea only in the light, in the fiery shadow, of the Holocaust as the central event of our lives." "The Holocaust has an all-pervasive effect on us whether we want it or not." The Holocaust involves so much guilt and mystery that all roads lead to it. "No Jew can be fully Jewish today, can be fully a man today, without being part of the Holocaust." The Holocaust is a unique and incomparable event that has never happened before and will never happen again. "Only if you take the Holocaust as a measure can you understand what is taking place today," Wiesel asserted in 1973. Contemporary literature is dominated by the timeless man of the concentration camp: "dehumanized, naked or in rags, weaned from society and civilization, somebody's victim always, a corpse on reprieve, groping in the dark, drained of hope and dreams." The Holocaust is the anti-Sinai, the anti-nomian law, remarked Wiesel in 1975, the greatest event in his life, that of his people, and of mankind. We the witnesses are the link between yesterday and today, wrote Wiesel in 1979, and that is why we are so deeply involved with today's tragedy in Asia. "If the fate of the boat people does inspire a vast movement of solidarity and compassion throughout the Western world, it is because the life and death of another people, only some forty years ago, were met by society's indifference."[9]

Wiesel sees the Holocaust as a Jewish and human tragedy with universal lessons and consequences, but he is most strongly opposed to universalizing the Holocaust event itself by adding in the 5 million non-Jews who also were murdered. No other people was ontologically threatened, even the Gypsies being exposed to a death sentence only to a limited extent. At one of the ceremonies of the President's Commission on the Holocaust, Wiesel took President Carter to task when he used the figure 11 million, which he had gotten from other Jews. Always remember, Wiesel said to him, "that not all victims were Jews, but all Jews were victims." That by no means makes the Holocaust just a Jewish concern; for in it man was pushed to his limit and beyond and the human condition shattered. It is for this reason that whatever happened since must be judged in its light. "The event has altered man's perception and changed his relationship to God, to his fellow man, and to himself. The unthinkable has become real." "Thanks to this event the world may be saved, just as because of it the world is in danger of being destroyed."[10]

> Nothing should be compared to the Holocaust, but every-thing must be related to it. Because of what we endured then we must try to help victims everywhere today: the Bahais who are being murdered by the dictatorship in Iran; the Miskitos on the border of Nicaragua; the boat people who are still seeking refuge; the Cambodian refugees; and the prisoners, so many of them, in Communist jails.[11]

At a certain level all human dramas are linked. Because one people was marked for slavery and "final solution" in the past, others are so marked today. Auschwitz and Treblinka mark the beginning of the planetary peril, for in them humanity leapt across a fearful threshold. The tragedy of tragedies is that the Holocaust has not evoked a salutary change on the ladder of history. It has taught us instead that it is possible to live and die under a permanent question mark. Although all analogies with it are false and blasphemous, it represents an aberration and culmination point of history from which all today's dehumani-zation, terror, isolation, and murder of language stem.[12]

Wiesel's essay "Uprooting and Taking Root: Hasidism," in his book *Words of a Stranger*, affords us a remarkable glimpse into the way the Holocaust has operated for Elie himself as a touch-stone of reality. The essay centers on the Hasidic communities displaced from Europe to the Williamsburg section of Brooklyn, New York, particularly the Satmar and the Lubavitcher. On a visit to Williamsburg, Wiesel meets a childhood friend who has become a Williamsburg Hasid in no way different from what he and Wiesel were as children in Sighet. "Has nothing changed, then?" Wiesel asks his childhood friend, and the latter responds, "The Torah is above changes."

> —And Auschwitz? And Treblinka?
> —Auschwitz proves that nothing happens without the will of God, praised be His Name. Treblinka proves that human beings have need of God: without Him, they kill or die.

. . .
—You have never doubted?
—Never.
—Not even *down there?*
I flared up. I should not have, but I could not help it.
—You are not human!
He regarded me with an infinitely serious air:
—Why should my faith be less human than your absence of
faith? I did not respond: why did he reproach me with my lack
of faith? I never said that I did not believe in God, I only said
that our generation has the right to bring God to trial.
—You have known horror, I too, said my friend. You are
deceived in God? Me, I give him my trust. And I am only
mistrustful of men.[13]

At the end of his discussion of the Hasidim of Williamsburg,
Wiesel, who has seldom shown less than enthusiasm for anything
Jewish, and especially anything Hasidic, draws a melancholy conclusion that shows that when the chips are down it is the Holocaust that is his touchstone of reality:

Of all these people I alone know that this miraculous survival
takes its inspiration from a misunderstanding: the Hasidic
movement has lost more than it dares admit. We are despite
all in Brooklyn and not in Sighet, Wizhnitz, Lublin or Satmar.
. . .
As for me, I leave the room, I leave my childhood friend, I
leave my childhood and return home, to Manhattan, pursued
by a sentiment of defeat.[14]

The Holocaust is also a touchstone of reality for religious life
and for prayer, which Wiesel holds to be central to all human
beings but particularly so for the life of the religious Jew. Wiesel
begins by giving us an incomparable picture of what prayer used
to be for the Hasid and the religious Jew in general—before the
Holocaust:

One defies chastisement and catastrophe by prayer. It suffices
to pray—to pray well, with fervor, in an élan of sincerity—in
order for God and man to be reconciled, in order for the Master

of the universe to offer his children courage and boldness, and a little happiness, and perhaps even a little peace. It is possible that God created man in order to hear him and to hear him chant.[15]

The Holocaust killed in man this capacity to adore, to become enthusiastic, to pray. He still feels the need, but he can no longer satisfy it. The talmudic adage "The destruction of the Temple has caused the gates of prayer to close" applies to the present even more than the past. "If our survival and our renaissance has not rendered us mad, mad with joy and mad with happiness, it is because we have not known how to weep."

> How is it possible for a person in the century of Auschwitz and of Maidanek to affirm and confirm the grandeur, the justice, the grace of our Father in heaven? . . . God participates in the destiny of man, in the good as well as in the evil. Whoever blesses Him for Jerusalem but does not question Him about Treblinka is purely and simply a hypocrite. . . . At the same time that one cannot conceive of Auschwitz with God, one cannot conceive of it without God.[16]

Wiesel ends *Words of a Stranger* with a short but poignant personal essay that affords us a still deeper glimpse into the Holocaust as his touchstone of reality and its effect on that unique mixture of testimony and silence that has marked his writings from first to last. Wiesel tells in this essay how after the war he entered a period of total disillusionment, silence, asceticism, and isolation. Disgusted with the West, he went to India and sought meaning in Indian mysticism, only to find that he could not look away from the great suffering that he encountered there, as did his Indian friends. Returning to Paris, he lived in total isolation and silence in a cell-like room not big enough for more than one.

> I felt myself above all a stranger. I had lost my faith, then my sense of belonging and of orientation. My faith in life: covered with cinders. My faith in man: derisory, puerile, sterile. My faith in God: disturbed. Things and words had lost their significance, their axis.[17]

Although Wiesel found himself always in the ghetto and the ghetto in him, in the course of the years he underwent a change. Still unable to talk about his experience in the Holocaust, he found himself able to talk:

> In order to protect the silent universe in me, I recount that of others. In order not to talk of that which makes me feel bad, I explore other subjects: biblical, Talmudic, Hasidic, or contemporary. . . . The stories that I tell are never those that I should prefer, that I ought to recount.
> The essential will never be said or understood. Perhaps I should make my thought more precise: it is not because I do not talk that you do not understand me, it is because you do not understand me that I do not talk.[18]

The survivors are a race apart. They await everything from God, yet they are conscious that that will not suffice:

> God Himself is incapable of changing the past; even He cannot make it come to be that the killer has not killed six million times. . . . Those who pretend that this or that constitutes a response to the Holocaust content themselves with very little.[19]

For me the Holocaust has become a touchstone of reality above all through my friendship with Elie Wiesel. If, as Ellen Fine says, "to listen to a witness is to become a witness," friendship with a witness adds a link which reading alone cannot do. Because of my friendship with Elie Wiesel, I, a Jew raised in the thinnest possible Reform Judaism in Tulsa, Oklahoma, and a conscientious objector in the Second World War, must to some extent imagine concretely what it is to be a Hasidic Jew raised in Sighet and undergoing the unimaginable horrors of life in Auschwitz and Buchenwald. It is not that Wiesel's works would not have spoken to me personally had I not known him personally. There are countless persons who will testify how close they feel to Wiesel as a person, through his novels and plays and essays, who have never met him or even heard him speak. The students in the course I taught in Wiesel's works at San Diego State University complained when they read *The Testament* that they no longer found in it Elie Wiesel's voice, as they did in novels where the hero was more easily identifiable with Wiesel himself! Nonetheless, I have read his books with different eyes, because I knew him first and cared for him as a person and a witness.

I first met Elie Wiesel twenty years ago in the Laurentian Mountains north of Montreal, where I had joined a group of rabbis, ranging from the most Orthodox to Reform, for discussion of Jewish theology and Judaism in general. Elie had just come from Cape Canaveral, where he had written a report for an Israeli newspaper of the launching of a rocket. He joined us late. My first memory of him was a story he told, one which I had heard from Martin Buber too, of an old Jew who sat in front of Hitler laughing because he knew Hitler would go the way of Haman and other oppressors of the Jews. I had just succeeded in cutting out over a hundred pages from my book *To Deny Our Nothingness: Contemporary Images of Man*. Yet I knew from that story that I had to add a section on Elie Wiesel. Although I had been assured by knowledgeable friends that Saul Bellow's *Herzog* was the contemporary image of the human that I was looking for, I did not even read it until after I published the book. I read everything Elie had written and everything he was writing until the time of publication of *To Deny Our Nothingness* and inserted a Wiesel section in my chapter on "The Dialogue with the Absurd," along with Franz Kafka and Albert Camus. I also published an article on Wiesel for the Catholic journal *Commonweal* at that time.

I found in Wiesel, indeed, what Kafka and Camus had only prefigured—that modern Job I had delineated in my book *Problematic Rebel: Melville, Dostoevsky, Kafka, Camus*. Even more than Camus, Wiesel showed the way through the alienation of modern man and the "death of God," the Modern Exile, the "Modern Promethean" (which I point to as the first, heroic, "either/or" rebellion against that exile), and the "problematic of modern man" to the second, quieter, and more courageous rebellion of the "Modern Job." It was Wiesel who showed, as no contemporary writer before him, what it means to combine trust *and* contending within the dialogue with God. Since God has to do with our actual life, the dialogue with God is also a "Dialogue with the Absurd." This does not mean, however, that I saw or see Wiesel only in universal Western terms or in the coloration of Camus's existentialist rebellion, as my friend Thomas Idinopolous and Michael Berenbaum imagine. In my book *The Hidden Human Image* I included a chapter in the section "Religion and Literature" entitled "Elie Wiesel: The Job of Auschwitz," and the Job of Auschwitz is precisely the *Jewish* survivor of the extermination camps. It is this which forms the kernel of the Wiesel section of *You Are My Witnesses.*

I shall not try to describe my friendship with Elie Wiesel at length, as I have that with Abraham Joshua Heschel. Only tiny snapshots. The night he came to dinner at our home in Bronxville, New York, he was telling Eugenia and me about a stormtrooper who helped a two-year-old child to get into the crematorium since the child was too small to make it on its own. Suddenly Elie was overcome by such a terrible headache that he had to leave the room and literally fell on the bed I pointed him to.

Another story about Elie that Wiesel himself later retold is one told us by my old friend Rabbi Zalman Schechter, who is widely known for his "Aquarian" New Age Hasidism but who was once a faithful follower of the Lubavitcher rebbe. Once Elie went to attend a huge gathering of the Lubavitcher Hasidim at Crown Heights in Brooklyn. He was standing in the doorway in his raincoat when, to his astonishment, the rebbe asked for him. He was lifted hand over hand above the crowd until he stood on a table facing the rebbe. When Elie declared himself a Wishnitzer Hasid, the rebbe challenged him by saying that here in Lubavitch we drink our vodka straight. Not to be outdone, Elie followed suit and drank one glass of vodka after another, until finally the rebbe let him depart, almost totally drunk. Zalman later stood outside and explained to the curious Hasidim the deep kabbalistic mysteries which had transpired during this interchange![20]

When Elie became a favorite lecturer of the United Federation and of Jewish synagogues and universities all over the country, I often found myself thinking of what he had told me about his first lecture in America. The president of the sisterhood of a Long Island temple called him and asked him to lecture just after the publication in America of his first book, *Night*. Elie demurred and said he was going to Europe for several months. When he returned from Europe, she called him again, and he finally yielded to her persistence. When he actually stood in front of the audience, he could not believe these people really wanted to hear about Auschwitz and Buchenwald. So instead he made up a romantic love story such as they might expect of a French novelist. Not a single person rose and protested that that was not the book she had read. When it was over, Elie turned to the beautiful and charming chairwoman and said, "Tell me honestly. Did you read *Night*?" "No, but I mean to read it," she replied. "Then why did you invite me to speak?" he countered. "There was a good review of your book in *The New York Times*, and we needed a speaker," she replied without the least embarrassment!

When I went to Israel for seven months in 1966 to do research on my Buber biography, Elie wrote me and put me in touch with a journalist friend of his with whom I spent time. At the same time as I was doing research at the Jewish National and University Library, I was also the official consultant for a National Educational Television film, *Buber and Israel: A Dialogue*. The director of the film, Mike Roehmer, had also directed a prize-winning film about an unemployed black man in the South—*Nothing But a Man*—and was seriously considering making a film of Wiesel's novel *Dawn*. Mike insisted to me that *Dawn* proved that Elie was in sympathy with the Jewish terrorists, and I insisted the opposite. We were about that close on the subject of Buber, too. Elie had criticized Buber before I left, because he thought that he had pled for the Arabs who were sentenced to death by the British under the Mandate but not for Dov Gruner, a Jewish terrorist. I made a point of checking that out with a Mapam and IHUD leader in Israel who had worked closely with Buber during all those years and discovered that Elie was wrong, as I later told him. Although Elie was consistently helpful with my biography, he was always somewhat critical of Buber.

In the late 1950s and the 1960s I was on the Executive Committee of the Association for Existential Psychiatry and Psychology. We regularly had our meetings in the office of Rollo May on the top floor of an apartment hotel on 103rd and Riverside Drive. By a curious chance, Elie was living in the apartment exactly below Rollo's office, so I sometimes went down to see him after our meetings. In 1968, I was astonished that Rollo's *Love and Will* and Elie's *A Beggar in Jerusalem* had both been on *The New York Times* best-seller list for a great many weeks at the same time, yet neither of these men, who occupied quarters just one floor from each other, had ever heard of the other. I asked Elie, who was still unmarried, why he chose to live in New York City rather than in Paris. After all, he wrote all his books in French and identified himself in many ways with French culture. "Because New York City is the loneliest place in the world," he replied.

Once two years before, when I was lecturing at Antioch College, Elie's and my mutual friend Rabbi Jacob Riemer came out to see me from Dayton, Ohio, where he had a pulpit. "Elie is about to get married," Jack announced to me. "To whom?" I queried. "Oh, to no one in particular," Rabbi Riemer replied. "I can tell from his book *The Jews of Silence*." When Elie dedicated *A Beggar in Jerusalem* "To Marion," I knew that he was indeed about to be married. When sometime later Elie and Marion had a son, my then wife, Eugenia, and I gave him a little cowboy outfit. "He will be the first Hasidic cowboy," Elie remarked to me, much amused.

I was particularly pleased in 1974 when Elie wrote a letter for me to the University of California at Santa Cruz, which was considering me as director of its History of Consciousness Ph.D. program—not only because it was from him, but also because in his short statement he said that I had "surprising insights." I took this as confirmation that I had glimpsed something of where he was coming from, despite the abyss that must yawn between one who actually experienced *l'univers concentrationnaire* and one who did not.

I was even more deeply touched when Elie asked Bill White-head, my editor at Dutton, to come to talk with him about my projected three-volume biography, *Martin Buber's Life and Work*, which at that time seemed in danger of floundering. After the death of Hal Scharlatt, the editor in chief who originally suggested it to me and believed in it deeply, there was no one who understood what it was really about. "I told him what Maurice Friedman is," Elie later said to me, and added the (for me) immensely comforting words "There should be a limit to suffering."

Once when Elie was lecturing in San Diego, I gave him a couple of hundred pages from the second volume of *Martin Buber's Life and Work* to take with him and read. I was astonished when he called me the next morning on his way to Los Angeles to tell me that he had read it all the previous night. He must have been totally exhausted from the series of lectures that he had given, yet he stayed up much of the night as an act of friendship. "It reads very well," he said. "It will make you rich." That hardly proved true, though the three volumes were very well received. Friendship is one thing Elie not only believes in but commits himself to. Whenever there is a friend of his in the audience, he is likely to mention that friend by name, and even something about him, no matter how large the crowd and how auspicious the occasion, in order to give that friend a boost in his hometown!

At some point in the late sixties Elie invited me, along with a number of other Jewish intellectuals, to a meeting at his apartment in Manhattan with Israeli Prime Minister Golda Meir. I sat beside her and found that she was, indeed, as great a woman as she is pictured in the long movie that Ingrid Bergman made of her just before Ingrid's own death. As a strong opponent of the Vietnam War, I was not happy with her views on the subject, which struck me as too close to that of the American administration. But she was direct, forthright, clear, warm, and above all very human. It was clear that she and Elie were close friends. In *Against Silence*, Irving Abrahamson's three-volume selection subtitled "The Voice and Vision of Elie Wiesel," there is reprinted a long dialogue between Elie and Golda Meir entitled "Golda at 75" and a short memoir of Golda. In the dialogue Golda said that she was convinced that Jerusalem is the place for Elie to live and the place where he eventually would be:

WIESEL: Do you think that I would be as moved every time I come to Jerusalem if I lived here?

MEIR: I do not believe that Jerusalem should be a place where one comes occasionally to be moved. Jerusalem is a real place, with everything that it has in it, and everything that will be. When you live here, it does not become less exciting and less important. Jerusalem is not a thing of the past.[21]

I think what moved me most, given Elie's long-standing concern for the plight of Soviet Jewry, was Golda's memory of visiting the Soviet Union in 1948, just after the founding of the State of Israel, which the Soviet Union was one of the first to recognize. Elie linked the amazing response of Soviet Jews to Golda and what she represented with Stalin's paranoid drive to destroy Soviet Jews. In a 1981 lecture, "The New Anti-Semitism," Wiesel spelled out this link:

I think it was *Rosh Hashanah* that she went to the synagogue on Arkhipova Street. Somehow the Jews in Moscow got word that Golda would appear there. Within an hour the street was filled with Jews; thousands had come to see the first representative of the sovereign Jewish State. Arkhipova Street is near the Lubyanka prison, headquarters of the secret police, now the KGB, then the NKVD. Beria, then head of the secret police, saw the Jewish throng and asked, "What is this?" And they told him, "Golda is inside." So he went to Stalin and said, "Look at these Jews. Forty years after the Revolution and they are not Russian. They are not Communist. They are Jews. Their loyalty is to the Jewish people." And that is how it began. The Jews and the Communists were no longer at peace.

Golda felt guilty about that synagogue visit—she told me so, many times—because that was the turning point. Suddenly the Russian government became anti-Semitic, anti-Jewish. Even worse, much worse, the police had taken pictures of the crowds. All the Jews who could be identified were shipped off to Siberia.

Stalin was furious and literally became crazy. In 1950–1951, he ordered the arrest of a group of physicians, mostly Jewish, for allegedly plotting to kill him and the entire Politburo. Stalin's scenario was to hang publicly in Red Square all those involved in the "Doctors' Plot." The next day there would be a pogrom, and a day later all Jews would be shipped off to Siberia. Whole villages were emptied to receive the Jews. Why didn't this happen? Everything was ready. Stalin had prepared the decree. But he died before he could sign it.

Unfortunately he lived long enough to order the murder of more than four hundred Jewish poets, novelists, thinkers, and artists. On one day, August 12, 1952, each of them was shot in the neck. Suddenly all the Yiddish papers ceased publication, and the printing shops were destroyed. Stalin himself directed the operation.

Why did he want to kill the spirit of Judaism, the spirit of Jewish culture? Because he realized that we represented the living symbol of his defeat. The fact that Jews who had grown up under communism still wanted to remain Jewish meant the Revolution had failed.[22]

In April 1985 I was astonished to pick up the *Los Angeles Times* and find on the front page a picture of Elie standing talking with President Reagan and Vice President Bush seated behind him. The occasion was Elie's receiving the Congressional Medal of Honor for his activities in connection with the Holocaust, including chairing the Presidential Commission and planning the national Holocaust Memorial. But in the speech that he gave and which the *Los Angeles Times* reprinted in full, Elie pointed to another, even more pressing occasion. The West German Prime Minister had invited President Reagan to come to a cemetery at

Bitburg for a memorial celebration when he visited Germany in May. Even after it was discovered that a number of SS men were buried in that cemetery, Reagan refused to cancel his plans and the profitable ties with West German arms that went with them! "The Nazis were victims, too," rationalized Reagan, who also visited Bergen-Belsen.

"This is no proper place for you, Mr. President," Elie said to him in his speech.

> This medal is not mine alone! It belongs to all those who remember what SS killers have done to their victims. . . . I know of your commitment to humanity, and therefore I am convinced as you have told us . . . that you were not aware of the presence of SS graves in the Bitburg cemetery.
>
> May I . . . implore you to do something else, to find a way, to find another way, another site.
>
> That place, Mr. President, is not your place. Your place is with the victims of the SS.
>
> Oh, we know there are political and strategic reasons. But this issue . . . transcends politics and diplomacy. . . .
>
> Mr. President, there was a degree of suffering and loneliness in the concentration camps that defies imagination. . . . Terror, fear, isolation, torture, gas chambers, flames, flames rising to the heavens.
>
> . . . I, too, wish to attain true reconciliation with the German people. I do not believe in collective guilt nor in collective responsibility. Only the killers were guilty. Their sons and daughters are not.
>
> . . . We must work to bring peace and understanding to a tormented world that as you know is still awaiting redemption.[23]

I heard that Elie was on national TV as a result of this issue, and I surmised that he was besieged by reporters. But on the very day that Reagan flew to Germany I left this country for a celebration in Israel of *Martin Buber's Life and Work: The Later Years* winning the National Jewish Book Award for Biography. As a result I was not able to talk with Elie until June 7 in New York, where I had returned for the official award ceremony. When

I did I told him I had received an hour-long long-distance call from a former student from the New School for Social Research who desperately wanted me to suggest to Elie that Reagan go to Beethoven's grave instead of Bitburg! This same student told me that the *New York Post* had carried a story that Reagan had asked Elie and Simon Wiesenthal, Director of the Simon Wiesenthal Center in Los Angeles (justly famous for seeking out Nazi war criminals), to accompany him to Bitburg. I dismissed this as mere rumor, but Elie said it was true. In fact, Reagan approached sixteen different leading Jewish figures to go with him, happily without success. Just after the award ceremony, Reagan took Elie aside and implored him to come with him. Elie, of course, refused. Later a United States senator approached Elie again on the same subject: "President Reagan says you are the gentlest person he knows. He cannot understand why you refuse to go with him." How little President Reagan understands the true strength and courage of the Job of Auschwitz!

I shall conclude with two other snapshots, both from the sixties. I was the first non-Catholic Professor of Philosophy in the 140-year history of the Manhattanville College of the Sacred Heart in 1966–67. Elie came to speak there as a favor to me and refused to take any money for his speech. During the course of his talk, he mentioned that this was the first or second Catholic institution he had ever been in. As a child he looked away whenever he saw a Catholic church—not out of hatred, but out of fear. Now, he affirmed, if we cannot have the same answer, we— the Jew and the Catholic—can have the same question. After the lecture, attended by four hundred (almost the whole of the college), the students in my M.A. course, mostly nuns, met with Elie in a separate room. One of the nuns in my class asked Elie what the question was that Jews and Catholics had in common. My friend Mother Elizabeth McCormack, the president of Manhattanville College, stepped in and answered for him: "Meaning." "Meaning, yes," said Elie with a wave of his hand, "but also fervor."

It is because of his fervor that Elie is a witness for God and a witness for me. I conclude the chapter "Hasidism and the Contemporary Man" in my book *Touchstones of Reality* by pointing to fervor as the central quality that is lacking in American Judaism:

> Martin Buber's own conversion to Hasidism came, he tells us, when as a young man he read the saying of the Baal Shem's, "He takes unto himself the quality of fervor. He arises from sleep with fervor, for he is hallowed and becomes another man and is worthy to create." For all the moral idealism of contemporary Judaism there is little in it that could call out the highest allegiance and devotion of Jewish youth. The quality that is lacking in American Judaism, as in American religion in general, is fervor. One of the statements that is quoted in "Hasidism Reexamined" as characteristic of the extravagance of our current romantic neo-Hasidism is Buber's assertion in the Preface to *The Legend of the Baal Shem*, "No renewal of Judaism is possible that does not bear in itself the elements of Hasidism." Whether or not the mature Buber himself would have stood behind this statement of his youth, *I* would—at least as far as the element of fervor is concerned. The unprecedented success of organized Jewish religion in America threatens to leave it a movement in search of a meaning unless it is caught up within genuine movement of the soul. As Abraham Heschel has said, "Jewish belonging has taken the place of Jewish living." We do not need a "religious revival" in the sense of Billy Graham, nor certainly any turning away from study or from the full and, where possible, improved, use of the powers of reason. But we do need genuine fervor if the quantitatively greatest body of Judaism in the world is not also to be the thinnest and most meaningless.[24]

How close Wiesel is in spirit to what I wrote he expressed just the year before I published *Touchstones* in a discussion of the alienation of Jewish youth. "Why should young Jews in America be enthusiastic over the kind of Judaism we here are trying to give them?" Wiesel asked. "Jewish life in America today is boring. Even the quarrels are boring." Wiesel's conclusion from the many synagogues he visited was that "Jewish life in America lacks elevation." Two years later, in his commencement address at the City College of New York, Wiesel urged the young people who were graduating to treasure fervor: "Whatever the road you have followed and you are about to take, whatever you do, do it with fervor. Fervor is the most precious of gifts—and of rewards as well."[25]

As a storyteller, Elie speaks with a quiet intensity that holds the audience totally attentive. No one can adequately or fully appreciate Wiesel the writer who has not heard him tell a story; for his writing, in the end, is nothing other than a mosaic of tales, a written embodiment of the living voice. But what I have appreciated equally as much as Wiesel's gifts as a storyteller is his wonderful, genuine, and subtle sense of humor. Although his present life is a happy and full one—an all too full one—he bears the unimaginable burden of his memories of the Holocaust as a touchstone of reality for our time. That precisely he should live and speak with such a rich interweaving of humor is a grace for which those of us who know him can only be grateful in the fullest and most religious sense of that term. If it were not for his humor, he would not be thoroughly genuine, and his witness would not be as compelling as it is. Humor is the milk brother of faith, Martin Buber said when speaking of his friend Franz Rosenzweig. This is equally true for Elie Wiesel.

Sometime in the late sixties I was asked to speak on Hasidism at the 92nd Street Young Men and Young Women's Hebrew Association in New York City. Elie, whose lectures there became such a staple that several of his biblical and Hasidic books grew out of them, sat in the audience. When I spoke about how the Hasidim loved to dance and sing, I said, "There is someone here who could sing for us the genuine Hasidic songs if he would." I was thinking in particular of a song Elie had sung for us that, according to legend, was a tune of David the King's and was acquired by a Hasidic rebbe from a shepherd whom he heard sing it. "You didn't think I was going to sing there in that auditorium," Elie said to me afterward when we were having dinner together. "Of course not," I replied. Yet that melody threads its way through all that he has written and said and through his existence, in which I have been privileged to be his contemporary, associate, and friend. In the *niggun*, the wordless melody of your life, you are our witness, Elie Wiesel.

"Peddler of Night and Agony"

Religion at the deepest level might be described as a basic *attitude* or relationship arising in the encounter with the whole reality directly given to one in one's existence. From this standpoint, many works of literature are as close to religious reality as any work of theology, for both may be products of some genuine religious encounter. This means taking seriously the full address of literature to the wholeness of the human. The most fruitful approach to the meeting of religion and literature, therefore, is not to treat literature as if it were covert theology but to discover in our meeting with it that image of authentic human existence that is implicit in the very style of most great literature.

In contemporary literature the meeting of literature and religion stands under the sign of that pervasive existential mistrust that Martin Buber has described as the "eclipse of God." This literature must not be misunderstood as merely atheist, pessimistic, or absurd, as is so often thought. Part of our existential and religious hope lies in our confrontation with that contemporary literature which in its depth asks us *the* religious questions of our time. In our day the only way to the positive, perhaps, is through the tension of the absurd, the contradictions of modern existence, through the absence of a modern image of meaningful personal and social existence and the attempts to create such an image in response.

The most impassioned complaint, the most stubborn and faithful Dialogue with the Absurd, the most moving embodiment of what Buber has called the "Job of the gas chambers" is found in the work of Elie Wiesel. His slim volumes form one unified outcry, one sustained protest, one sobbing and singing prayer. It is difficult to classify Wiesel as a writer, for, of the twenty-three books he has published so far, one is an autobiography, eight are novels, two are collections of stories and dialogues, two are books of essays, one is a prose book on the "Jews of Silence" (the Jews of Soviet Russia), three are interpretations of biblical stories, three interpretations of Hasidic masters, two are plays, and one a cantata. Above all else, however, Elie Wiesel is a member of the oldest profession in the world—that of the storyteller, the person who preserves the awesome life of the tribe in the form of myths and legends—dramatic events—rather than of connected historical accounts. The art of storytelling was an oral one for countless millennia before it became a written one as well. Wiesel retains this oral quality both in his speaking and in his writing. In a series of poignant and powerful writings, he has woven together words and silence into tales of unexampled beauty and terror. In each successive work he has wrested an image of humanity from his Dialogue with the Absurd—his contending with the Nazi Holocaust and the monstrous shadow which it cast on his life.

"God made man because he loves stories," says Wiesel in the motto to his novel *The Gates of the Forest*. The story is not just the possession of the storyteller. It is the joint creation of the one who tells and the one who listens—the product of a dialogue. "Do you know that it is given to us to enrich a legend simply by listening to it?" says Katriel in *A Beggar in Jerusalem*. "It belongs as much to the listener as to the teller. You listen to a tale, and all of a sudden it is no longer the same tale." Katriel's counterpart, David, elevates this dialogue of storyteller and story listener into a new midrash upon "You are my witnesses"—the saying from Deutero-Isaiah that gives the title to this book: "Let's say He also needs witnesses. In the beginning there was the word; the word is the tale of man; and man is the tale of God." A closely similar spirit informs the motto of *Souls on Fire*, Wiesel's portraits and legends of Hasidic masters:

> My father, an enlightened spirit, believed in man.
> My grandfather, a fervent Hasid, believed in God.
> The one taught me to speak, the other to sing.
> Both loved stories.
> And when I tell mine, I hear their voices.
> Whispering from beyond the silenced storm,
> they are what links the survivor to their memory.

In "The Storyteller's Prayer" Wiesel links listening to a tale to Buber's I-and-Thou: "When one tells a tale, one relives it. One does not talk to the listener. One talks with the listener." The quality of an exchange depends, in fact, upon the listening; for the storyteller is just the messenger who creates links between word and being.[1]

If storytelling is the oldest form of literature, it is also peculiarly appropriate for the most modern—the literature of the Holocaust. As Robert McAfee Brown points out in *Elie Wiesel*, the storyteller and the storyteller alone inhabits both worlds—that of the Holocaust and that of those who have not and can never experience the Holocaust from within. The task of the storyteller, Brown asserts, is not to entertain us but to engage us and draw us into the "mad logic of the story from another world":

> This is disturbing. It means that we cannot dismiss his stories from one world as though they were unrelated to our world. What happens (unless we are immensely clever at safeguarding ourselves) is that the story not only confronts us; it also implicates us, involves us, *draws us into it*. Not very far. But far enough so that we can no longer live as though Auschwitz had never happened.[2]

Holocaust literature indeed is literature without analogy, as Wiesel has stressed: "By its nature, the Holocaust defies literature." The implications of this statement are "frightening in the extreme," as Alvin Rosenfeld has pointed out; for the whole of our literature rests upon the foundation of its antecedent. "Our whole fund of literacy . . . comes into play in reading"; for we read and understand literature with implicit reference to the poems, novels, or plays that preceded it. Not so with Holocaust literature and, by extension, with all the writings of Elie Wiesel. "Without our expected moorings in a familiar literary landscape, we no longer know how to proceed: Lost in a place whose dimensions we cannot easily recognize, let alone acknowledge as our own, we strive for orientation through intimacy with the common and familiar things of the world, but grasp only fog."[3]

At the same time, as Sidra Ezrahi has pointed out, Wiesel's fiction differs from other "lamentation literature" in that it does not dwell on the sordid facts but focuses instead on the function of the events in raising questions and generating legends. For this reason, too, "the balance between reality and legend is a very tenuous one, and Wiesel's narratives are often in danger of being subverted by too much or too little realism."[4] Wiesel's fiction must be judged by the delicate balance between the horror on which it is laid and the stories, protests, and affirmation that emerge from the confrontation with that horror. This is not ultimately a question of the amount of realism, as Ezrahi asserts, but of Wiesel's special polyphonic dialogue. Wiesel himself, in his conversations with Harry James Cargas, has pointed to his writings as a dialogue—a dialogue between writer and reader and just thereby between man and God:

> Between author and reader there must be a dialogue. When man speaks to God there is a dialogue. The creative process is a strange one: it comes from solitude, it goes to solitude and yet it's a meeting between two solitudes. It is just like man's solitude faced with God's solitude. Once you have this confrontation, you have art and religion and more. You have a

certain communion in the best and purest sense of the word. Exactly the same thing happens when you write and someone reads you; your solitude is faced with the reader's and you join with that solitude. When both are sincere, God is there. Whenever one man speaks to another, ultimately he involves God.[5]

Ellen S. Fine in *The Legacy of Night*, the finest literary study of Wiesel's works that has as yet appeared, links this dialogue between writer and reader to a very special dialogue between Wiesel and his own characters, one through which they transform their author from mute sufferer into eloquent witness:

> Elie Wiesel has chosen to reach out: he has given birth to a literary universe in which his protagonists testify for him. They tell his story, the story of how a young survivor, mute and passive, transforms himself into an articulate messenger. It is these characters—*the witnesses of the witness*—who provide insights for both the reader and the author. "Novelists ought not to speak," he observes. "Their mission consists in listening to other voices, including those of their own creations, of their own characters." . . . to listen to a witness is to become one.[6]

Wiesel describes the literary form that he has chosen as a linking of the past to the present through which the ordinary logic of time is set aside in favor of a past-present and a present-past in which past and future are interchanged. This follows the tradition of Hebrew, with its sense of imperfect verbs that can be both at once. It also follows the tradition of the novel: "The time of a novel is not the real time and yet it is the substances of a lifetime." Both past and future are contained within a limited time and a closely confined space in Wiesel's fiction:

> Most of my time periods last one night in all of my novels. And most take place in a closed location. It's either in the camp (*Night*), or in a cellar (*Dawn*), in a hospital room (*The Hospital*), in a cell (*The Town Beyond the Wall*), in a cave (*The Gates of the Forest*), or near to the wall (*A Beggar in Jerusalem*).[7]

The literary critic Robert Alter has pointed out that the arguments of Wiesel's novels repeatedly crystallize in wisdom-statements, most often in the form of memorable aphorisms ("The lack of hate between executioner and victim, perhaps this is God"). This method of writing is natural for Wiesel, Alter remarks, because he writes in French. French has a long tradition of the aphorism, going back to Pascal and La Rochefoucauld, and that blends into the philosophical novels of Sartre, Camus, and Malraux. Wiesel's rich knowledge of midrashic, talmudic, and Hasidic lore is equally a source for his use of the concise tale as a relevation of spiritual truth, Alter concludes.[8]

Wiesel's choice to write all of his works in French is an anomaly, and a very important one for understanding his literary production. French is neither Wiesel's native language (Yiddish), his scholarly language (Hebrew), nor the language of his adopted country (English). Why, then, has Wiesel restricted his entire literary output (excluding his first, long Yiddish work and his early journalism) to French? Alter suggests that Wiesel may have been "attracted to French because of its readily available heritage of stylistic classicism that makes possible the expression of serious emotion with a chaste conciseness quite unlike the effects of pathos and effusion to which Hebrew and Yiddish easily lend themselves." Wiesel himself says that he chose French, which he only learned when he was sixteen, because it meant to him a new home, but also because it challenged him to express the mystical in the language of *clarté*.

> The language became a haven, a new beginning, a new possibility, a new world. To start expressing myself in a new language was a defiance. The defiance became even stronger because the French language is Cartesian. Reason is more important than anything else. Clarity. French is such a non-mystical language. What I try to transmit with or in and through that language is mystical experiences. So the challenge is greater.[9]

Ellen Fine elaborates on this explanation, at the same time linking Wiesel's French writing to the later stylistic techniques of a specific contemporary French tradition, the *nouveau roman*, "which interrogate reality and question systems of time and causality found in established narrative forms." The adoption of French as his written language meant "a distancing from the brutal experience of the Holocaust, a rejection of the past. Yiddish, his mother tongue, and Hebrew, the language of his early educational training, evoked painful emotions, while the Hungarian and German languages were those of the oppressors." Yet it meant, finally, no rejection of the past—either the ancestral past of Judaism or the immediate past of the Holocaust—only a distancing. Wiesel's style is unique, Fine points out, in its fusion of aspects of the French novel with Jewish lore:

> His narrative structure is often fragmented: characterized by shifts in points of view, disjointed images, contradictory statements, and a blending of fact and fiction, of history and imagination. The effect produced is similar to the mode of the *Nouveau Roman* and, at the same time, is in keeping with the tradition of the Jewish storyteller who weaves folktales, anecdotes, and parables into the fabric of his texts, transmitting messages that are highly ambiguous.[10]

Whatever the reasons for Wiesel's writing in French, he became a great writer at the point where he moved from his first published work written in Yiddish, *Un di Velt hot Geshvign* (*And the World Was Silent*), an 800-page witness of his life in Auschwitz and Buchenwald, to the 80-page condensation in French of *La Nuit*. Wiesel himself tells the story of how once a friend who had just had a baby said to him, "You can't know what it is to be awakened in the middle of the night by a baby." "Perhaps I can't," rejoined Wiesel, who had not yet married and had a child of his own. "But you can't know what it is like when the nine-tenths that I have cut out of my writing during the day comes to me at night and complains, asking why I have cut it out!"

Wiesel gives us further insight into his approach to writing in some of his lectures and interviews. Only those writers who in all of their books relate to the same world, the same theme, the same obsessions have an *oeuvre*, a body of work, Wiesel stated. He himself is clearly that sort of writer, and he sees all of his books as the same. To Wiesel the writer is responsible not only for the language but for the silence, the spaces between the words. "The less you write, the more true the message and story. . . . One useless word and the whole structure falls apart and becomes a lie."[11]

Wiesel always works from six to ten in the morning, and he always works on two projects at the same time, one fiction and one nonfiction. During the rest of the day, he prepares for the morning writing hours by doing research, reading, and studying related to it. "I work sixteen hours a day, and I work every day except Jewish holidays and Sabbaths." He knows no dry periods, but he often throws away what he is doing if he does not like it or turns from a novel to nonfiction or from nonfiction to fiction. In his room he has a picture of his house in Sighet from the American television program on his town, and whatever he does, he remembers that house. Thus he justifies each moment of his life as a witness, a survivor. "Not to transmit the experience is to betray the experience." "Though I want to celebrate the sun, to sing of love, I must be the emissary of the dead," rebuilding with memories, ruins, efforts, and moments of grace.

In his novels it is the first line, which comes mysteriously, that determines the whole. But before that first line, Wiesel hears the melody that sets the tone for the whole book. He always writes three drafts. The first flows according to the melody—hundreds and hundreds of pages, most of which he throws out. The choice of each word is an act of freedom, a decision internally consistent with the novel. The second draft creates the structure, cutting, reorganizing, changing; and the third represents stylistic changes, concentration and condensation, "though the symphony is already there." In all of this there is the silence which Wiesel first endures and then allows to break out before there are any words. "If one of my novels is only words, without silence, I do not even reread or publish it. The unspoken is as important as the spoken: the weight of silence is necessary." Silence, as we shall see, is an essential theme in all Wiesel's books.

Writing, for Wiesel, is pleasure and agony, a chosen obsession by one who feels chosen, one who writes because no one else could write what he does. It is expiation and suffering, faith in something indestructible within oneself, compulsion, all based on a personal universe and a particular message. It carries with it great responsibility for what is said and what is not said, a vast and infinite responsibility. The words of the writer are endowed with meaning and power, able to push a person to despair or salvation. "If I am a good writer . . . I take your life . . . into my hand . . . touch it, caress it, soothe it, perhaps break it."[12]

In his first book, *Night*, Wiesel tells the story of how he was deported with his family from his Hungarian-Jewish village when he was a child of fourteen, how his mother and sister were metamorphosed into the smoke above the crematories, how he and his father suffered through Auschwitz, Buchenwald, and forced winter marches until finally, just before liberation, his father died. For Wiesel the "death of God" came all at once, without preparation—not as a stage in the history of culture, but as a terrifying event that turned the pious Hasidic Jew into a Job of Auschwitz whose complaint against the "great injustice in the world" can never be silenced.

> Never shall I forget those flames which consumed my Faith forever. Never shall I forget that nocturnal silence which deprived me, for all eternity, of the desire to live. Never shall I forget those moments which murdered my God and my soul and turned my dreams to dust. Never shall I forget these things, even if I am condemned to live as long as God Himself. Never.[13]

On a later day, when he watched the hanging of a child with the sad face of an angel, he heard someone behind him groan: "Where is God? Where is He? Where can He be now?" and a voice within him answered: "Where? Here He is—He has been hanged here, on these gallows." When after the liberation of Buchenwald he looked at himself in a mirror, a corpse gazed back at him. "The look in his eyes, as they stared into mine, has never left me."

From these passages one might conclude that Wiesel had emerged from the Holocaust an atheist, a nonbeliever, or, at the very least, an implacable enemy of God. Yet not only Wiesel's interpretations of the Bible and of Hasidism are suffused with Jewish religiousness but also his novels, plays, stories, and essays. Practically every one of his works is steeped in the atmosphere of some aspect of Judaism—biblical, kabbalistic, Hasidic, or modern. What is more, there is a strong emphasis upon the plight of the Russian Jews under Soviet persecution, the importance of the State of Israel, and, throughout but especially strongly in his novel *The Testament*, a ceaseless stress on Jewish identity. All this might raise the question of whether Wiesel has used his writings as a propagandistic or at least quasi-theological medium to convey ideas and positions and has thereby contributed to the *mis*meeting of religion and literature. *Does* Wiesel misuse literature to convey a theology? No, because Wiesel transmutes it into his own attitude toward life and makes it integral with the literature that he creates. It is not the messianism of traditional Jewish theology, insofar as there is one, but the inverted messianism of a cursed century.

At the heart of the work of Elie Wiesel are the unresolved tensions between witness and rebellion, speaking and remaining silent, keeping faith with the past and honoring the present. The true greatness of Wiesel lies in the creative interaction of these opposites—sometimes opposed, sometimes identical, sometimes moving from one life stance to another and back. So far from wishing to anticipate a resolution of this tension, we must wish that it be maintained with all the integrity of Wiesel himself.

Israel's side of the covenant has again and again been as witness to God precisely through contending—through wrestling with the nameless messenger until dawn and receiving the blessing of a new name, Israel—one who has fought with God and with one's fellows and has prevailed. But what is the blessing that comes to the witness of "night," who finds himself caught again and again in the double pull of speaking and remaining silent? What of Elie Wiesel himself, who, after ten years of silence, became a witness and a messenger to bring the world of the Holocaust to contemporaries who had not even begun to grasp its enormity, let alone its threat to the past, present, and future of Israel and mankind? What blessing has enabled Wiesel to live with the past and yet not forsake the present? What room is there for affirmation in a witness such as his? What portion of rebellion is necessary that the witness remain true and the affirmation real?

Contending with God and with man is an essential ingredient of the witnessing of Wiesel—our modern messenger. The thick silence between the words in Wiesel's works is also integral to this witnessing. Wiesel's works give repeated evidence of an all-too-understandable temptation to give up altogether the retelling of the story of the Holocaust because of the repeated realization of the futility of such a witness. Yet to do so would itself be a despairing rebellion which would be still more futile. Thus Wiesel's witness stands in a double tension—a tension with rebellion, on the one side, and a tension with keeping silent, on the other. In this dialectic, both rebellion and keeping silent may be affirmation and both may be negation—just as witnessing to the Holocaust may itself be simultaneously negation and affirmation. The third, doubly dialectical tension that runs through all that Wiesel has written and is integral to the other two is that between past and present. Here a double temptation has to be overcome— that of denying the present out of loyalty to the Holocaust past and that of gliding over the Holocaust too easily for the sake of affirmation and response in the present.

These unresolved tensions are meaningful in their very unre-solvedness. That unresolvedness is, in fact, the only possible meaning; for witness and rebellion, speaking out and keeping silent, remaining faithful to the past and being present to the present must necessarily go together. We shall explore the tension between witnessing and rebelling in our chapter "The Job of Auschwitz," and that between past and present in our chapter "The Messianism of the Unredeemed." Before we come to either of these, however, we must focus on the tension between wit-nessing and keeping silent and its corollary—"Silence, Madness, and Laughter."

To Witness or Keep Silent: The Unresolved Tension

In a 1963 memorial for his home city, Sighet, Wiesel protested:

> How, then, does one eulogize a martyred community which the wind of human cruelty has dispersed like smoke? Something inside me rebels against the traditional manner of observing *Yahrzeit*. I seek a new prayer, one which will transcend ceremony and express more than words can express—a mighty protest against man and God, both of whom participated in the cosmic burial.
>
> So for now, I lock the mourning inside me and lock myself inside it. Instead of going to memorial meetings, I go to the river and watch the waves dig graves for each other, one beneath the other. There is sadness and restlessness in their soft stirring. I listen intently, and from far and near there comes to me not the sound of *Kaddish*, but the sound of that night when the Angel of Death sat on the throne of Almighty Creation.[1]

In *Legends of Our Time* Wiesel describes his writing as "often nothing more than the secret or conscious desire to carve words on a tombstone: to the memory of a town forever vanished, to the memory of a childhood in exile, to the memory of all those I loved and who, before I could tell them I loved them, went away."[2] In the title essay of *One Generation After* a strong note of ambivalence appears concerning this testimony of messengers who hope that other persons will benefit from their report of

123

their experience "under a totalitarian regime, when the line be-tween humanity and inhumanity becomes blurred." Looking back after twenty-five years, Wiesel expresses pity for those guileless witnesses and confesses discouragement and shame on his own part. Nazism is on the rise in Germany, and former Nazi killers hide under the respectability of eminent citizens. A French pol-itician accuses the Jews of peddling their suffering; Jews are slandered in the Soviet Union, persecuted in Poland, and live in constant fear in the Arab countries. "Was it not a mistake to testify, and by that very act affirm their faith in man and word? I know of at least one who often feels like answering yes." "Noth-ing has been learned," he adds. "Auschwitz has not even served as warning. For more detailed information, consult your daily newspaper."

The result is that the storyteller witness is left with a sense of impotence and guilt, and his writing itself is called in question. To try to bring back the life of even one human being in a single camp borders on sacrilege. "We think we are describing an event, we transmit only its reflection." Words lose their innocence; the myth becomes tarnished. "By its uniqueness, the Holocaust defies literature." No one, not even the survivor, has the right to speak for the dead. "No image is sufficiently demented, no cry suffi-ciently blasphemous to illuminate the plight of a single victim, resigned or rebellious, walking silently toward death." Yet, de-spite all this, Wiesel concludes that the story had to be told "for the sake of our children," even though he ends the essay with the sad statement: "Soon there will be no one left to speak of them, no one left to listen." In the story "First Royalties," Wiesel tells how a story of his childhood evoked the childhood of his hearers in his concentration camp and won him two bowls of thick soup *and* the nauseating sense that it was his story itself he was swallowing—"a story impoverished and diminished for hav-ing been told; its source a memory grown dim and less and less my own."[3]

At the heart of Wiesel's novel *The Oath*, which he wrote after

One Generation After, is precisely this tension between the powerful urge to keep silent and the equally powerful call to witness. *The Oath* is structured around a dialogue between an old man with a terrible secret protected by a solemn communal vow and a young man contemplating suicide who just thereby tempts him to break his vow. Witness to the ultimate destruction of his community, the narrator has not been silent by choice. Rather, silence has been his master, drawing "its strength and secret from a savagely demented universe doomed by its wretched and deadly past." If, despite this, the old man reveals all to the youth, it is because of a residue of responsibility which forms the final state of every encounter even in the era of "night" and the eclipse of the human. "Whoever says 'I' creates the 'you.' Such is the trap of every conscience. The 'I' signifies both solitude and rejection of solitude."[4] Azriel tells his story to the young man and by transmitting his experience thus makes the young man, too, into a messenger who will have no alternative but to stay alive until he has transmitted his message. Even so, Azriel's father had doomed him to survival by entrusting to him the *Book of Kolvillàg*, the chronicle of his doomed village. By making him a repository of their tragic truths, Azriel's father and his mad teacher, Moshe, had made him into a perpetual exile, a *Na-venadnik*, who reveals and attaches himself to no one, becoming the link, the hyphen between countless communities. In his daydreams it is not he but his village that is roaming the roads in search of help and redemption. There is nothing paradoxical in this; for Azriel's message is the message of silence—of events too monstrous to be told, too bewildering to be imagined. It is the silence of the Holocaust, the burden of which the youth of today have inherited without its mystery.

Set in two time periods, before and after the Holocaust, *The Oath* only gradually reveals itself as the most terrifying of Wiesel's works in its suggestion of the possibility of the permanent eclipse of the hidden human image. It is, by the same token, a powerful comment on the Holocaust itself—not just as a sickness of the

Nazis or of modern man but of humanity. In the first instance, this is European, Christian humanity, but in the end it is the human as such that is tainted by senseless hatred and ultimate stupidity. *The Oath* begins and ends with visions of apocalyptic terror and of the dread beast of the Apocalypse. The beast at work was "alternatively savage and attentive, radiant and hideous . . . reducing to shreds whoever saw it at close range," turning the town into a "desecrated, pillaged cemetery," crushing all its inhabitants into a twisted and tortured monster with a hundred eyes and a thousand mouths, all of which were spitting terror.

Before the destruction of the Jews of Kolvillàg (every village) and later of Kolvillàg itself, Moshe is allowed to summon the whole of the Jewish community to an extraordinary session where he sweeps everyone up into his own rebellion against the traditional Jewish task of pleasing God by becoming the illustration of his own tale of martyrdom. Jewish memory, it was held, robbed the executioner of his final victory, by preventing his attempts to erase the evidence of his cruelty, haunting his conscience, and warning humanity present and future of his crimes. Murdered, plundered, humiliated, oppressed, expelled from society and history, forbidden the right to laugh or sing or even cry, the surviving Jews turned their ordeal into a "legend destined for men of good will." But now, says Moshe the Madman, the time has come to put an end to this Jewish role of being mankind's memory and heart. "Now we shall adopt a new way: silence." By refusing to testify anymore, we can break the link between suffering and the history of suffering, thereby forestalling future abominations. Moshe leads the whole community to take an oath that whoever may survive the massacre and humiliation which await the Jews of Kolvillàg will go to their graves without speaking of it, and he seals this oath by placing the entire people of Israel under the sign of the *Herem*—the dread word of excommunication and damnation!

Azriel, as we have seen, finally breaks his vow to save the young boy; for he was not afraid of a *Herem*, only of indifference. Yet

the last notes of the book suggest that the tension between witness and silence is still unresolved: "The Book, said my father.
The *Herem*, said Moshe. . . . Memory, insisted my father, everything is in memory. Silence, Moshe corrected him, everything is
in silence." Azriel's father and Moshe the Madman are the two
voices in Elie Wiesel, two voices that "merge into one and remain
a secret."

In 1970 Wiesel seemed to have resolved the tension in the
direction of witnessing and "against silence":

> To forget is to go mad, to die, to give up faith in language,
> in art, in man, in the past, in all that links man to his world,
> to his past, and to others. To write, therefore, is not to forget:
> It is to call people not only to remember but to affirm their
> faith in themselves and their future.[6]

Yet in 1973 the unresolved tension is clearly manifest again:

> The anguish of the writer stems from his attempt to com-
> municate something in words that defies words. His is the
> anguish of somebody who has collected tales and testimony
> and knows that whatever he does with them will be wrong.
> To speak may be to distort. Not to speak may be to betray and
> conceal. To question is already an admission of weakness but
> to answer is an admission of defeat. . . . How do you deal with
> a subject which transcends the personal being . . . without
> exploiting it . . . cheapening it? How do you deal with it and
> still remain faithful to what you have been and whatever your
> friends have been?[7]

At the same time, Wiesel admitted that, in spite of the survivor's
inhibitions and apprehensions, his need to testify proved stronger
than his awareness that his testimony might not be understood.
But that does not remove the difficulty of translating into words
an experience that transcends them. Again, in spite of this, one
must write in order to remember, precisely because the Germans
did not want their crimes to be remembered. Whoever forgets
or moves others to forget becomes thereby an accomplice of those
murderers. Those who recorded what happened while it was

happening or took part in armed rebellion did not want to survive but to tell the tale. To forget would be to betray them again. Yet thirty years after, we must wonder whether the testimony was ever received or even told, this tale "shattered into six million fragments, each with anguish and anger enough for seven times seven generations, a tale . . . about . . . death-producing factories burning a people drunk with eternity into a people of ashes." "The dead are in possession of a secret that we, the living, are neither worthy of nor capable of recovering."[8]

Linking the Akeda to all future holocausts, Wiesel declares in *Messengers of God*, his biblical portraits and legends, that each of the pogroms, crusades, persecutions, slaughters, massacres, and liquidations that followed were Abraham leading his son to the altar all over again. And here, too, the unresolved tension reappears: "We have known Jews—ageless Jews—who wished to become blind for having seen God and man opposing one another in the invisible sanctuary of the celestial spheres, a sanctuary illuminated by the gigantic flames of the Holocaust." Yet Isaac had no choice but to survive in order "to make something of his memories, his experience, in order to force us to hope." Not that suffering in the Jewish tradition confers any privileges. Isaac knew how to transform his suffering into prayer and love, rather than into rancor and malediction.[9]

In *A Jew Today* Wiesel explains his ten-year vow of silence as an effort to learn how to describe the indescribable: "Long enough to learn to listen to the voices crying inside my own. . . . Long enough to unite the language of man with the silence of the dead." In the face of the startling appearance of sixty books all over the world that declared that the exterminations never even took place, Wiesel declares in this same book that silence is not and never was the answer, and that that is the reason why the survivors chose to bear testimony.[10]

In an imaginary dialogue between father and son, the dead father says to his son that the winds of night have swept away his words, their story and its heroes. The father hears the son, but no one is left to speak for mankind, to save him from himself, and the son is "weary of trying, of fighting, of speaking." Surely a cry of Wiesel himself. In the eloquent "Plea for Survivors" with which *A Jew Today* concludes, Wiesel again asserts that a "Holocaust literature" is a contradiction in terms. Someone who has not lived through the event can never know it. "And whoever has lived through it can never fully reveal it." The words of the survivor "are feeble, stammering, unfinished, incoherent attempts to describe a single moment of being painfully, excruciatingly alive—the closing in of darkness for one particular individual." Not only is there an unbridgeable gulf between the survivor's memory and its reflection in his words, but any attempt to capture the Holocaust is pure illusion: a theology of Auschwitz is blasphemous for both nonbeliever and believer; a novel about Auschwitz is not a novel, or it is not about Auschwitz:

> Auschwitz signifies death—total, absolute death—of man and of mankind, of reason and of the heart, of language and of the senses. Auschwitz is the death of time, the end of creation; its mystery is doomed to stay whole, inviolate.[11]

Knowing this, the survivor is burdened with obsessive helplessness coupled with guilt. Yet this knowledge does not relieve him of the duty to testify and thus rob the executioner of his second murder, when he tries to erase the traces of his crimes.

The autobiographical documents of the Sonderkommando members who chose not to finish the killer's work by contributing to oblivion all seem pale in relation to their content: "What they did not say surpasses—in intensity, in truth—everything they thought themselves capable of verbalizing."

> The killers' laughter and the hallucinatory silence of the condemned; the distant look of old men who knew; the dull lament of children afraid to know; the screams, the moaning, the beatings; the thirst inside the sealed wagons; the terror inside the barracks during the *selections*; the silent, almost solemn processions marching toward the mass graves or the flames; the lucidity of some, the delirium of others . . . the torpor, the

> despondency, the distress and shame of people who . . . think
> of bread more than of God, more than of honor, more than
> of life. . . . It is as impossible to speak of them as not to
> speak of them. . . . One would have to invent . . . a new
> language to say what no human being has ever said.[12]

The spare statements of the Sonderkommando were not written
with words but against them, and what they communicated was
their sense of helplessness in the face of the impossibility of
communicating.

Today, Wiesel insists, the Holocaust is a desanctified theme,
robbed of its passion and its mystery by novelists and politicians
who cheapen and exploit it. This does not mean that the con-
centration-camp phenomenon ought not be studied. Wiesel himself was the center of an important international conference in
which scholars from many disciplines met to share their responses
to Wiesel's works and their studies of the Holocaust. Wiesel's
conclusion, rather, is that the Holocaust should be approached
with fear and trembling and, above all, with humility.

Even in *The Testament*, a novel which centers on the Jewish
poets murdered by Stalin, the theme of witness and silence is
resumed—with a surprising twist. The father has left a testament
to his son, one which he hopes will give meaning to his own
experiences, even though he has no reason to believe it will ever
reach him. And the son, who has made himself into a mute rather
than talk about his father with a man whom he suspects of being
an informer, becomes a messenger precisely through his silence.
Through his father's life and his own duty to bear witness to it,
his silence is given a meaning. This theme enters, too, into the
conclusion of Wiesel's portrait of the prophet Jeremiah in his
Five Biblical Portraits:

> And what are we doing, we writers, we witnesses, we Jews?
> For over three thousand years we have been repeating the same
> story—the story of a solitary prophet who would have given
> anything, including his life, to be able to tell another kind of
> tale, one filled with joy and fervor rather than sorrow and
> anguish.

> But he transmitted only what he received—and so do we.
> And so do we. And if God was angry at him for not weeping,
> we are not. Quite the contrary: we are proud of him. The
> world was not worthy of his tears. Or ours.[13]

In the end the survivors have no choice but to go on witnessing.
Yet, as Wiesel stressed in 1981, they do so with awareness that
their numbers are steadily declining, that the next generation may
be one without memories, and above all of being tired.

> First ignored, then resented, we have seen our message dis-
> torted, cheapened, trivialized, commercialized so much that we
> do not know what to do: to speak or not to speak, to give
> more words or to take them back. For years we have tried to
> tell the tale, but now we feel more misunderstood than ever.
> The survivors are weary of whispering, alerting, warning, pro-
> testing, compelling others to remember, weary of trying to
> preserve the sacred dimension of a certain experience, a certain
> despair, a certain defiance. Oh, yes, we *are* weary.[14]

In their commitment to life and truth, the survivors recall ultimate
violence in order to prevent its recurrence. Since they are incapable of revealing the event, the admission of this becomes an
integral part of testimony. "This is what I have been doing in
my own work," wrote Wiesel in 1983. "I write to denounce
writing. I tell of the impossibility one stumbles upon in trying
to tell the tale. I need only close my eyes for my words to desert
me, repudiate me." In a lecture that same year, Wiesel stressed
that their desire was not to make people sad but to make them
more aware, open, and sensitive. It was insensitivity and indifference that led to the great massacre. "We have learned that
indifference to evil is evil." If evil strikes one people and others
do not react, the dynamic of evil continues.[15]

In conversation with Harry Cargas, Wiesel spoke of literature
and human destiny together as endeavors by man to redeem
himself, to take responsibility for one's own suffering, rather than
be condemned forever to a meaningless solitude.[16] In conversation with Lily Edelman, in contrast, Wiesel not only spoke of
the guilt and ambivalence surrounding writing of the Holocaust

("Only one of my books, *Night*, deals directly with the Holocaust; all the others reveal why one cannot speak about it"), but also laid bare the motive for *The Oath* as his reaction to the way in which others began to misuse, misunderstand, misinterpret, and distort the Holocaust after the survivors succeeded in creating a certain awareness of it:

> As a result, I often tell myself that in 1945 all of us, all the survivors, should perhaps have gathered in a conclave in a forest somewhere and decided that whoever survived should not speak. . . . That's why I put so much stress in the book on the oath of silence.[17]

In "Why I Write" Wiesel speaks of a contrary oath: "If, by some miracle, I emerge alive, I will devote my life to testifying on behalf of those whose shadow will fall on mine forever and ever." Wiesel writes to remain faithful to those to whom he owes his roots and his memory, the million massacred Jewish children, hungry, thirsty, and afraid, with no one to comfort or reassure them. These haunt his writings, and even when Wiesel writes about other things, it is in order to keep the essential—the personal experience—unspoken. Nor does the fact that he has written only one book about the Holocaust mean that it is absent in his other works. The presence of the dead affects even the most removed characters in even the most foreign of settings: "When I speak of Abraham, Isaac, and Jacob, when I evoke Rabbi Yohanan ben Zakkai and Rabbi Akiba, it is the better to understand them in the light of Auschwitz." "I never intended to be a philosopher, or a theologian," Wiesel says earlier in the same essay. "The only role I sought was that of witness." And even when the survivor feels remorse because his witness seems all in vain, he must continue to speak, whether his song is heard or not. "What matters is to struggle against silence with words, or through another form of silence . . . and thus justify the faith placed in you, a long time ago, by so many victims." Wiesel writes to help the dead vanquish death.[18] "*Thanatos thanatan,*" it says of Christ in the Greek Orthodox Easter service—"Dead, he vanquished death." This is what Wiesel—the Holocaust survivor who died to life and returned to it to witness—has done, in an entirely human way and yet one that must inspire awe in all who know him or have heard him lecture or have really read one of his books.[19]

Silence

Wiesel has not only refused to choose between witness and silence and held the tension between them. He has also confronted silence with silence, penetrating and permeating his words with a thick silence from which they receive both their depth and their resonance. It behooves us, therefore, to understand silence not only as an alternative to Wiesel's witness but also, along with madness and laughter, as an integral part of it. I have cited the three basic attitudes that befit the Jew, according to the Hasidic master Menahem Mendel of Vorki: "Upright kneeling, silent screaming, motionless dance." Who more than Elie Wiesel in our day has embodied these basic attitudes?

In Wiesel's early novel *Dawn*, before young Elisha executes the British hostage at the behest of the Jewish terrorist movement, for which he works in pre-state Palestine, he goes over to the little boy that he used to be and asks him why he, along with all the other family, teachers, and friends who have gathered around him, is judging him. They are all silent, the boy replies, because "silence is not only our dwelling place but our very beings as well. We *are* silence. And your silence is us." It is not they who judge him. "Your silence is your judge."[1] In *The Town Beyond the Wall*, two novels later, the hero Michael reflects that it is when he is silent that he is alive. "In silence I define myself."[2]

In Wiesel's next novel, *The Gates of the Forest*, the hero, Gregor, moves much more deeply into silence as his true realm. In the cave in which he hides out in spring, he had become used to silence, and he loved it. There his companion had told him that people talk because they are afraid, because they are trying to convince themselves that they are still alive. "It's in the silence after the storm that God reveals himself to man. God is silence." Now in summer under the protection of his family's servant Maria in her native village, Gregor masquerades as a mute (what Grisha in *The Testament* literally becomes), and he comes to love the silence still more deeply. His muteness allows him to glimpse a universe which has nothing in common with words, and in the future he lives for the purpose of putting together the scraps of this universe that he kept. "Sometimes he fancies he is succeeding and then the sounds of the faraway night become voices and he shuts his eyes in order to hear them."³

But Wiesel does not let us forget that there is silence and silence. After his visit to the Soviet Union, he wrote a book, *The Jews of Silence*. Later he came to regret that he had given them that sobriquet; for they sang and danced and, with the meagerest of means, celebrated their Jewishness in a manner that would befit the most fervent Hasid, whereas the Jews of the free world for the second time in a single generation committed the error of silence in regard to their endangered brethren. "What torments me most is not the Jews of silence I met in Russia, but the silence of the Jews I live among today."⁴ In Wiesel's next novel, *A Beggar in Jerusalem*, the co-hero Katriel warns that not all silences are pure or creative, for some are sterile and malignant, and it is not easy to distinguish between them. Katriel prefers not the silence which preceded creation, the one that contains chaos and solitude, but the silence which accompanied the revelation, the one that suggests presence, fervor, plentitude. "I like silence to have a history and be transmitted by it." Like Martin Buber, who spoke of a silence that is dialogue and told of a three-hour walk that he took with a friend in Berlin without either of them saying a word, Katriel affirms that he can spend a whole evening with his father or his wife without saying a word, yet know when it is over that each has told the other all there is to tell.[5]

Wiesel concludes his book of essays *One Generation After* with a message to the victims of the Holocaust, a message of silence: "Tell them that silence, more than language, remains the substance and the seal of what was once their universe, and that, like language, it demands to be recognized and transmitted."[6] Yet silence, as Mendel of Vorki has told us, is also the language of the Jew, and above all of the true Hasid. The great Hasidic rabbi Nachman of Bratzlav could scream silently in the midst of a crowd, and his cry was heard in the far corners of the earth. Menahem Mendel of Kotzk, realizing that the most pure and beautiful concepts were losing their weight of silence through smug repetition, tried to save Hasidism by redefining its objectives. His way of saying his prayers was to remain silent. When asked to recite Psalms for the dying Seer of Lublin, his former master, he was the only one to refuse. "The cry that one holds back is more powerful," he later explained, adding that there are certain experiences that can be transmitted only by silence and some that cannot be transmitted at all. Truth must be sought. It is not necessary to reveal it. "Silence in Kotzk is so heavy, so dense that it tears the nights," Wiesel reports in his portrait of the Kotzker rebbe in *Souls on Fire*. "Kotzk is neither philosophy nor social system; Kotzk is a narrow and solitary road whose beginning touches its end; a road where silence enters the word and tears it apart the way the eye tears apart what it sees."[7]

"God is not silent; God is Silence," Wiesel quotes the thirteenth-century Hebrew poet Eleazar Rokeah, and adds himself, "Without the thought that behind the words we say there is another word we do not say, our words would be empty." "The greatest poetry comes from words that are coated in silence," Wiesel said elsewhere. In still another place Wiesel confessed himself obsessed with silence because the world was silent when we needed its outcry and because God was silent. If God is present in history, His presence must be felt.[8]

In *Four Hasidic Masters*, Wiesel tells us of Rabbi Naftali of Ropshitz, who always found the right word for every situation, but behind whose words there were other, inaudible, imperceptible words, and behind even these words silence. Rabbi Naftali died without speaking, opposing to the anxious questions of his sons an absolute silence, signifying by gestures that his muteness was nothing mystical, but confessing on his last day, in a slow, burning whisper, that he did not want to speak because he was afraid![9] In *Somewhere a Master*, Wiesel devotes a whole chapter to the School of Vorki, Hasidic masters who placed silence at the center of their service of God. In this chapter Wiesel confesses that as a child he yearned for the "mystical silence that evokes faraway secrets and forbidden truth." His kabbalistic teachers had taught him "how to cleanse language and thought by refusing to indulge in language and thought, thereby hastening the coming of the Messiah." God not only loves silence, said Rabbi Eliezer of Worms. "God *is* silence." The silence that comes at Sinai after the tempest and thunder and lightning signifies that God is present, ready to be heard. People come to Vorki simply to be silent, Wiesel tells us, "to discover living silence—the newest and most disturbing aspect of the Hasidic experience." Silence is good even if it is empty, said Rabbi Mendel of Vorki, whereas words if they are empty remain empty. Rabbi Mendel was obsessed with silence not in order to withdraw from language but to amplify and deepen it with silence, Wiesel suggests. There are zaddikim, Just Men, Mendel suggested a week before he died, who possess the powers to bring the Messiah but who, since God is silent, choose to remain silent, too.

Another reason he is obsessed with silence, Wiesel confessed in 1979, is that he is afraid of the written word. While the practical silence of indifference can be misinterpreted, mystical silence, the creative, poetic silence, which is itself a mode of language, cannot. Silence has shades, layers, dimensions, colors, tones which, if you are worthy of its using you, are conveyed as a secret. Words are a horizontal approach, while silence offers a vertical one into which you plunge. "To speak about silence is to reduce it, but in every book I do speak about silence," for silence is the universe itself. "You must break silence in order to communicate silence." This is especially true now when, for the first time in history, we feel unworthy to use words. We know that in speaking about the Holocaust we diminish it. In the beginning was not the word, but silence. Yet even some words contain more darkness than light, for language, too, can be exiled and uprooted—"the sudden dichotomy between the word and its meaning."[10]

When divine silence is answered by human silence, it is tragic for both, Wiesel comments. At the same time, he confesses that he feels close to Vorki because of its silence, which symbolizes for him *l'univers concentrationnaire*, a universe that *was* dominated by silence. What haunts us is the silence of the victims, all those who walked into their death and left behind them a silence that attained the level of the absolute, if any silence ever did.

> We have so far failed to decipher or even to confront God's silence in a universe empty of God—or worse: filled with God.
> Now, in this generation, we have learned at least one lesson: that some experiences lie beyond language, that their language *is* silence. For silence does not necessarily mean absence of communication. . . . The silence of the victim is one thing, that of the killer, another. And that of the spectator, still another. There is creative silence, there is murderous silence. To a perceptive human being the universe is never silent—but there exists a universe of silence, and only perceptive human beings are aware of it.[11]

The silence of Vorki can be understood in the light of the silence of *l'univers concentrationnaire*. It was "an appeal, an outcry to God on behalf of his desperate people and also on His behalf, an offering to night, to heaven . . . to mark the end of language—the outer limits of creation—a burning secret buried in silence."[12]

In the beginning of *The Oath* Azriel warns his young friend: you "risk stumbling over a people engulfed in silence and protected by it." Moshe the Madman tells Azriel's father that though the words pronounced at Sinai are so well known that they have been distorted and exploited, the silence communicated from atop that same mountain has not. It has been transmitted only among the initiated like a secret tradition that eludes language. There is another, secret tradition that only the Messiah can speak without betrayal, and it remains to be seen whether he will speak at all. Speaking of God so as not to speak of ourselves, Moshe tells the assembled Jews, whom he forces to take an oath of silence, What will remain of us will be only something of our kinship and our silence.[13]

Paltiel Kossover, in his testament in the novel of that name, writes that he is beginning to believe in the word "mystery": "The words you strangle, the words you murder, produce a kind of primary, impenetrable silence. And you will never succeed in killing a silence such as this." But Paltiel also sees silence as the ultimate torture, invented by a poet of vengeance. As a child and adolescent, he had begged God for a mute master who would impart his truth wordlessly, and he spent hours with a disciple of the Hasidic school of Worke, whose rebbe had turned silence into a method and with Rebbe Mendel the Taciturn, who helped him listen to the song of the silence of Jerusalem—"a celestial and yet tangible silence in which both voices and moments attain immortality." Now in solitary confinement in prison, he has learned that silence can be nefarious and evil, driving the human being to lies and treason. Silence is the prison which isolates one not only from mankind but from oneself as well. "Silence was more sophisticated, more brutal torture than any interrogation session," because it unsettles the senses and the nerves, sets the imagination on fire, and fills the soul with night and death. Silence kills impulse and passion, desire and the memory of desire, invading, dominating, and reducing the human being to a slavery in which one is no longer human. He learns that it is possible to die of silence, as one dies of pain, sorrow, hunger, or illness. He understands now that God fashioned man in His image and conferred on him the right to speak, because God, too, was afraid of silence![14]

Speaking of the ten years in which he traveled the world and found his own area of possibilities, Wiesel reported: "I explored the dimension of silence in me. There were weeks and weeks and weeks when I didn't speak, not a word, voluntarily—not one single word. I wanted to see what one does with silence." This dimension of silence entered into Wiesel's writings so that even what is cut out remains in the density of those pages that he preserved.[15] Commenting on the power of silence in conversation with Lily Edelman, Wiesel distinguished between the silence of indifference and that of the person who has too much to say:

> Of course, my silence is meant to be a very eloquent silence, a screaming silence, a shouting silence. . . . Before going to his post, Israel's first ambassador to Russia was told by President Weizmann, "You will not be able to speak to the Jews in Russia. But there is one thing you can do, and that is to remain silent. Let your silence be heard from one corner of the world to the other."[16]

In conversation with Harry James Cargas, Wiesel spoke of the penetrated, inspired silence which can be an expression of gratitude: "When I hear a beautiful trio by Beethoven or Mozart, I feel gratitude . . . and I keep quiet, and then I feel that I share, I participate in the playing with my silence." André Neher speaks of the "energetic dimension of silence" in his profound essay "*Shaddai:* The God of the Broken Arch," published in a book of essays, *Confronting the Holocaust: The Impact of Elie Wiesel.* Wiesel himself embodies that dimension as also that "diagonal bar of silence" which, says Neher, is drawn across the Book of Job.[17] Robert McAfee Brown speaks of a "silence of communicative power." That, too, is Elie Wiesel.[18]

The most sustained commentary on silence in the literary universe of Elie Wiesel is found in Ellen Fine's *Legacy of Night.* Comparing the silence of Michael and the spectator in *The Town Beyond the Wall,* Fine points out that while both are voiceless, Michael's voice is choked, whereas the indifferent spectator's voice is absent. Michael's silence is coerced, the spectator's the product of evasiveness and non-involvement. The muteness of both means resignation to society as it is, but there is a movement from the absence of the word to its presence:

> Michael's transformation from the silent stranger to the messenger of the dead occurs during the course of his confrontation with the spectator. His verbal assault on this man who has come to personify the indifferent world is a cry of defiance that releases him from his silent exile, his isolation and state of anonymity.[19]

This movement from the absence to the presence of the word has made Wiesel, too, a messenger of the dead, but a messenger whose voice is often that of the "silence after death." Wiesel "has made silence go beyond its limits and, from another level of reality, cry out," says Fine.[20] A mediocre person surrounds silence with empty words, said Wiesel in his conversation with Lily Edelman, "but a poet surrounds his silence with words containing layers of silence, dramatic tension, visions of horror, acts of gratitude." Wiesel is a poet in just this sense:

> If words structure Wiesel's literary universe, silence envelops it and lies at its deep center. . . . The witness seeks to make this legacy of unheard voices speak. He wants to transform the absence of the dead into a presence that transcends the finality of death. If words dissolve into darkness, the density of silence emanating from the extermination camps accumulates to the point of exploding, and it is just at this intersection of extremes, where language and silence are pushed to their limits, that the survivor-writer finds himself. This meeting place of words and non-words is what he tries to capture in his art. . . . The unutterable resonates through the selection of certain words and the exclusion of others. And these cautiously chosen expressions, chiseled into monuments, are imbued with a sacred stillness that takes form.[21]

THIRTEEN

Madness and Laughter

"You will find madness, laughter, and silence in all of my writings," Elie Wiesel once hinted in conversation with me. The reader of Wiesel's works will indeed find these motifs interspersed throughout. They are so omnipresent and scattered that they serve as a sort of ground. Focused on as the figure, they become an impressive theme in their own right. Madness and laughter are often expressed in silence in Wiesel's writings, but even more, as we shall see, laughter is often a form of madness, as madness itself is eloquent silence and the sanest speech.

> In all my books I stress certain themes: the theme of madness—because it was an era of madness; the theme of silence—because maybe only silence can transmit some fragment of the fire each of us took with him; and the theme of laughter. Maybe the whole thing was a farce, a theological farce. Maybe someone is laughing. It is not even a tragedy. It is a huge comedy, a divine comedy.[1]

MADNESS

"Madmen have always occupied me," confessed Wiesel in 1974. "Not madmen who kill but mystical madmen intoxicated by God. Rather than provoke solitude, they try to combat it." In the same year, Wiesel extended madness to the whole of the Jewish people—from their beginnings, when they chose the worst geographic spot in the Middle East—a crossroad of caravans—through the twenty centuries in which Europe tried to uproot and exile them, to today, when the entire world is in danger. Yet Maimonides said that the entire world exists thanks to some madmen. After the war Wiesel spent two years studying psychiatry, because he was so interested in madness. But Wiesel distinguishes between three sorts of madmen—the clinical madman whose madness is self-destructive, isolating himself and others; the mystical madman, whose madness brings people together, striving to make evil disappear and the Messiah come; and the evil madman, like Hitler, who is both clinical and mystical, but in an antinomian way.[2]

"Who is mad?" asks Wiesel, and replies: "Someone who tries to see God. Because then either he dies—according to the Bible he must die; he who sees God dies—or if he doesn't die, he must go mad, and maybe he goes mad in order not to die."[3] In *Messengers of God* Wiesel describes Job as a "moment of obsession, a gleam of anguish, a cry contained but not stifled trying to pierce our consciousness, a mirror a thousand times shattered reflecting the image of a solitude bursting with madness."[4] And in *Five Biblical Portraits* he reminds us that because the people of his time rejected Jeremiah's words, they called him a false prophet and a madman. Like the sufferer in Wiesel's novel *The Accident*, Jeremiah is a person who causes those around him to lose all impulse to live. Though surrounded by people, he is alone with and against God.

> Wherever he goes, he breathes misfortune, he shatters serenity. Like all prophets before him, he is constantly in the opposition, forever fighting the establishment, ridiculing power and those who hold it, emphasizing the fragility of the present, the uncertainty of the future.[5]

Wiesel's "mystical madness" is close to the moral madness of the Hebrew prophets, Robert McAfee Brown asserts. Hosea, warning of the approach of the days of punishment, calls the prophet a fool and the man of the spirit mad (9:7); Elisha is referred to as "this mad fellow" (2 Kings 9:11, *RSV*); and Jeremiah is threatened with being in the stocks as befits "every madman who prophesies" (29:26, *RSV*). Ranging Wiesel with them, Brown writes:

> No prophetic annunciation in Wiesel is announced simplistically by pat formulas. It receives no vindication by assurances or proofs. Its survival will always be in spite of massive evidence to the contrary. To believe in others will remain an act of madness in a world like ours. To believe in God will compound the madness.
> But it may be the only road toward true sanity.[6]

Wiesel finds an even richer precedent for his fascination with madness in Hasidism.

> All the first Hasidic masters were mad, and therefore I love them. . . . They had to be mad to try to transmit a message of humanism, a message of beauty, a message of compassion in a world that had none. Hasidism is an act of madness—sacred, mystical madness. I discovered in the very beginning with shock, and then with exaltation, that from the Besht to the Kotzker Rebbe, all of them—Rebbe Nachman of Bratzlav, Elimelekh of Lizensk, and the Shpoler Zeide, even Levi Yitzhak of Berditchev—at some point in their lives played with madness or were tempted by madness.[7]

In his portrait of Israel Baal Shem Tov, the great founder of Hasidism, Wiesel goes out of his way to tell us of a madwoman who understood the Baal Shem's powers and his great future long before any of the town's devout and erudite men because she *spoke his language*. The great Hasidic rabbi Levi Yitzhak of Berditchev admired King Solomon because he understood the language of madmen. Rabbi Nachman of Bratzlav, the great-grandson of the Baal Shem, outwitted Satan by playing the careless, carefree madman. And madness figures prominently in the fantastic tales that Rabbi Nachman loved to weave as his special form of teaching. Once when a king learned that whoever ate of the next harvest would be struck by madness, he elected to join his people rather than protect himself: "When the world is gripped by delirium, it is senseless to watch from the outside: the mad will think that we are mad, too." Rather, he and his advisor should eat and become mad themselves, hoping that through them the others might find the strength to resist later. But he said that each should mark the other's forehead with the seal of madness, so that every time they look at each other, these two will know that they are mad. In another tale of Rabbi Nachman's, a mad king who imagined he was a rooster was cured by an unknown sage who pretended to be a rooster himself. Wiesel also tells a variant of the earlier tale in which the king who knows that the next harvest will make him and all his subjects mad entrusts to a friend the key to a granary in which all of the last, nonschizophrenogenic crops were stored. Spared from the common madness, the friend's mission was to become a messenger covering the whole earth and telling tales and shouting at the people that what is at stake is their life, their survival![8]

But the *source* of Wiesel's fascination with madness is neither biblical nor Hasidic. It is the experience of the Holocaust, of a world gone mad, in which madness of a different sort is the only way to preserve one's sanity. "Anyone who was in the camps came out deranged. . . . To remain normal would itself be mad." Asked by Cargas why he is not mad, Wiesel replied, "Maybe I am and I don't know it. If I am, I try to know it." Looking at what has happened and what is going to happen, Wiesel finds himself haunted by madness. "Then in order to save myself from *that* madness, I go back to another madness—a holy madness— the one that became a victim, the one that kept us alive for so many centuries, for thousands of years." But the madness that Wiesel embraces is not insanity, against which we should fight, but a "mystical madness," one that is essential if one is going to have children and essential to communicate to them if one is *not* to be insane. "One has to be mad today, in this time and age,

to say certain things and believe that they could make a difference."[9] In conversation with Lily Edelman, Wiesel again spoke
of a mystical, as opposed to a clinical, madman whose madness
is that he becomes one with the world, man, and God. In the
face of the rationalism that led to the Holocaust, madness is the
only sane alternative:

> If there is one word that can include all other words about
> the Holocaust that word is madness—madness from the vic-
> tim's point of view, madness from the executioner's point of
> view, madness from God's point of view, from man's point of
> view. The winds of madness were blowing. Creation itself was
> contaminated.[10]

But the madness of the characters that Wiesel portrays is of a
different order. It is the madness of those who want to survive
intact in an evil world—pure and beautiful madmen who try to
save the world, not destroy it. Captured by the evil forces, Wiesel
tries to give them back to the pure forces. "All the messengers
are mad, all the saints are mad."

> If we were to tell the story and remind the world of our
> madness, some things might change. We are mad to go on
> believing in what we believe—in mankind. We are mad to go
> on praying and worshipping and remaining Jews. We are mad
> to go on believing in words. We are mad to believe something
> can be done. . . . Even in an era of madness man is capable of
> humanity. In spite of the cruelty, the ordeals, and the agonies,
> we are still capable of dreaming strange and marvelous dreams,
> of strange and marvelous victories.[11]

Enlarging on Wiesel's statement that if Eichmann was sane,
he preferred to be mad, Robert McAfee Brown points to the
"sane" people in charge of burning babies alive in camps at the
behest of the "reality" that dictated that Jews be exterminated by
every and any means. Such "sanity" left no alternative to those
who challenged these assumptions other than "to embrace an
unacceptable view of reality, i.e., to be mad."[12] Emil Fackenheim
puts Wiesel's madness theme into a traditionally Jewish category

by suggesting that he has offered us a "mad Midrash." Midrash, the traditional Jewish commentary on the Bible by way of legends and stories, suffuses everything Wiesel has written, Fackenheim points out. Wiesel's Midrash is mad, as Wiesel himself has hinted, because, in contrast to insanity, it dares not flee from the horrifying reality to some more palatable illusion. It is a Truth transcending the world of which it is a victim; yet it is not a mysticism that rises above the contradictions of human existence toward some divine ecstasy. The mad Midrash "cannot but hold fast to *its* world, the anti-world." In opposition to this anti-world, of which it can be neither part nor heir, it wishes to restore the world and thus "turns into a Kaddish for all the victims of the anti-world, 'that solemn affirmation full of grandeur and serenity, by which man returns to God His crown and sceptre.' " Midrashic madness is thus redemptive. It points to an existence in which the madness is transfigured. "After Planet Auschwitz, there can be no health without *this* madness, no joy, no life. Without this madness a Jew cannot do—with God or without him—what a Voice from Sinai bids him to do: choose life."[13]

"The 'mad' persons in Wiesel's writings," summarizes Brown, "are those who see things in a way radically different from other persons, and have the effrontery to speak out, no matter what the cost."[14] The most important of such persons is Moshe the Madman, who threads his way through many of Wiesel's novels and even some of his nonfiction, since Wiesel really did know such a man. "Rather than reject his madness, Moshe evoked it. It served him as a refuge, as homeland," wrote Wiesel in an essay devoted to him in *Legends of Our Time*. This figure from his past exerts a strange power over him, Wiesel confesses, a power which he cannot escape.

> I want to run away, but Moshe guards all the exits. Armed with unknown power, he commands and I obey: it is my life against his. To escape him, I would have to destroy him. But how does one assassinate an angel gone mad? . . . The idea occurs to me at times that I myself am nothing but an error,

a misunderstanding: I believe I am living my own life, when in fact I am transmitting his.[15]

This possession goes back to Wiesel's childhood in which he knew a broad-shouldered, heavyset, and always starving beadle with red bushy beard and frequently bleeding, swollen lips. "I can still feel the bite of his fierce, frightened eyes, which, unseen but seeing, lurked behind the two narrow slits carved in his untidy face." Persecuted by the schoolchildren during his summer months of madness (he regained his sanity before the High Holidays and conducted services and taught), he sometimes sought refuge in the Wiesel home, where he drank and sang to forget his pain. The young Elie tried in vain to get him to describe what was tormenting him. "As I listened to him, I felt myself turning into someone else. He frightened and fascinated me; I knew that he moved in a universe all his own." Wiesel's later fascination with psychiatry and the insane stemmed, he suspects, from Mad Moshe; for the insane, too, "are alone and they sing—their silence sings," and they see things we do not. Managing to escape from the first deportation, Moshe the Beadle comes back to Sighet to tell people of what is really happening. Transformed into a tireless messenger, he is no longer the gentle, shy stutterer but a public speaker and agitator, impatient and irascible. But his speaking brings him no credence. In response to tales that made their skin crawl, people said to one another, "Poor beadle, he has lost his mind." Lapsed into silence, a muteness bordering on madness, "only his burning eyes revealed the impotent rage inside him." Finally, after two years, he disappears forever.[16] It is this story that Wiesel tells in *Night*.

When young Elie goes at his father's behest to awaken an old man to tell him to prepare for deportation, he too is regarded as mad. On the train on the way to Auschwitz, Madam Schachter goes mad, and it is she who sees in her mind's eye the terrible fire that the others behold only when they arrive! Terrified by her incessant screaming until they feel that madness is taking possession of them all, the others beat and gag her into silence until they themselves arrive at Birkenau, the reception center for Auschwitz, where they see flames gushing out of a tall chimney and smell the abominable odor of burning flesh. "In one ultimate moment of lucidity," comments Wiesel, "it seemed to me that we were damned souls wandering in the half-world, souls condemned to wander through space till the generations of man came to an end, seeking their redemption, seeking oblivion—without hope of finding it."[17] In the kingdom of night, as Michael Berenbaum observes, madness is a correct perception of reality in a world gone mad.[18]

"I have a plan—to go mad," Wiesel quoted Dostoevsky in the motto to his third novel, *The Town Beyond the Wall*, and madness figures strongly in this novel. Michael's father tells him that the real Moishe, who hides behind the madman, is a great person who sees worlds that remain inaccessible to us, one whose madness is only a wall erected to protect those for whom such far seeing would be dangerous. Moishe himself asserts that in these days honest men can do only one thing: go mad—stay human and preserve their wholeness through spitting on logic, intelligence, sacrosanct reason! "God loves madmen. They're the only ones he allows near him," Michael says to his friend Pedro when telling him about Moishe, who wept when he sang because he was heartbroken, but laughed when he silently mused that nothing is as whole as a broken heart.[19] The old man Varady, who wishes to be immortal by opposing God, is also mad in this novel. But Michael, looking back on his community in those years, tells Pedro that all of them were mad:

> In those years, nineteen forty-three, nineteen forty-four, you had to be crazy to believe that man has any control over his fate. You had to be crazy to hope for a victory of the spirit over the forces of evil, to imagine any possibility of redemption, of consolation; you had to have lost your reason, or sacrificed it, to believe in God, to believe in man, to believe in a reconciliation between them.[20]

Pedro in response teaches Michael what Michael calls a "madman's prayer": "Oh God, give me the strength to sin against you, to oppose your will! Give me the strength to deny you, reject you, imprison you, ridicule you!"

The meaning of the motto becomes clear in the "Second Prayer"—the second day Michael must stand unmoving before the wall as the Hungarian police try to get him to betray Pedro, who has used the black market to get him behind the Iron Curtain into his hometown Cerenczavaros, the "city of luck." To revolt against the absurd means to break through the other side of the wall, to give up holding the tension in favor of abandoning oneself to madness. The death of the "little prince," the boy Yankel, who survived the extermination camps only to be crushed by a truck in Paris, brings Michael to the verge of madness. The death of this child becomes for him a negative touchstone of reality which tests and judges all things and which tempts him to liberate himself from his self through choosing madness. One leap, one yes, one acquiescence and he would be in that pool in the valley in which fear is banished forever. But this is a temptation to which Michael does not give in; for this is no longer the madness that sees reality but the one that denies it. Even though one simple step would have enabled him to enter into the kingdom of madness, where there is no torment, problems, or anguish, and to bathe there in the divine source, Michael cannot use his freedom to destroy freedom. Pedro laughingly applauds Michael, saying he is trying to drive God mad. But Michael thinks, "God too is trying to drive me mad."[21]

Michael does not conquer once and for all the temptation to go mad. In an imaginary dialogue between Michael and Pedro in the "Third Prayer," Pedro says to Michael, "You frighten me. You want to eliminate suffering by pushing it to its extreme: to madness." Back in the prison cell in "The Last Prayer," Michael is confronted by Menachem, a pious Jew who pleads with him "not to surrender to the breakdown of sanity, of your person, of your soul. In a word, to madness."[22] This motif reappears in the last pages of the novel:

> For Michael madness was a door opening onto a forest, onto
> the liberty in which anything is permitted, anything is possible.
> . . . The universe frees itself from the order in which it was
> imprisoned. Appearance snaps its ties with reality.[23]

Michael is obsessed with King Lear, "who preferred suffering at
the hands of men to flight into a trackless desert," who faced
treason and cowardice directly and said, "I am here and nowhere
else!" Yet he berates him for not going mad as a way of spitting
in their faces, protesting against pain and injustice, rejecting their
life and their sanity. Later Michael complains to Pedro that his
soul is blotting up madness and night, that the whole universe
has gone mad. Yet by restoring the sanity of a boy in the cell
with him, he saves himself, as Pedro adjures him to do, and
resists the temptation to go mad.

In Wiesel's next novel, *The Gates of the Forest*, Gregor's grandfather tells him not to be afraid of madmen, for they are wandering messengers without whom the world could not endure,
messengers who preserve surprise on the earth and who even
surprise the Creator by escaping from Him and regarding Him
with pity. Later shut up in a cave with the mad laughter of
Gavriel, Gregor reflects that madmen believe themselves alone
in the world, as though they were holding it in the hollow of
their hand. "And they are right." He resolves that if he lives he
will give the rest of his life to finding out if Gavriel was crazy.
"I'll become him in order to understand him better, to understand
and love him, or to love him without understanding." The mad
Gavriel is the one who bears the message of the Holocaust that
no one knows, that no one wants to know. When Gregor carries
this message to Leib the Lion, the leader of the partisans whom
Gregor joins in the forest, Leib rejects it as "pure madness," and
angrily retorts that if what Gregor says is true, then both of them
are mad. Leib refuses to admit that the earth and sky of Europe
have become great, haunted cemeteries, but Gregor insists that
they are living in a time of madness, a universal eclipse in which
everything falls apart, and past, future, present, hope, humanity,
progress are nothing but words. Tomorrow has already been

extinguished; for "time only exists in the measure to which man is there to endure or bless or deny."[24]

When David goes back to his native town in *A Beggar in Jerusalem*, he meets a young madman in the sanatorium, one of the three or four remaining Jews, whose madness consists precisely in the fact that he sees reality as it is. Confronting a city emptied of all its Jews and of the Jewish life that once peopled it, he tells himself that these are the hallucinations of a sick and tortured mind: "I am not so mad as to suppose that my vision reflects any reality but my own."[25] On the other hand, Dan, one of the beggars whom David joins at the Wailing Wall in the old city of Jerusalem after the Six-Day War, is a prince of men whose madness is a proud rejection of the sanity of a civilization gone mad.

> Man has become dehumanized, horror is piled on horror, evil on evil. . . . Your entire universe is crumbling with violence and hatred. Old against young, white against black, poor against rich. Yesterday's holocaust will be followed by tomorrow's, and *that* one will be total! . . . Not all your scientists put together could guarantee the serenity of a single human being, yet they could easily destroy the last man's last breath on our planet. . . . You're all rushing into collective suicide, and you'd like to have me there with you as an accomplice?[26]

The response of the President to this statement is "mad, absolutely, incurably mad," and this is the reason the cabinet seizes on to explain Dan's refusal to return. Truth is dismissed as madness because it is too unpalatable, as the Nazi officer warns the Jew who refuses to die in *A Beggar in Jerusalem*. This statement (written by Wiesel in 1967) has proved prophetic, as Brown has pointed out, citing the more than sixty books that have been published attempting to prove that the Holocaust never happened. Yet *A Beggar* ends with a quite different, affirmative madness. When the Wailing Wall is being captured and everyone is rushing toward it, David sees all of them as "in the midst of a demented hell, with heaven and earth gone insane." "Have we all gone mad?" he screams into the ear of his friend Gad, the Israeli army officer. "I warned you, didn't I," responds Gad. "The madmen have taken things into their hands."[27]

The double positive and negative character of madness recurs in Wiesel's novel *The Oath*. One must be mad to hope to save someone, one must be mad to hope, thinks the old Azriel, whose "madness" frightens his young friend more than death. This is a positive madness, but the apocalyptic vision of horror in Kolvillàg, when the Master of the Universe seemed to have gone mad, is the quintessence of the negative—"the eruption of total violence, the rule of madness in the absolute sense, as though the absolute had become unhinged.

> As though the Creator, in a fit of joyous and destructive rage, had granted full freedom to His creatures . . . and these creatures, crazed by their burden of divinity, driven to madness and nothingness, suddenly resembled one another in their passionate hatred and vengefulness.[28]

The true hero and central character of *The Oath* is Moshe the Madman, and his madness enables him to see the future with clarity and to have compassion on an Israel and a humanity condemned by a mad world to destruction and decimation. "Moshe in *The Oath* is a composite of all the mad Moshes who have appeared throughout Wiesel's works," writes Ellen Fine. "His painful journey to the dark kingdom of Night has propelled him beyond the bounds of history" and turned him into a visionary. "Mystical in his attachment to humanity, righteous in his attempt to redeem mankind, a martyr who sacrifices himself for the sake of community, he is a 'madman turned saint, or the saint gone mad.' "[29]

If Wiesel's previous works center on the madness of man, Wiesel's play *Zalmen* (1974) centers on the "madness of God," and this is its subtitle. Zalmen, the beadle in the Soviet synagogue who finally succeeds in pushing the rabbi to a mad rebellion against the regime that puts them down, cries out to the rabbi:

> We are the imagination and madness of the world—we are imagination gone mad. One has to be mad today to believe in God and in man—one has to be mad to believe. One has to be mad to want to remain human. Be mad, Rabbi, be mad![30]

Become mad and fear will shatter at your feet, Zalmen tells the rabbi. Formerly, a rabbi was one who taught humility and forgiveness and brought wisdom and serenity. Today, suggests Zalmen, he is someone who drives you to pain, torture, and madness. Later, when the inspector is interrogating the rabbi because of the sermon he gave, the rabbi responds to the inspector's exclamation "Sheer madness!" with an affirmation of madness: "sheer madness, pure and impure madness, dark madness, liberating madness, salutary madness." Later, the inspector dismisses the rabbi's gesture of martyrdom as the "dream of a madman," declaring that his "revolt quite simply *did not take place!*" and the play ends with the laughter of Zalmen the mad beadle. Brown explains the play's subtitle, "The Madness of God," as "the decision of God to be found among the weak—with those who always seem to be put down (the Jews, to take a not-so-random example), to exhibit the divine presence where least expected and most easily discounted (among madmen, to take the least random example of all)."[31]

In his own comment on the play, Wiesel focuses on Zalmen's madness rather than God's:

> Zalmen, in my world, in my place, is the wisest of men; he knows the limits of our despair, he wants to deny them, to break them. To him madness is an answer to man's evil and to God's silence. One has to be mad, he says, to go on believing in justice, in history, in man's future.
>
> One has to be mad to want to go on telling the tale to a world which refuses to listen.[32]

LAUGHTER

The mad laughter of Gavriel in *The Gates of the Forest*, the laughter of the mad Zalmen in *Zalmen, or The Madness of God*, already demonstrate the link between madness and laughter in Wiesel. But laughter is also a motif in itself that, often in close relation to madness, threads its way through most of Wiesel's writings.

In Wiesel's first novel, *Dawn*, the young hero tells the story of how he owes his life to a laugh. A Nazi was about to choke him to death at Buchenwald for hiding in a barracks when the sight of this miserable clown appeared so comical that he lost his grip and burst out laughing. Later, Elisha tells Ilana that he is afraid that Captain John Dawson, the hostage whom the Jewish terrorist movement has ordered him to execute, will make him laugh.[33] In *The Accident*, Wiesel's next novel, the hero reflects that his mistress, Kathleen, like Christ, believes too much in the power of love to protect man from suffering. He, in contrast, can only laugh at the thought of love or death, so absent is hope, so pervasive indifference. Later he thinks back to his teacher's statement that God needs man and thinks of the pious men who walked to their deaths singing that it is we, with our fire, who will break the chains of the Messiah in exile. Now the symbolic implication of what his teacher said comes clear. What philosophers and poets have refused to admit is that God needs man because, "condemned to eternal solitude, he made man only to use him as a toy, to amuse himself." "In the beginning there was neither the Word, nor Love, but laughter, the roaring, eternal laughter whose echoes are more deceitful than the mirages of the desert."[34]

In *The Town Beyond the Wall*, after he leaves the asylum, Michael encounters mad Martha, who, twitching her naked belly obscenely, urges Michael to carry his revolt to the end and break through to the other side of the wall. "Take me and I'll teach you absurd love, imbecile love, eternal love. Take me to take revenge, to revolt yourself. To laughter you can only oppose laughter." To the laughter of God, who amuses Himself at our expense, we can oppose our laughter! When Menachem warns Michael in prison that he is headed straight for perdition, Michael responds, "That's possible. But I prefer to go down laughing."[35]

In the opening of *The Gates of the Forest*, shut in a cave with a nameless companion to whom he gives his Hebrew name Gavriel, Gregor finds himself loving and hating Gavriel's "laugh, which was like no other, which did not even resemble itself."

> Imagine a life-and-death struggle between two angels, the angel of love and the angel of wrath, the angel of promise and the angel of evil. Imagine that they both attain their ends, each one victorious. Imagine the laugh that would rise above their corpses as if to say, your death has given me birth; I am the soul of your conflict, its fulfillment as well.
> The laugh of the man who had saved his life.[36]

When Gregor first heard that laughter, it seemed not the laughter of one man but of seven times seven hundred, a laughter that threatened to drive him to insanity. When Gregor commands the man to stop laughing, he responds in Yiddish, "I'm listening to the war and I'm laughing." When Gavriel gives himself up to the Hungarian soldiers to save Gregor, "in the face of the soldiers and the stupefied dogs, he burst suddenly into overwhelming laughter." In "summer" Gregor tells Maria that Christ was crucified because he never learned to laugh: "If from the cross he hadn't appealed to the Father that had forsaken him, if he'd simply laughed, then he would have triumphed over the others and himself as well."[37]

In *Messengers of God* Wiesel ponders why Isaac, the most tragic of our ancestors, had a name which evokes and signifies laughter and answers that "as the first survivor, he had to teach us, the future survivors of Jewish history, that it is possible to suffer and despair an entire lifetime and still not give up the art of laughter." The Holocaust had marked Isaac and continued to haunt him; yet, in spite of everything, he remained capable of laughter.[38] Wiesel's cantata *Ani Ma'amin*, in which Abraham, Isaac, and Jacob complain to the Creator of the Holocaust, ends with the chant: "Blessed are the fools / Who go on laughing, / Who mock the man who mocks the Jews."[39] In Hasidism, too, Wiesel finds echoes of laughter at the Holocaust—mad, bitter laughter and triumphant, saving laughter. He recounts a story of Rabbi Nachman of Bratzlav's in which a sage and a messenger laugh at everyone who claims to know the king. "And they laugh," comments Wiesel:

> They laugh with such despair that in the end, they will understand that there must be a link between the voice and the call, between man and his road; in the end they will understand that their feeling of despair is not absurd, for it may well be the link that binds them to the king.[40]

The key to Rabbi Nachman's enigma, Wiesel suggests, is his ability to laugh, and it is in connection with the laughter that occupies such an astonishingly important place in the work of Rabbi Nachman that Wiesel offers us his own most sustained excursus on laughter:

> Laughter that springs from lucid and desperate awareness, a mirthless laughter, laughter of protest against the absurdities of existence, a laughter of revolt against a universe where man, whatever he may do, is condemned in advance. A laughter of compassion for man who cannot escape the ambiguity of his condition and of his faith. To blindly submit to God, without questioning the meaning of this submission, would be to diminish Him. To want to understand Him would be to reduce his intentions, His vision to the level of ours. How then can man take himself seriously? Revolt is not a solution, neither is submission. Remains laughter, metaphysical laughter. . . .
>
> In one of his tales we read: "Once upon a time there was a country that encompassed all the countries of the world. And in that country, there was a town that incorporated all the towns of the country; and in that town there was a street in which were gathered all the streets of the town; and on that street there was a house that sheltered all the houses of the street; and in that house there was a room, and in that room there was a man, and that man personified all men of all countries, and that man laughed and laughed—no one had ever laughed like that before."
>
> Who is that man? The Creator laughing at His creation?

Man sending Him back His laughter as an echo, or perhaps
as a challenge? Will we ever know.[41]

At the end of the chapter on Rabbi Nachman, Wiesel retells
the story about the king who enjoins his friend not to eat of the
harvest that will make the others mad but to become a messenger
to cry out to the people not to forget that their life, their survival,
is at stake. Wiesel finishes with an adaptation to legends and to
his own role as messenger of Nachman's story about the man in
the room who laughs:

> And the friend in question could not help but obey. He
> entered the legend with fiery shadows. And this legend en-
> compasses all other legends. It is haunted by a creature that
> reigns over all others, and this creature is laughing, laughing
> and crying, laughing and singing, laughing and dreaming,
> laughing so as not to forget that he is alone and that the king
> is his friend, his friend gone mad—but the king, is he laughing
> too? That is the question that contains all the others and gives
> life to its own tale, always the same tale, the tale of a king and
> of his friend separated by madness and united by laughter, fire
> and night.[42]

Rabbi Naftali of Ropshitz is another Hasidic master for whom
laughter performs a philosophical, quasi-religious function and
becomes an integral part of the Hasidic experience. Wiesel tells
a story in which the powers of the Holy Maggid of Kozhenitz,
including all his tears, prayers, and litanies, are set at naught
because God is listening to the funny stories of Rebbe Naftali.
And God, too, was laughing. "Naftali, Naftali, are you aware of
your own strength?" the Maggid of Kozhenitz would say to his
friend and disciple. "What I cannot accomplish with my tears,
you can accomplish with laughter!" Yet there is also a sad side
to Naftali's laughter which makes him one of the most misunderstood figures of Hasidism. "People saw his laughter but not
the torment beneath it." Indeed, he wanted them not to understand, not to pity him: "He laughed so as not to cry; he chose

exhibitionism so as to hide his anguish, his lack of confidence in himself, in his own powers, in his own words.[43]

In Wiesel's novel *The Oath*, it is laughter that unites the old man Azriel with Mad Moshe, his dead friend. Asked by villagers to perform a miracle and cure the insane and crippled, Azriel laughs, and in doing so dreams of a dreamer who haunts his dreams:

> I am present while my "I" explodes, I shall be present when it disappears. I brush against nothingness almost stealthily. And I shall penetrate the void. I am Azriel. I am not Azriel. I come face to face with his victims and I laugh. I come face to face with naked misery and I laugh. Sitting here, I contemplate injustice at its ugliest and I laugh. Suddenly I remember the features and expressions of my mad friend Moshe. Moshe in prison. Moshe facing me. As he faced me long ago. I open my mouth to give free rein to laughter. I am dreaming your dream, Moshe. It is you who are laughing. . . . Bravo, Moshe. Now I understand your teachings. In the valley of tears we are left one weapon, the last. Now I understand you. I will laugh like you. I am laughing louder and louder, louder than the noise of the mob and of the valley below, the noise of life and of heaven, I laugh with all my strength and I know that this time it is not your doing, it is mine. With my laughter I bring together earth and sea, hell and redemption, enigma and light, my self and its shell.[44]

Later in the novel, Azriel tells of a father who in the face of the imminent destruction of Kolvillàg was overwhelmed by an irresistible urge to laugh: "Laugh about life and man, laugh about his people so foolishly determined to survive in a twisted, perversely evil world, and about himself most of all."[45]

One of the principal characters of *The Testament* is the night watchman Viktor Zupanev, who tells little Grisha that he has never laughed in his life, that he has never been able to laugh even when he was kidding around and playing, even though he wanted to roar with laugher until he croaked. His parents, his neighbors, his adversaries, "life and death, intertwined like drunkards," did everything they could to make him laugh—without success. "I had no real friends, no real enemies, no mistresses, no illegitimate children—I had no one, I was no one. And all because I didn't know how to laugh." But at the end of the novel, Zupanev tells Grisha that on the day the Soviet officials learn that he has saved Paltiel Kossover's testament and the poet's song comes to haunt them from all corners of the globe, he will laugh at last, laugh for all the years he tried so hard and could not succeed.[46]

Wiesel's comment on laughter in *The Testament* becomes a commentary on laughter in all his novels and tales:

> We may even say that this is the story of laughter. In the beginning Zupanev cannot laugh. At the end he laughs. Why does he laugh? Because the story that was meant to be stifled, that was meant to be dead comes to life elsewhere—in Jerusalem. What a laughter! What a victory!
>
> The element of laughter plays an important role in all my tales. There is something about laughter that makes man more human or less. It all depends on what we do with it. When someone is sad, and he laughs, then there is strength in him. When someone is sad, and I laugh, then I am less human than before. . . .
>
> Often, in my novels, I make people laugh. Although the tragedy around them is tremendous, all-powerful, they laugh. That is their victory. . . .
>
> When I think of Paltiel Kossover, I feel he has all the right to join his friend, his unknown friend, Viktor Zupanev, and laugh at the world, but not only at the world: with the world and for the world.[47]

Laughter is the bridge between death and life in Wiesel's novels, writes Robert McAfee Brown, the laughter of madness, the laughter of despair acknowledging that all doors are closed, the laughter of anticipation that new doors are opening.[48] In conversation with Harry James Cargas, Wiesel speaks of laughter in his works not as comedy but as defiance and as a victory: "The only way to be victorious over God is to laugh, not at Him, but with Him." But laughter is also a sort of anguish in times of despair, the fear that maybe God simply created man to laugh at him. "So laughter again has all the possibilities in my tales to open all the avenues and explore all the hypotheses of God and Man, and man and Man."[49]

FOURTEEN

The Job of Auschwitz I

"How is life with God still possible in a time in which there is an Auschwitz?" writes Martin Buber.

> The estrangement has become too cruel, the hiddenness too deep. One can still "believe" in the God who allowed those things to happen, but can one still speak to Him? Can one still hear His word? . . . Dare we recommend to the survivors of Auschwitz, the Job of the gas chambers: "Give thanks unto the Lord, for He is good; for His mercy endureth forever"? . . . Do we stand overcome before the hidden face of God like the tragic hero of the Greeks before faceless fate? No, rather even now we contend, we too, with God. . . . We do not put up with earthly being; we struggle for its redemption, and struggling we appeal to the help of our Lord, who is again and still a hiding one.[1]

The Job of Auschwitz begins with the scientific extermination of six million Jews, a million Gypsies, and four million other human beings, *and* with those who have had to continue living with the memory and in the face of those unimaginable horrors. It is Elie Wiesel who, at the center of an ever-growing literature on the Holocaust, has given classic expression to the Job of Auschwitz. It is he above all who has become the voice and the protest of those who were exterminated and of those who survived the extermination and who have had to contend for forty years with the blight it has thrown on their lives and that of their wives and children and all of those who stand in close contact with them.

For most people, Job is associated with suffering, patience, and piety. For Wiesel, as for Buber and myself, Job is associated above all with trust *and* contending, with wrestling with God within the dialogue with God. "The dialogical leads inevitably to Job's question to God," wrote Martin Buber. "My God will not allow to become silent in the mouth of his creature the complaint about the great injustice in the world, and when in an unchanged world his creature yet finds peace because God has again granted him his nearness . . . that is a peace that is compatible with the fight for justice in the world."[2] In *Problematic Rebel: Melville, Dostoevsky, Kafka, Camus* I present Job as the paradigm of the biblical rebel:

> Job never gives up his trust in the creator who is also his redeemer, but he can only recognize him as the God of the real world in which the innocent suffer while the wicked prosper. Were Job to experience an evil so terrible that he could not recognize the voice of God in it, he would no longer be able to trust in God; for trust in God, at its deepest level, means trust in existence. Job's "temptation" is that he may . . . find it impossible to bring his suffering, his loathing, and his horror into his dialogue with God. Job's temptation is equally, however, that he will not stand his ground and witness for his own innocence when no one else will do so. . . . In the end Job withstands *both* temptations—that which comes to him from his bitterness and that which comes from his dread: he neither denies God nor ceases to contend with him. . . . He holds fast to his trust in the real God whom he meets in the dreadful fate that has befallen him, and he holds fast to the facts of his innocence and his suffering. At the heart of the Book of Job stands neither "blind faith" nor denial of God, but trusting *and* contending, recognizing his dependence on God yet standing firm on the ground of his created freedom.[3]

The combination of trust and contending within the dialogue with God goes back to Abraham. In *Fear and Trembling* Søren

Kierkegaard puts forth Abraham as the paradigm of unquestioning faith in his readiness to sacrifice Isaac. In so doing Kierkegaard ignores the Abraham who, in pleading for the people of
Sodom, says to God, "I who am dust and ashes have taken it
upon myself to argue with the Lord. Shall the Lord of justice
not do justice?" (Genesis 18:25, 27). Before he must confront
his brother Esau, whom he has wronged, Jacob wrestles all night
with a nameless messenger who blesses him with the name Israel,
he who has contended with God and man and has prevailed. In
Messengers of God Wiesel says of Jacob's fight with the "angel":
"No man before him had revealed to other men the battle God
wages against them; no man before him had compelled God into
open contest with man; and no man before him had ever established relations of provocation with God." Even Moses becomes
for Wiesel the prototype of the Jew rebelling against God for
the sake of life. Wiesel suggestively interprets the midrash which
tells of Moses' reluctance to accept God's decree of death as "his
way of protesting heaven's use of death to diminish, stimulate
and ultimately crush man," "his way of teaching Israel . . . that
life is sacred—always and for everyone—and that no one has the
right to give it up . . . that to live as a man, as a Jew, means to
say yes to life, to fight—even against the Almighty—for every
spark, for every breath of life."[4]

> Abraham was the first true rebel against God. . . . The very
> first encounter between Abraham and God was a good dia-
> logue, a dialogue of anger . . . Moses broke the first tables not
> only because he was angry at the Jews for having created the
> Golden Calf but also because he was angry at God. And, of
> course, we have Job, the modern rebel. Each of us can be a
> Job. . . . One Midrash says that Job became the Messiah despite
> his anger toward God, despite his accusations. . . . The real
> joy of God is to be defeated by man.[5]

It is Job whom Wiesel signals out among his biblical "Messengers of God" as "our contemporary." Tragedies do not cancel
each other out, Wiesel asserts. "On the contrary, they multiply

and accumulate, becoming more unjust with every blow." Job's anguish is not given meaning by Abraham's: "Every individual is both beginning and end; that is why he deserves an answer, not a consolation, unless the consolation itself becomes an answer."[6] Job demanded an answer that would show him unequivocally that the human being is not God's toy, that he is defined only in relation to himself:

> That was why Job turned against God: to find and confront Him. He defied Him to come closer to him. He wanted to hear His voice, even though he knew he would be condemned. He preferred a cruel and unjust God to an indifferent God. . . . On a deeply human plane, his revolt ultimately was directed against his own solitude, which he knew to be irreducible, for it concealed God's face beneath that of a man.[7]

Wiesel identifies Job with the Jewish people, who are also alone and whose best friends commiserate without helping. "Israel too maintains an endless dialogue with God or on God. Israel too is persecuted by men who, after inflicting pain, denounce its people for attempting to bear suffering in a proud and dignified way." Job had nothing but words, but he knew how to make them quiver and scream. He discovered within himself unequal power and reversed the roles with God. "Though accused, condemned and repudiated, he defied the system that kept him imprisoned."[8]

Wiesel confesses that he is deeply troubled by Job's hasty abdication. Job is more human when he is crushed and grief-stricken than after his prosperity is restored. Wiesel prefers to think that the book's true ending was lost: "That Job died without having repented, without having humiliated himself; that he succumbed to his grief an uncompromising and whole man." Wiesel was preoccupied with Job during the early years after the war, when Job could be seen on every road of Europe, wounded, robbed, mutilated, but not happy or resigned. Job's resignation was an insult to man. "He should have continued to protest, to refuse the handouts: for the sake of his children if not of himself. That

Job agreed to go back to living as before and welcomed happiness despite himself is God's true victory." Wiesel prefers to see Job as someone who continues to interrogate God (the text bears him out!). He personified man's eternal quest for justice and truth. He did not suffer in vain; for "thanks to him we know that it is given to man to transform divine injustice into human justice and compassion."[9]

On the basis of the ending of the Book of Job to which Wiesel objects and of Wiesel's interpretation of Jeremiah in *Five Biblical Portraits*, Robert McAfee Brown asserts that it is not Job but Jeremiah, who never accepted answers from God but kept hurling back new questions and challenges, who is the true prophetic counterpart of Elie Wiesel. Brown comments at length on Wiesel's own portrait of Jeremiah as a "victim of injustice," a "survivor, a witness," who "after being singed by its flames went on to retell it to any who would listen," someone who shatters serenity and forces us to look at what we refuse to see, someone who teaches his contemporaries the lesson that one must look away from death and rebuild life even before the tragedy has ended, someone who taught his people of God's suffering in their exile and of their own responsibility for their fate, a reluctant messenger who had to deal with suffering and death, who survives just to give his testimony, and who knows that for all tellers of tales to transmit is more vital than to invent.[10]

Brown makes such a good case that I was tempted, for a moment, to retitle this chapter "The Job of Auschwitz and the Jeremiah of New York"! The parallels which he finds between Jeremiah, as Wiesel portrays him, and Wiesel himself are unexceptionable—and not particularly surprising, since Jeremiah, the great lamenter, offers Wiesel an irresistible temptation to discover his own fate as "peddler of night and agony." But I cannot accept Job as "cop-out," and neither, I think, ultimately does Wiesel. Job does not repent of his contending but only of putting God in the wrong to justify himself (Job 40:8). Job's repentance does not mean the end of his dialogue with God but its real beginning.

> " 'Hear, and I will speak,
>   I will question you, and you declare to me.'
> I had heard of thee by the hearing of the ear,
>   but now my eye sees thee." [*RSV*, 42:4–5]

This is the real answer which Job receives and not the Epilogue, which restores to him his health, his riches, and another set of children. When God comes near to Job again, this suffering, without being any less real, is taken up into the dialogue that stands at the center of his existence.[11]

By 1985 Wiesel himself no longer saw Job as capitulating to God at the end. The very fact that he did not say to God, "You are right on such and such points and wrong on others," but instead "bowed his head," meant that he did not bow his head! Also, the end of the Book of Job with its "happy ending" of a dime novel and Job dying "full of days," a phrase which is only used in the Bible otherwise of Isaac, means, in fact, that like Isaac he had had more than enough of life! Although on the surface Job seems to accept what God offers him, as if it were possible to replace one human life by another, one set of children by another, in fact there was no way to indemnify suffering and grief. Job is "full of days" because he no longer wants to live after the catastrophe, yet has no choice because suicide is not acceptable.[12] Scholars might properly object that here Wiesel is reading himself into Job, but at the very least we can conclude, as I do, that Job remains a central figure for Wiesel that he is unwilling to give up.

The trust and contending of Job within the dialogue with God is carried forward into Hasidism, and particularly in the figure of Levi Yitzhak of Berditchev who, according to the legend, called God to trial for His treatment of the Jews and God lost! In *Souls on Fire* Wiesel portrays Levi Yitzhak as the protector of Israel who pleaded for any and all Jews unjustly accused and unjustly punished.

> His most beautiful adventures, the most beautiful accounts and stories of his adventures, are those that show him in his role of attorney for the defense, challenging and remonstrating

the Judge. As a child, I loved them and saw in them nothing but love and friendship. Today I feel their weight of despair and revolt—and love them even more. I often look at them; I owe them much. Sometimes I dip my pen into their wealth before I write.[13]

Levi Yitzhak was the first rebbe to take man's defense against the Judge, on the High Holy Days, in the presence of the entire community, speaking Yiddish or Polish lest someone fail to understand. Others have carried on dialogues with God and maintained I-Thou relations with Him. Only Levi Yitzhak dared to take a stand against God, threatening to break off relations and leave it to "Ivan" to praise God.

Levi Yitzhak demonstrated that "one may be Jewish with God, in God and even against God; but not without God." He went beyond Abraham and Job, who asked God questions: he demanded answers and, in their absence, drew his conclusions. He wanted "to accede to holiness against God." Thus he showed that "Jewish tradition allows man to say anything to God, provided it be on behalf of man." "Man's inner liberation is God's justification," provided that the rebel stands inside the community not outside it. The believer and the renegade do not revolt in the name of the same anguish. Although he lived more than a century and a half ago, Levi Yitzhak is our teacher in confronting and contending with the Holocaust: "The questions of the Berditchever Rebbe, and his challenges too, flung at the face of a sky in flames . . . give us the strength and courage to claim them and retell them as if they were our own."[14]

Levi Yitzhak is not the only Hasidic rebel whom Wiesel admires. The Baal Shem's grandson, Reb Barukh, understood that in a world filled with violence love was not enough to assure the survival of his people. "Perhaps he thought that a certain measure of anger, of rage, was necessary for the people of Israel. . . . Hence his sadness, hence his despair: how can one not despair of a world where rage is needed for redemption?"[15] Reb Moshe Leib of Sassov translated the Psalmist's "Happy is the man who is chastised by God" as "Happy is the man who is chastising God, who is questioning Him, and taking Him to task for not fulfilling His obligations toward His people."[16] And Menahem Mendel of Kotzk, a stranger to his own generation, is seen by Wiesel as belonging to ours: "He is our contemporary. His anger is our anger, our revolts reflect his." Wiesel even reflects that when Mendel shut himself away from everyone for the last twenty years of his life, it was because he anticipated the role of the Job of Auschwitz a century later:

> Could he have foreseen that one hundred years after his retreat another fire set the continent ablaze, and that its first victims would be Jewish men and women abandoned by God and by all mankind? Could it be that from that moment on he planned to fight fire with fire—attempting to prepare us, demanding that we be strong, intransigent, capable of resisting evil no matter what form it takes, the comfort of faith included: capable of resisting even God and the hope in God?[17]

Wiesel saw Hasidism in general as a protest against divine indifference, an attempt to shake God out of His seventh heaven and bring Him closer to man. There was so much persecution, evil, sadness, and despair in those days that they had every reason to believe that God was indifferent. But the Besht said, "It is not so. You can speak to God so that he will listen and lessen your suffering."[18]

Wiesel is Job, Jeremiah, and Levi Yitzhak rolled into one. But for me it is Job above all who remains the touchstone for his writings. In 1968 Wiesel quoted a Jew in a concentration camp as saying to God, "Perhaps I am guilty, perhaps we all are, and all deserve punishment. But what are *You* guilty of in meting out to us this terrible punishment?" In Auschwitz one of Wiesel's "teachers" taught him to sing the song "Because of our sins we have been exiled." "I sang it then. I sing it now, but I resent it," Wiesel confesses. "I refuse to believe that there could have been so many sins to provoke such a punishment." "I am possessed by a *dybbuk* because of the children," Wiesel said elsewhere. "I will not forgive mankind, nor will I forgive God." When the camps were finally liberated, the inmates, who had not eaten in six days, formed *minyanim* and said Kaddish for the dead. "I would say this in front of the *Sefer Torah* itself: God did not deserve that *Kaddish*."[19]

Elie's 1956 Yiddish book, *And the World Was Silent*, the much longer precursor of *Night*, gives us a glimpse of the Jobian spirit in which the latter book was written, too. At the opening of that book Wiesel points to the naïve faith, the foolish trust, the terrible illusion of faith in God, and the holy spark in every soul which was the source, if not the cause, of the misfortunes that befell them. Two days after his liberation, he tells us in that book, he fell terribly ill with food poisoning and for two weeks hovered between life and death. One day, mustering all his strength, he got up, looked in a mirror for the first time since leaving the ghetto, and saw a skeleton of skin and bones gaze back at him— himself after death. At that moment, Job's protest arose within him, and he expressed his will to live by raising his fist and breaking the mirror. He fainted, but from that moment on his health improved, and during the few days more in which he stayed in bed he wrote the outline for *Night*.[20]

In *Night* Wiesel tells that he did not recite the Kaddish, the traditional mourner's prayer, on the day of his father's death, because he felt empty and barren and because to do so "in that stifling barracks, in the very heart of the kingdom of death, would have been the worst of blasphemies." "In *Night* I had to voice my protest," said Wiesel in 1975, and added that anyone who did not protest was not a true believer. Having started as a pious *yeshiva* boy, he could not become a rabbi but had to say to God what he thought about God. All of his other books contain the same themes of protest, testing faith, testing the absence of faith; testing the necessity of maintaining some values. "Too many people talk about the Holocaust," said Wiesel in 1976. "To find the authentic voice I must give the more complete experience of being a Jew. It is not really about suffering. It is about defiance

of suffering." "I felt that the Covenant was broken," Wiesel amplified in 1978. "I had to tell God of my anger. I still do so."
God is present in all his books, but that presence is always accompanied by a protest. "I hope that as long as I live I shall
somehow be able to formulate, to articulate, that protest. But
from within and not from without."[21]

Wiesel's novels are continuous with *Night*. In *Dawn* Wiesel
places what is recognizably the Eliezer of *Night*, now called Elisha,
in the position of a Jewish terrorist, killing English soldiers in
an effort to secure the independence of the Jewish state in Palestine. Elisha had wanted to study philosophy at the Sorbonne
in order to rediscover the image of man that had been destroyed
for him by the extermination camps: "Where is God to be found?
In suffering or in rebellion? When is a man most truly a man?
When he submits or when he refuses? Where does suffering lead
him? To purification or to bestiality?" Instead, Elisha gives his
future to the "Movement," the first group in his knowledge which
changes the destiny of the Jew from that of victim to executioner.
It is he himself who must execute the English hostage, Captain
John Dawson, whom the Movement has sentenced to die as a
reprisal for the hanging by the British of one of their number.
In taking upon himself an act so absolute as killing, he comes to
realize, he is making his father, his mother, his teacher, his friends
into murderers. He cannot rid himself of the impression that he
has donned the field-gray uniform of the Nazi SS officer.

Elisha rediscovers the presence of God when he spends the
last hour with the hostage before shooting him. His victim-to-
be is sorry for Elisha and troubled by him—an eighteen-year-old
turned terrorist—while Elisha tries in vain to hate him, as if the
coming of the Messiah were dependent upon the Jews finally
learning "to hate those who have humiliated and from time to
time exterminated them." But when he kills John Dawson, he
feels that he has killed himself, that he himself has become the
night.

In *The Accident*, this same child of *Night*, somewhat older and

now an Israeli correspondent at the United Nations, is almost
killed by a taxi, and in the course of a long and painful recovery
confronts the fact that he had seen the taxi, that he wanted to
die, that he did not fight to stay alive even in the hospital but
left the burden entirely on the doctor. Even "love" gives him no
incentive for living in the present. He is one of the "spiritual
cripples" whom the world does not dare to look in the eye,
amputees who have lost not their legs or their eyes but their will
and their taste for life. The sufferer is the pariah, the modern
exile who must live apart from men because he tells them something about their common humanity that they cannot bear.

> Suffering pulls us farther away from other human beings. It
> builds a wall made of cries and contempt to separate us. Men
> cast aside the one who has known pure suffering, if they cannot
> make a god out of him; the one who tells them: I suffered not
> because I was God, nor because I was a saint trying to imitate
> Him, but only because I am a man, a man like you, with your
> weaknesses, your cowardice, your sins, your rebellions, and
> your ridiculous ambitions; such a man frightens men, because
> he makes them feel ashamed. . . . He poisons the air. He makes
> it unfit for breathing. He takes away from joy its spontaneity
> and its justification. He kills hope and the will to live.[22]

The accident occurs the day after he has entered into an agreement
with his mistress, Kathleen, that he knows is meaningless—an
agreement to let her make him happy and to forget the past.

When the doctor tells the I of the story that he should thank
God that he is still alive, he thinks to himself, "Why thank him?
I had not been able to understand for a long time what in the
world God had done to deserve man." This attitude pushes the
central character ever closer to active rebellion. He rejects a tri-
angle that only succeeds in making one another miserable because
he has never been interested in sterile suffering. "Other people's
suffering only attracts me to the extent that it allows man to
become conscious of his strength and of his weakness, in a climate
that favors rebellion." He laments the fact that human beings

prefer to blame themselves for all possible sins and crimes rather than coming to the conclusion that God is capable of the most flagrant injustice. "I still blush every time I think of the way God makes fun of human beings, his favorite toys."

In Paris he encounters a half-crazed girl named Sarah whom the Nazi officers used for their pleasure when she was a twelve-year-old in a concentration camp. "Maybe I had only lived for this meeting, I thought. For this meeting with a prostitute who preserved within her a trace of innocence, like madmen who in the midst of their madness hold on to a trace of lucidity." Appalled by her story, told in a monotonous voice, he is unable to make love to her. Instead, she becomes for him the embodiment of the Job of Auschwitz, the focal point of rebellion against God and the world. "Whoever listens to Sarah and doesn't change, whoever enters Sarah's world and doesn't invent new gods and new religions, deserves death and destruction." Now it becomes clear to him why it says in Exodus that no one can see God and live. "Why should he want to kill a man who succeeded in seeing him? . . . God was ashamed. God likes to sleep with twelve-year-old girls. And he doesn't want us to know."[23]

In the last chapter of *The Accident*, the I of the story introduces the Hungarian painter Gyula, who is at once foil and image of the human and who provides the final judgment on the hero.

> Gyula was a living rock. A giant in every sense of the word. Tall, robust, gray and rebellious hair, mocking and burning eyes; he pushed aside everything around him: altars, ideas, mountains. Everything trembled, vibrated, at his touch, at the sight of him. . . . We encouraged each other to stick it out, not to make compromises, not to come to terms with life, not to accept easy victories.[24]

Gyula visits the hospital room repeatedly to do his portrait. He tries to tell Gyula his secret—that the accident was no accident, that on the deepest level he wanted to die—but Gyula will not listen. Yet when Gyula shows him the completed painting, he knows that he has guessed. The eyes are those of a "man who had seen God commit the most unforgivable crime: to kill without a reason." Gyula confronts his friend's will to death with a silent offer of friendship—a proof that if God is dead, man is alive. Man's duty is to make suffering cease, not to increase it, Gyula tells him. This means a rejection of the lucidity that exchanges the light of hope for the clear darkness of the absurd.

> Lucidity is fate's victory, not man's. It is an act of freedom that carries within itself the negation of freedom. Man must keep moving, searching, weighing, holding out his hand, offering himself, inventing himself. . . . The dead, because they are no longer free, are no longer able to suffer. Only the living can. Kathleen is alive. I am alive. You must think of us. Not of them.[25]

Gyula poses the choice of life or death, but to the I of the story, only lies can make happiness possible, while the truth is on the side of death. Sensing his decision for death by the intensity with which he looks at the painting, Gyula puts a match to the canvas and burns it up. "No!" he exclaims in despair. "Don't do that! Gyula, don't do it!" For a long time after Gyula has closed the door behind him, he weeps. Gyula's angry act of friendship brings tears to the eyes of the man who cannot weep and brings him one step forward toward the Job of Auschwitz.

Next to Camus's *The Plague*, the clearest presentation in literature of what I describe in *Problematic Rebel* as the progression through the "Modern Promethean" to the "Modern Job" is Wiesel's novel *The Town Beyond the Wall*. The plot of the book is the return of Michael after the war to his native Hungarian city. Entering by means of the Black Market, the only organization that can get through the Iron Curtain, he is arrested by the police and forced to say "prayers," i.e., to stand eight hours at a stretch before a wall without moving, eating, or drinking. The police hope to extract from him a confession as to who helped him get into the country—a confession that would condemn his friend Pedro to death or imprisonment—but they have reckoned without his tenacious loyalty to his friend and his capacity to endure by going inward to the sources of memory.

After the war and the extermination camps, Michael went to Paris and lived in utter solitude in order to seek His God, to track Him down. Even in his determination not to give in so easily as Job, even in his insistence that he will be a match for God and will defy His inhuman justice, he still remains within his dialogue with God. "He took my childhood; I have a right to ask Him what He did with it." Michael combines the Modern Promethean and the Modern Job, and he shows the link between them: in our time man *has* to go through the first to reach the second, but he may not remain in the first. At the death of the "little prince"—a Jewish boy pampered by the Nazis in the concentration camps only to die under a truck in Paris—Michael's suffering leads him to the verge of madness.

> An immense wrath, savage, and destructive, welled up suddenly in Michael. His eyes flashed. The little prince's death—this death—was too unjust, too absurd. He wanted to pit himself against the angel as Jacob had: fell him with a blow, trample him. One gesture, just one, but a gesture in proportion to his misery.[26]

In prison Michael complains to his friend Pedro that he wants to blaspheme but has not concentrated his strength sufficiently to do so. He not only remains in dialogue with God, like Job; his protest turns into praise despite himself: "I go up against Him, I shake my fist, I froth with rage, but it's still a way of telling Him that He's there, that He exists, that He's never the same twice, that denial itself is an offering to His grandeur. The shout becomes a prayer in spite of me."[27]

Michael recognizes that greater than the mad revolt of the Modern Promethean is the tension of the Modern Job who refuses to go mad. "The man who chooses death is following an impulse of liberation from the self; so is the man who chooses madness. . . . To keep our balance then is the most difficult and absurd struggle in human existence." Madness is an easy, comfortable escape, a once-for-all act of free will that destroys freedom. Michael understands that madness represents a moral choice as well as psychological compulsion. Michael's friend Pedro, "a living rock," like Gyula, warns him against the mad revolt which tempts him.

> To say, "I suffer, therefore I am" is to become the enemy of man. What you must say is "I suffer, therefore you are." Camus wrote somewhere that to protest against a universe of unhappiness you had to create happiness. That's an arrow pointing the way: it leads to another human being. And not via absurdity.[28]

These, of all Pedro's words, are the ones that later come to Michael's aid.

Only after he has already come back to his native city does Michael discover what has impelled him to return—the desire to find the man who watched impassively from the square above during the whole week in which the Jews of the "City of Luck" were gathered in the synagogue and deported to their deaths. In Michael's desperate need to understand and to confront this indifferent observer shines forth the trust and the contending of the Modern Job. The spectator's "presence is evasive, and commits him less than his absence might. . . . He is there, but he acts as if he were not. Worse: he acts as if the rest of us were not." He reduces himself and us to the level of objects. The man who insists that he felt nothing when he saw the Jews deported and who resolutely refuses to let himself be humiliated, nonetheless suffers visibly under Michael's contempt, under his refusal to dignify him with hatred. Realizing that this man has become human again, Michael realizes too that "down deep . . . man is not only an executioner, not only a victim, not only a spectator: he is all three at once." It is this man who turns Michael in, in order to force Michael to hate him rather than simply despise him.

Like Ivan Karamazov, Michael wants "to turn his ticket in"—to reject not God but his world. Madness is, indeed, the way of the Modern Promethean—Melville's Captain Ahab and Dostoevsky's Kirilov and Ivan. To resist it without glossing over *or* submitting to the suffering that gives rise to it is the way of the Modern Job. The Pedro whom Michael now imagines coming to speak with him in his cell points this latter way and shows it for the sober, courageous revolt that it is:

> The only valuable protest, or attitude, is one rooted in the uncertain soil of humanity. Remaining human—in spite of all temptations and humiliations—is the only way to hold your own against the Other, whatever it may be. . . . To see liberty only in madness is wrong: liberation, yes; liberty, no.[29]

Michael finds the alternative to going mad, as we have seen, in making himself responsible for his prison cellmate, a young boy who is completely silent and, until he responds to Michael's heartbreaking efforts, completely out of touch. In bringing Eliezer back into dialogue, Michael brings himself back to humanity. Pedro has taught Michael and Michael teaches Eliezer the necessity of clinging to humanity. "It's in humanity itself that we find both our question and the strength to keep it within limits." To flee to a Nirvana through a considered indifference or a sick apathy "is to oppose humanity in the most absurd, useless, and comfortable manner possible." Like Dr. Rieux in *The Plague*, Michael recognizes that "it's harder to remain human than to try to leap beyond humanity." The real heights and the real depths of humanity are found "at your own level, in simple and honest conversation, in glances heavy with existence." Man asks the question within himself ever more deeply, he feels ever more intimately the existence of an unknowable answer, and he brings both of these into the dialogue with his friend, into the Dialogue with the Absurd.

God and man exchanged places, the legend at the end of the novel tells us, and remained so for centuries, perhaps eternities—

until the drama quickened and the past for one, and the present for the other, were too heavy to be borne. This interchange of God and man is hinted at throughout the novel: "In prison, under torture, man becomes powerful, omnipotent. He becomes a God. That's the secret: God is imprisoned." God suffers with man and in him. The Modern Job does not contend with an entirely alien Other, hostile and indifferent, such as Captain Ahab's white whale or Caligula's absurd. Even the absurd reality over against us has a meaning—a meaning which can only be revealed in our trusting and contending. The dialogue, or duel, between man and his God does not end in nothingness: "As the liberation of the one was bound to the liberation of the other, they renewed the ancient dialogue whose echoes come to us in the night, charged with hatred, with remorse, and most of all, with infinite yearning.

Malach, the Hebrew word that is unusually translated "angel," actually means "messenger." *The Gates of the Forest* is the story of the lasting effect of two "messengers" on the life of Gregor, a young Jewish refugee. Gavriel, the nameless messenger to whom he gives his own Hebrew name, and the much more tangible Leib the Lion, accompany him—in person or in memory—through the spring, when he hides from the Nazis in a cave in the forest; through summer, when he plays the role of a feebleminded mute in the village where Maria, the former family servant, passes him off as her nephew; through autumn, when he joins the partisans fighting under the leadership of his childhood friend, Leib the Lion; through winter, when he seeks a way forward in postwar New York, where he has gone with his wife, Clara, once the girlfriend of Leib.

Gavriel tells Gregor that the Messiah has already come, that he is among men, that nonetheless the horror has taken place, and that all that is left is to learn to laugh in the face of the horror—a terrible, mad laugh that defies the absurd. It is the laugh of a man poised midway between the Modern Promethean and the Modern Job and holding the tension of both. The message which this messenger brings Gregor is that of the "final solution," the unsuspected extermination of the Jews. His father will not come back. No one will come back. His family has left without hope of return.

The curse that Gregor fails to pronounce on this occasion breaks out of him when he is forced to play Judas at the school play and is almost killed in the frenzy of the crowd. "Miraculously" casting off his dumbness and speaking with the voice of a prophet, he forces the people, including the priest, to beg Judas's pardon—for it is *he*, not Jesus, who is the crucified one. Yet Gregor resists his desire for vengeance and does not tell any of the secrets that have been imparted to him. When he announces that he is not the son of Illeana but a Jew, a smile not of victory but of pity illuminates his face.

Escaping to the forest, he makes contact with a band of Jewish partisans and rediscovers his childhood friend Leib the Lion. When they were boys, Leib had taught him to fight the gang of children that descended on them on their way to school with cries of "Dirty Jews!" and "Christ-killers!" on their lips. The mythic proportions that Leib took on then in Gregor's eyes are now realized in fact in his role as leader of the Jewish partisans, a latter-day Bar Kochba. Gregor informs Leib of what was known for a long time already in Washington, London, and Stockholm but which no one had taken the trouble to radio to the Jews of Transylvania—that the deported Jews were not being taken to factories or labor camps but to extermination centers. The shocked and almost unbelieving Leib orders an attempt to liberate Gavriel from prison to ascertain the truth of Gregor's report and is captured himself in the process. It falls on Gregor to inform the other partisans that their leader is taken and to discover through their dismay and grief the image of man that he represented for them—the Modern Job:

> Every one of his words and gestures enriched their hope by giving to it simplicity and humility: we shall prevail, for inasmuch as it has any meaning, victory is within the domain of man and of that which elevates rather than denies him.[30]

Gregor makes the Promethean laughter of Gavriel and the Jobian courage of Leib his own, and they sustain him and give strength until that distant day in postwar New York when he is confronted by a Hasidic rabbi who recognizes both his suffering and his pride. When Gregor admits that what he wants is that the rebbe cease to pray and that he howl instead, the rebbe, with a movement of revolt, says to him, slowly, accentuating every word and stopping after every phrase: "Who has told you that force comes from a cry and not from a prayer, from anger and not from compassion? . . . The man who sings is the brother of him who goes to his death fighting." The dancing, the singing, the joy of the Hasid is *in spite of* the fact that all reason for dancing, singing, and joy has been taken from him.

> He's guilty; do you think I don't know it? That I have no eyes to see, no ears to hear? That my heart doesn't revolt? That I have no desire to beat my head against the wall and shout like a madman, to give rein to my sorrow and disappointment? Yes, he is guilty. He has become an ally of evil, of death, of murder, but the problem is still not solved.[31]

The revolt of the Modern Promethean is unmasked by the rebbe as only a romantic gesture. It still leaves the question of what to do, of how to live, of the direction from which salvation and hope must come.

In 1980, as a testimonial to Rebbe Menahem Schneerson's thirty years of leadership of the Lubavitch movement, Wiesel stated that this dialogue in *The Gates of the Forest* was based on his first conversation with the Lubavitcher rebbe. At one point during this interchange, which lasted for hours, he asked him point-blank, "Rebbe, how can you believe in *Hashem* after the *Khourban*?" to which the rebbe responded, "And how can you not believe after the *Khourban*?" Wiesel confessed that that simple dialogue was a turning point in his writing.[32]

Unable to bear any longer the way his wife, Clara, betrays him by remaining faithful to her first lover, the dead Leib, Gregor has resolved to leave her. Now, after joining a minyan in reciting the Kaddish, he knows that he will return to Clara to take up again the battle of winning her back to the present, to life.

Gregor's last Kaddish is for Leib the Lion, his old comrade in battle, who, while alive, incarnated in himself what is immortal in man. This prayer for the dead is also a prayer for life—a prayer that the dead Leib will allow Gregor and Clara to live, but also that, despite their loyalty to the past, Eliezer, Elisha, the "I" of *The Accident*, Michael, Gregor, and Elie Wiesel himself will be able to live for the living and not for the dead. It is a prayer for all of us—for we are all the inheritors of Auschwitz—that we work our way through to the trust and contending of the Job of Auschwitz who meets the living present, including the absurd, with the courage that these "messengers on high" have bequeathed.

FIFTEEN

The Job of Auschwitz II

"In the very shadow of the flames there were God-fearing Jews who demanded with broken hearts an answer from God." To Wiesel the question of God's existence is no longer a theological but purely a moral problem. How can we call to God in the era of Auschwitz? More than any other people in the world, the Jews have the duty to be angry about Creation and the Creator; for the betrayal they suffered has been universal, even cosmic. "All gates were shut tight to us and all eyes full of daggers." If God chose to question man through the Holocaust, then it is man's right and duty in turn to question God. One can argue with the God of Israel, provided it is for the sake of the people of Israel. Man is allowed to say no even to God's system when he believes God to be inhuman. One becomes a renegade, not by saying no but by turning away, becoming another. "A Jew is someone who does not turn away."[1]

The original title of Wiesel's book *Chants des Morts*—"Songs of the Dead"—might well be the title of all his books. But so also might be the English title, *Legends of Our Time*. In *Legends of Our Time*, Wiesel tells how each year anew he must decide whether he will say Kaddish for his father:

> Stretched out on a plank of wood amid a multitude of blood-covered corpses, fear frozen in his eyes, a mask of suffering on

the bearded, stricken mask that was his face, my father gave back his soul at Buchenwald. A soul useless in that place, and one he seemed to want to give back. But, he gave it up, not to the God of his fathers, but rather to the imposter, cruel and insatiable, to the enemy of God. They had killed his God, they had exchanged him for another. How, then, could I enter the sanctuary of the synagogue tomorrow and lose myself in the sacred repetition of the ritual without lying to myself, without lying to him? . . .

Perhaps, after all, I should go to the synagogue to praise the God of dead children, if only to provoke him by my own submission.[2]

Those who lived through the Holocaust will always take the side of the human being confronted with the Absolute, writes Wiesel. The survivors know that God's presence or absence at Treblinka or Maidanek poses a problem which will remain forever insoluble.

Loss of faith for some equalled discovery of God for others. Both answered the same need to take a stand, the same impulse to rebel. In both cases, it was an accusation. Perhaps some day someone will explain how, on the level of man, Auschwitz was possible; but on the level of God, it will forever remain the most disturbing of mysteries.[3]

On Yom Kippur, the Jewish Day of Atonement, Wiesel fasted even in Auschwitz—not out of obedience, but out of defiance, to make his indignation heard: "Not for love of God, but against God."[4]

In "The Guilt We Share" Wiesel comments that "it is by a strange irony of fate that the only ones who were, who still are, fully conscious of their share of responsibility for the dead are those who were saved, the ghosts who returned from the dead." Originally their feeling of guilt was a religious one, the belief that they were being punished for their sins and that through their sufferings they were expiating them. The prisoner sacrifices his own freedom for God's, preferring "to believe himself guilty rather than think that his God is the god of Job, for whom man is a mere example—a means of demonstrating a thesis in a verbal duel with Satan." The revolt against God comes only later, at the final stage. The tragedy of the survivors is the tragedy of Job before his submission. They believe themselves to be guilty even though they are not, and in their eyes no one, either human or divine, has the authority or power to relieve them of their burden.

> Therefore they prefer, in this condemned world, not to hurl their defiance at men and their anger into the face of history, but to keep silent, to pursue the monologue which only the dead deserve to hear. Guilt was not invented at Auschwitz, it was disfigured there.[5]

"Man defines himself by what disturbs him and not by what reassures him." Elie Wiesel lets himself be disturbed, and he disturbs us by insisting, in the face of *all* who turn away from it, on the "guilt we share." Witnessing the trial of Eichmann, Wiesel conducts a worldwide trial: of the indigenous populations of Hungary and Poland, whose eagerness to become *Judenrein* alone made it possible for "the cattle trains with their suffocating human cargo" to "roll swiftly into the night"; of "the whole outside world, which looked on in a kind of paralysis and passively allowed" the murder of six million Jews, a number that could never have been reached had Roosevelt, Churchill, and the Pope let loose an avalanche of angry protestations; of the American Jewish community, which did not use its political and financial powers to move heaven and earth to save five to ten thousand Jews from murder each day; of Chaim Weizmann, who put off for two weeks the messenger of the Holocaust who had told him that "every passing day meant the lives of at least ten thousand Jews" ("How did Brand not go stark raving mad?" Wiesel asks); of Gideon Hausner, Ben-Gurion, and the Israelis who tried Eichmann without crying out "in a voice loud enough to be heard by three generations: We never attempted the impossible—we never even exhausted the possible." From this trial,

Wiesel concludes that "with the advent of the Nazi regime in Germany, humanity became witness to what Martin Buber would call an eclipse of God."

Wiesel has a different view of the victims of the extermination camps from those of Bruno Bettelheim and Hannah Arendt, who rushed to judge them for not resisting and revolting. Their torturers shrewdly knew how to push to the extreme the emotions of shame and humiliation that those who were still alive felt toward the dead. "*I am happy to have escaped death* becomes equivalent to admitting: *I am glad that someone else went in my place.*" Finally, these Jews came to believe that "to die struggling would have meant a betrayal of those who had gone to their death submissive and silent."

It is Auschwitz that will engender Hiroshima and perhaps that extinction of the human race by nuclear warfare that "will be the punishment for Auschwitz, where, in the ashes, the hope of man was extinguished." At the time of the Holocaust, those outside did not speak out. Nor were the inmates of the camps ignorant of this. Their seemingly weak "acceptance" of their death became, in consequence, "an act of lucidity, of protest," not only against their torturers, but also against the rest of humanity, which had abandoned, excluded, and rejected them. "It is as though every country—and not only Germany—had decided to see the Jew as a kind of subhuman species" whose disappearance did not weigh on the conscience since the concept of brotherhood did not apply to him.

From the Holocaust Wiesel extracts a bedrock image of the human, even of that person who wants to speak and to judge, to be strong and invulnerable: "The lesson of the Holocaust— if there is any—is that our strength is only illusory, and that in each of us is a victim who is afraid, who is cold, who is hungry. Who is also ashamed." But Wiesel also finds in the Job of Auschwitz an image of what the human being *can* become after one has reached bedrock:

The Rebbe in Warsaw who stood erect, unyielding, uncon-
querable before a group of SS; they were amusing themselves
by making him suffer, by humiliating him; he suffered, but did
not let himself be humiliated. One of them, laughing, cut off
his beard, but the Rebbe stared right into his eyes without
flinching; there was pain in his expression, but also defiance,
the expression of a man stronger than evil, even when evil is
triumphant, stronger than death, even when death assumes the
face of a comedian playing a farce—the expression of a man
who owes nothing to anyone, not even to God.[6]

Every time that image comes to his mind, Elie Wiesel is silent,
but it is an image that he carries with him, that he cannot part
with and does not want to part with, "as though wanting always
to remember there are still, there will always be, somewhere in
the world, expressions I will never understand."

The most masterful expression of Wiesel's fight for the hidden
human image is his haunting and compelling novel of the Six-
Day War, *A Beggar in Jerusalem*. In *A Beggar in Jerusalem* the
Holocaust and the threat of extermination that seemed to hover
over the people of the State of Israel on the eve of the Six-Day
War fuse into one reality. "They were alone," writes Wiesel, "as
earlier in Europe in the time of Night." In the face of this alone-
ness and of the threat of a second holocaust, Wiesel puts into
the mouth of a zaddik, a person who has proved righteous and
just before the eyes of God and humanity, words that might well
be a continuation of those of the Hasidic rebbe in *The Gates of
the Forest*—transformed and intensified into a plaint worthy of
Job:

> Elsewhere, a *tzaddik* locked himself up in study, and ad-
> dressed his plea to God: "I have never questioned Your justice,
> Your mercy, though their ways have often confounded me. I
> have submitted to everything, accepted everything, not with
> resignation but with love and gratitude. I have accepted pun-
> ishments, absurdities, slaughters, I have even let pass under
> silence the death of one million children. In the shadow of the
> Holocaust's unbearable mystery, I have strangled the outcry,
> the anger, the desire to be finished with You and myself once

and for all. I have chosen prayer, devotion. I have tried to transform into song the dagger you have so often plunged into my submissive heart. I did not strike my head against the wall, I did not tear my eyes out so as to see no more, nor my tongue so as to speak no more. I told myself: It is easy to die for You, easier than to live with You, for You, in this universe both blessed and cursed, in which malediction, like everything else, bears Your seal. I invented reasons, causes for rejoicing, to create a link to You and also to myself. But . . ."

Despite his resolve to hold back his tears, he felt them flowing through his hands. He let them flow. "But that's all over," he continued with redoubled strength. "Do You hear? It's all over, I tell You. I cannot go on. If this time again You desert Your people, if this time again You permit the slaughterer to murder Your children and besmirch their allegiance to the covenant, if this time You let Your promise become mockery, then know, O Master of all that breathes, know that You no longer deserve Your people's love and their passion to sanctify You, to justify You toward and against all, toward and against Yourself; if this time again the survivors are massacred and their deaths held up to ridicule, know that I shall resign my chair and my functions as guide, I shall fall to the ground, my forehead covered with ashes, and I shall weep as I have never wept in my life, and before dying I shall shout as no victim has ever shouted, and know that each of my tears and each of my shouts will tarnish Your glory, each of my gestures will negate You and will negate me as You have negated me, as You will have negated Your servants in their dazzling and ephemeral truth."[7]

Perhaps it was the overwhelming feeling that Wiesel himself was the first to articulate—that we could not allow this extermination to happen twice in one lifetime—that gives this book a different time sense than all his other novels. In all of them there are flashbacks and the easy—and enormously painful—intermingling of what has been and what is. But only in *A Beggar* are all the ages present simultaneously. One of the circle of "beggars" who sit before the Wall during the long and story-laden nights after the Six-Day War tells of when he came up to the man Jesus as he hung on the cross and said to him, "They will kill millions of your people in your name," at which Jesus wept so bitterly that the man who stood beneath him wept, too. In *A Beggar*, and in *One Generation After*, there appears the bitter irony that alive, Jesus, the Jew, is the enemy of mankind; whereas once he is safely dead he becomes their God. "We have been crucified six million times," Wiesel seems to say, "and no amount of worship of the crucified ones will stay the hand of the next slayer who comes looking for a victim."

The plot of *A Beggar*, insofar as there is one, is the story of two men, David and Katriel, the one present throughout, the other both present and absent. We come to feel that David and Katriel are one person before David is recognized by Katriel's wife, Malka, whom he has never met before, yet who is his wife. Nor is it clear to David which one of them, himself or Katriel, is "the beggar of Jerusalem"—the man who will come and tell you your own story in such a way that you will recognize in it your life and death.

Commenting on those Jews who wished, before the Six-Day War, to define themselves simply as men and only accidentally as Jews, Wiesel neatly reverses the formula and suggests that in our day "one cannot be a man without assuming the condition of the Jews." "The Jew is the most exposed person in the world today," wrote Martin Buber in 1933. The inhumanity which has been unleashed upon the Jew since then so threatens the humanity of all men that only in sharing the exposure can any man today become man. Today we must all suffer with the "Modern Exile" or lose our birthright as men. When David recognizes himself as the permanently exiled stranger in a story of Katriel's, he speaks for every hero of Wiesel's novels and for Wiesel, too:

> Disguised as a stranger, I might have been living beside women who were mistaking me for someone else. The real me remained below, in the kingdom of the night, prisoner of the dead. . . . I was nothing more than an echo of voices long since extinguished. . . . I thought I was living my own life. I was only inventing it.[8]

At the heart of *A Beggar in Jerusalem* lies Wiesel's concern to bring forth from its concealment the hidden image of the human. If we human beings are created in the image of God, then the only way that that image can be transmitted is through transmitting the image of the human. It is for this that a whole people set out to march for a third time, and with the living marched the dead: "Israel conquered because its army, its people included six million additional names." The pull of the duty toward the living and the duty toward the dead is not so much resolved as transformed—into living unity. Only Elie Wiesel in our generation has been capable of uniting the Holocaust and the emergence and survival of the State of Israel without denying the mystery or reality of either, or turning one into historical cause and the other into historical effect. In this sense, all of Elie's other books were preparations for *A Beggar in Jerusalem*; for only here do the living fight *with* the dead and not against them, only here is it possible for David to stay with Malka despite their loyalty to Katriel.

In what he himself says is his final book on the Holocaust, *One Generation After*, Wiesel repeatedly asserts that in the Holocaust man betrayed his image and that, whether or not the murder of a million children makes any historical sense, it denies and condemns man. The Job of Auschwitz witnesses for those for whom he cannot witness—not only for the survivors, but also for the silent dead for whom alone, perhaps, Auschwitz was a reality.

But there is a positive witness contained in the negative. If Emil Fackenheim sees the new commandment that Auschwitz has laid upon the Jews as "not to give any more victories to Hitler," the Job of Auschwitz hears above all the command to witness to what has happened, recalling and telling every detail, writing down his testimony moments before dying in agony, surviving in order to be able to tell—to howl against the wall of death that crushed a whole people. The prayer of such a witness, like the prayer of Job, is only that God will listen to him, not that he might attain happiness or paradise. Although all roads led to the Night, those who managed to survive did so not just to subsist but to recount. It is only this—and the hope that someone might listen to this recounting—that enables the Job of Auschwitz to continue at all. Nothing so concisely sums up Elie Wiesel's mission as a person and as a writer than his own sentence "I do not demand of the raconteur that he play the role of master but that he fulfill his duty as messenger and as witness."

What it means to "hold fast to one's integrity" in this calling of messenger and witness Wiesel has shown us in every one of his novels and stories, and in *Night* and *The Jews of Silence*. He has also shown it in his "Rendezvous with Hate" in *One Generation After*, in which he tells how he could not remain on the soil of Germany for more than a day, although he had planned to stay for a month. The Nazis, who had seen the Jews not as human beings but as objects, or numbers, had earned the right to Wiesel's hatred, if one can hate a machine that devours men. But when he finally visited Germany years after the Holocaust, he was no longer able to hate them; for hatred, like all feelings, is transient. It was precisely that inability to hate that made it necessary for him to leave; for it seemed to him to betray the dead. "The God of the Jews is a God of anger, not of hatred," Wiesel reflects, and adds, "If we had to hate all those who have hated us, we should long since have lost all desire to survive."

Even Wiesel's concern with "the Jews of silence"—the Jews of the Soviet Union, the discrimination against whom Wiesel has done more than any other person in the world to make known—stands under the sign of the Modern Job. Simhat-Torah, the day of the rejoicing in the giving of the Torah, "will henceforth be associated with the Jews of silence," Wiesel testified after going to Moscow for a second time to see the thousands of young Jews, deprived of their heritage, publicly affirming and celebrating their existence as Jews. "For those who participate in their dancing, each moment becomes privileged: a victory over silence." From these Soviet Jews Wiesel learned that those who make of their

Judaism a song are of equal value with those who make of it a prayer. "The staunchest Hasid could learn from the most assimilated Jewish student in Moscow how to rejoice and how to transform his song into an act of belief and defiance." Out of a situation of constraint these young Jews made an act of choice, out of what should break and humiliate them they drew their force of resistance.

In *Entre deux Soleils* there appears a play—"Once upon a Time"— that does not appear in *One Generation After*, the English translation. The setting of the play is a ghetto, not unlike the Warsaw Ghetto. The plot is the fantastic but not at all uncommon choice that an innocent and idealistic young Jew is asked to make at the whim of a Nazi officer between the lives of two other ghetto Jews, neither of whom he knows, with his own life forfeit if he refuses. The leader of the resistance says bitterly, "I would advise all the Jews of the ghetto that is Europe to go to their death not raising their fist but laughing with roars of laughter in order that their laugh be transmitted like a cry in the night to the last of the generations to come." Whether Daniel had said yes or no to the impossible choice that was demanded of him, says the Witness who comments throughout, he would have been equally innocent—and equally guilty. "We fight not in order to conquer—it is improbable, impossible—nor to escape death—for what purpose?—but to shame those who have condemned us to solitude."

"Once upon a Time" is set during the time of the Holocaust, whereas the two essays "To a Young German of the New Left" and "To a Young Jew of Today" are very much of the present. Wiesel tells the German of the New Left that he confuses the lack of discipline with independence and that he indulges in tantrums and destroys everything in sight. He tells him that it is natural that he "should feel the need to challenge the regime— whatever it may be—and reject authority—whatever its source." He is, in short, the Modern Promethean. Wiesel wants him to be angry at being born "into the midst of a fanaticized and stubborn people that repudiated its Führer only after his military defeats and not for his crimes." If he does not despise his guilty fathers, he will become inhuman himself and unworthy of redemption.

> The important book of this era, a book of horror and malediction, you are the one who could write it; the son accusing the father of having mutilated and poisoned his future even before giving him birth.[9]

But he will not write this book, for his revolt, born out of trauma, leads to excessive goals which lose sight of its own limitations. Closed to humility, the young German does not "understand one essential point: that for a German today there is no possible salvation outside of his relationship with Jews. Your path will never lead to man unless it leads to us first." German writers such as Heinrich Böll, Alfred Andersch, Martin Walser, and Günther Grass understood that to gain self-respect as men, they first had to earn the respect of their fathers' victims. The young German of the New Left, in contrast, defines his position within the context of the Holocaust by siding with the Arab terrorists. His hatred of the Jews and its motivation is no different from that of his Nazi fathers. Wiesel demands that he face up to the reality of the past or become guilty of the Holocaust himself. "By agreeing to deliver to death the survivors of yesterday's massacres, you become, today, the executioner's accomplice and ally." "I shall not hate you," Wiesel declares in an echo of Camus's "Letter to a Nazi Friend," which he quotes from at the head of this essay, but "I shall denounce, unmask and fight you with all my power."

In "To a Young Jew of Today" God Himself is brought to trial, as he was by Abraham and Job and two and a half millennia later by the Hasidic rebbe Levi Yitzhak of Berditchev. "Rebellion is rooted in the very origins of Jewish history," Wiesel tells the young Jew of today:

> Abraham breaking his father's idols, Moses rejecting slavery, the prophets criticizing—most disrespectfully—kings and power-seekers: they were true rebels. As were those Jews who, though

exiled and oppressed, refused to join the ranks of their oppressors. By their stubborn faith, they contested the validity of the system. Their presence became protest and summons. Each Jew who did not take the easy road of conversion transformed his heresy into an act of defiance.[10]

This is the rebellion that the Job of Auschwitz continues. "If God is the answer," writes Wiesel, "it must be the wrong answer." There is no answer: "the agony of the believer equals the bewilderment of the non-believer." All there is is a question which man must live and formulate and in so doing challenge God. This challenge is permissible, indeed required. "He who says no to God is not necessarily a renegade. . . . One can say anything as long as it is for man, not against him, as long as one remains inside the covenant." Here contending means faithfulness; to betray the present means to destroy the past, whereas to fulfill oneself means choosing to be a link "between the primary silence of creation and the silence that weighed on Treblinka."

Auschwitz has led directly to Hiroshima and to genocide in Africa, and it is Auschwitz that has bequeathed to present-day youthful rebels, without their knowing it, the very vocabulary and terms of their rebellion: the distrust and rejection of authority, the urge to abolish uniforms and taboos, the rebellion against all those parents, philosophers, teachers, profiteers, leaders without ideals and preachers without souls responsible for this past.

> Factories and university buildings are "occupied." The Blacks rise up in the "ghettos." . . . The Watts and Harlem riots are compared to the Warsaw Ghetto uprising. Biafra is referred to as another Auschwitz. Political analysts talk of nuclear "holocausts." Racism, fascism, totalitarian dictatorship, complicity, passivity: words heavy with past significance. . . . That is why it is important to put society on trial. . . . By scorning its defenders, you place yourself on the side of the victims.[11]

The motif of the Job of Auschwitz recurs repeatedly in *The Oath*, as we would expect in a novel dominated by the figure of Mad Moshe. Even before he introduces us to Moshe, Azriel prepares us for that motif by reflecting: "How is one to worship a heaven splattered with mud? What is the good of prolonging a civilization wallowing in ashes? . . . This century is cursed." Later he relates how in the *Book of Kolvillàg* one chronicler records that "in these days exile is becoming ever harsher. To have hope in God is to have hope against God." Still farther on, Azriel tells of how Moshe said to Azriel's father that Jews "consider death the primary defect and injustice inherent in creation. To die for God is to die against God. For us, man's ultimate confrontation is only with God." To Azriel, Moshe says: "Let your words be shouts or silence but nothing else, nothing in between. Let your desire be absolute and your wait as well, for all yearning contains a yearning for God and every wait is a wait for God. . . . Whoever walks in the night, moves against night."[12]

"How can *God* be silent?" This is the question, Wiesel asserted in 1974, that has become ever deeper and more mysterious to him in the thirty years since the Holocaust. In the Holocaust years even God became a question mark. Commenting on his cantata *Ani Ma'amin*, Wiesel claimed, "What differentiates Judaism from other traditions and other religions is that we alone are allowed, indeed commanded sometimes, to question God and His ways." This was true of Abraham, Job, and Levi Yitzhak of Berditchev. Wiesel affirms that God was present to him both in *Night* and in *Ani Ma'amin*, but he does not know if it was as stranger, enemy, or friend. "Is God a friend to His Creation? The question remains a question. And I really have no answer." Since God is everywhere, He is present in evil, but that is not tantamount to saying that God *is* evil or that *evil* is God. "No faith is as pure as the broken faith." Any person who claims today to be at peace with herself and with God is estranged from both. If we believe in man, it is in spite of God and in spite of man. It is because God wants us to come in freedom and not as slaves that we contend with God.[13]

In *The Gates of the Forest* Gregor tells the Hasidic rebbe in New York the story of a trial of God in a concentration camp in which God was indicted and convicted of murder.[14] "The Scene" of Wiesel's play *The Trial of God* tells us that it had its genesis in that very event, and it is *The Trial of God* which marks the culmination of Wiesel's Job of Auschwitz and the transition to our chapter on Jewish identity. In the play itself, the innkeeper Berish declares that whoever kills in the name of and for the greater glory of God makes God guilty: "Every man who suffers or causes suffering, every woman who is raped, every child who is tormented implicates Him." Later in the play Berish violently rejects the notion that the justice of God is different from human justice:

> I don't want a minor, secondary justice, a poor man's justice! I want no part of a justice that escapes me, diminishes me and makes a mockery out of mine! Justice is here for men and women—I therefore want it to be human, or let Him keep it.[15]

After God's annihilation of Shamgorod, destroyed in a pogrom, Berish asserts that if God insists on going on with His methods, Berish will reject them even though God kills him. "Let Him kill us all, I shall shout and shout that it's His fault. I'll use my last energy to make my protest known. Whether I live or die, I submit to Him no longer."

And at the end of the play Berish makes still more explicit what has already become abundantly evident in our probing of the Job of Auschwitz: that Jewish identity is bound up with just this protest that the Job of Auschwitz must make:

> I lived as a Jew, and it is as a Jew that I shall die—and it is as a Jew that, with my last breath, I shall shout my protest to God! And because the end is near, I shall shout louder! Because the end is near, I'll tell Him that He's more guilty than ever![16]

What God was guilty of toward the Jews Wiesel tells us in simple and unmistakable terms in conversation with Cargas: "I believe during the Holocaust the covenant was broken . . . because of the clouds and because of the fire."[17]

Toward the end of *Words of a Stranger*, one of his most recent

works, Wiesel gives a magnificent portrayal of the Job of Auschwitz, precisely as we have seen him throughout—walking the
narrow ridge between blind faith and total denial, combining
trust and contending in the Dialogue with the Absurd:

> In the Jewish tradition, every situation is able to transform
> itself into defiance, every prayer into appeal. Despite faith, man
> revolts; man continues to revolt despite faith, to affirm faith
> despite revolt.
>
> Well, there has never been a confrontation between God and
> man equal to what took place *down there*. They have never been
> so totally put to the test. And never has the result been as
> nebulous.
>
> A great theological protestation was announced there, but
> it had nothing to do with atheism. On the contrary, the words
> indicate acceptance, submission and benediction. They say the
> kaddish in directing themselves toward the communal graves,
> the flames, and voluntarily or not, consciously or not, they
> have made an act of accusation of an unprecedented audacity.[18]

SIXTEEN

Jewish Identity

The task of the Job of Auschwitz is contending for meaning within the Dialogue with the Absurd. If he rakes over the ashes of the Holocaust, it is because "to be a Jew today . . . means to testify," to bear witness with fervent, if saddened, joy to the Israel that is and to bear witness with "restrained, harnessed anger, free of sterile bitterness" to the world of the six million Jews that is no longer. "For the contemporary Jewish writer, there can be no theme more human, no project more universal." To identify Wiesel with the Modern Job or the Job of Auschwitz in no way means to deny his concern with Jewish identity, as my friend Thomas Idinopolous suggests.[1] Jewish identity for Wiesel does not mean the particular as opposed to the universal, but the universal through the particular, the human through the Jew. "If Job was not Jewish to begin with, he became Jewish," wrote Wiesel in *Messengers of God*.

More than any other fiction writer of universal stature of our time, with the possible exception of Shmuel Agnon and Isaac Bashevis Singer, Wiesel writes in the fullest sense of the term as a Jew. Yet his work is permeated by the spirit of Albert Camus. Although he first attained fame when he was discovered by the French Catholic novelist François Mauriac, it is the spirit of Camus that Wiesel carries forward, as no other writer that I know.

Elie likes to tell a story that Camus told him about an event that Camus himself witnessed. During the Nazi occupation of France, a Nazi officer chanced to overhear the conversation of two young Parisians caught up in the current vogue of French existentialist literature. One said to the other that life is not worth living. The Nazi came up to the youth and asked him if he meant what he said. Swallowing hard, the young man stuck by his nihilism. The officer forced the young man to go into the courtyard, where, followed by the gaze of the people in the restaurant, including Camus, all of whom crowded to the window to see what was happening, he made the youth stand against a wall, pulled out his pistol, cocked it, and prepared to shoot him. At the last moment the officer lowered his pistol and said to the frightened boy, "It is worth living, isn't it?" Elie was a bit hurt when he heard the story, because it was a Nazi officer who made the point. But Elie, too, reaffirmed as a Jew, in spite and because of everything: "Life is worth living."[2]

Wiesel's close relationship to the spirit of Camus is illustrative of the paradox of Jewish identity in general. Since the Jew in the Diaspora always lives in a majority culture that is non-Jewish and, with the exception of those who live in exclusively Jewish communities, speaks, reads, and writes in the language of the country where he or she lives, he cannot have the sense of Jewish identity that comes naturally to the Frenchman as a Frenchman. This is one of the reasons that Sartre in his masterful essay, "Portrait of an Anti-Semite," sees the Frenchman who feels himself rooted in the land as bearing an impenetrable hostility to the relatively rootless and therefore "evil" Jew who may outdo him in academic competition but has no similar claim to an identity with French soil.

The problem of Jewish identity is complicated and permeated in our day by three factors—the more or less complete cultural, though not religious, assimilation of the Diaspora Jew into the dominant milieu, the Nazi extermination of six million Jews, and the identification of many Diaspora Jews with the State of Israel.

For these reasons, we must discuss the problem of Jewish identity for the contemporary Jew in order to understand it in the works of Elie Wiesel—the paradigmatic Diaspora Jewish writer of our time.

The problem of Jewish identity cannot be understood by recourse to a definition, such as the fruitless debates of earlier times as to whether being Jewish is a religious, racial, cultural, or national phenomenon. Rather, we must ask what, along with the simple fact of being identified as a Jew, the contemporary Jew responds to. For one modern Jew, Jewishness is a culinary matter. For another, it is a type of music and dance. For a third, it is a form of nationalism, very much "like all the other nations." For a fourth, it is the Hebrew language. For a fifth, it is the 1,100-year-old heritage of Yiddish language and culture. For a sixth, it is "ethical monotheism," a religious creed without any necessary cultural or national implications. For a seventh, it is a "civilization." The fragmented character of Jewish identity is no mere difference of opinion, but so many illustrations of assimilation. Even the post-World War II recrudescence of "Jewish" novels in America, like Philip Roth's *Portnoy's Complaint* and Saul Bellow's *Herzog*, is a new stage of assimilation in which fragments of Jewish culture—the Jewish mother, Jewish food, and Jewish humor—are themselves taken over by the general culture. It is significant that Saul Bellow and not Elie Wiesel was awarded the Nobel Prize in Literature; for the former's appeal is indeed more "universal."

The rise of officially sanctioned anti-Semitism in Nazi Germany, the Holocaust, and more recently the anti-Semitism, disguised as anti-Zionism, of the Soviet Union and the Third World has radically changed this situation for many Jews, as has the voluntary complicity of innumerable American businesses with the Arab boycott, not only of companies that do business with Israel, but also of companies with American Jews in key positions. Above all, it is the Nazi extermination of six million Jews that has demanded a new response of the contemporary Jew and with it a new understanding of Jewish identity. Even those who fear no repetition of what happened in Germany are appalled by the fact that it was Jewish identity, and nothing else, that brought so many millions to a grotesque and inhuman death. Some rationalize what happened by the fact that without it there might have been no State of Israel. But most are forced to question what positive meaning can exist in being Jewish that might alleviate the terrible absurdity of persons being put to death merely because others define them as Jewish. These questions have had a strong influence on the resurgence of temple and synagogue membership in America, on the readoption of many formerly cast-off religious forms, and on the tendency of intellectuals to identify themselves as Jewish even when they have little positive content to give this term.

Another decisive change that confronts the twentieth-century Jew is the existence of the State of Israel. Israel lives the "cultural pluralism" that American Jews talk of as the ideal. While Jewish culture in America is becoming an increasingly homogenized blend of East European food, synagogue membership, and suburban American values, Israel has become the melting pot that America once was. Israel shatters the illusions of those who wish to identify Jewishness with some particular cultural heritage in which they feel at home.

The contemporary Jew must also respond to the weakening of the old liberal certainties. Darwin, Marx, Einstein, and Freud have made it increasingly difficult for us to cling to our eighteenth- and nineteenth-century assumptions of enlightened values, universal order, benign and rational human nature, and inevitable progress. It is not just "universal values" that have been shattered, but the human image itself—the image which gave former ages and cultures some direction for meaningful personal and social existence. This loss is particularly devastating for the modern Jew. A great many twentieth-century Jews have inherited moral values from their parents without having inherited that Jewish way of life in which such values were originally grounded. Their children, as a result, do not even inherit the moral values, and it becomes increasingly clear that what we took to be the sure ground of liberal, rational, commonsense morality is really an abyss. In the face of Auschwitz, Hiroshima, Biafra, Vietnam, Arab-Israeli hostility, Third World terrorism, and the continued threat of nuclear war, the young Jew knows that much of what has been handed down to him is inadequate for confronting the concrete situations in which he finds himself.

Perhaps more than any other Jew today, Elie Wiesel embodies in exemplary fashion all these paradoxes of Jewish identity. For these reasons his writings are of enormous significance for those who must make their way forward in this tangled maze. It is his Jewishness above all that unifies all the ages into one for Wiesel. For Wiesel the Jew is haunted by the beginning, the kingdom of David and the prophet Elijah, more than the end. In fact, Wiesel defines a Jew as "someone who feels every blow that ever struck his ancestors," someone who "is crushed by their mourning and buoyed by their triumphs, someone for whom they were living men and women, not symbols, someone involved in all the legends and stories retold by the Bible and commented on by the Midrash. To be a Jew is to remember what Abraham and Isaac lived and endured and to tell their tale, not with tears but laughter."[3] Wiesel sees the sacrifice of Isaac as "a survivor's story":

> Here is a story that contains Jewish destiny in its totality, just as the flame is contained in the single spark by which it comes to life. Every major theme, every passion and obsession that make Judaism the adventure that it is, can be traced back to it: man's anguish when he finds himself face to face with God, his quest for purity and purpose, the conflict of having to choose between dreams of the past and dreams of the future, between absolute faith and absolute justice, between the need to obey God's will and to rebel against it; between his yearnings for freedom and for sacrifice, his desire to justify hope and despair with words and silence—the same words and the same silence. It is all there.[4]

In Wiesel's cantata, *Ani Ma'amin: A Song Lost and Found Again*, the Chorus says:

> To be a Jew is to believe
> In that which links us
> One to the other, and all to Abraham.
> Night calls dawn;
> The Jew is that call.
> Man calls man;
> The Jew is that call.
> God awaits man;
> The Jew is that wait.[5]

It is not surprising that Wiesel finds in Jonah the prophet whose task, like that of Wiesel himself, is "to bring God's word to the Gentiles—without forsaking his own people, his own memories and beliefs." Not only is Jonah to teach the Gentiles without ceasing to be Jewish; it is the Jew in him who will teach them.

> The more Jewish the poet, the more universal his message. The more Jewish his soul, the more human his concerns. A Jew who does not feel for his fellow Jews, who does not share in their sorrows and joys, cannot feel for other people. And a Jew who is concerned with his fellow Jews is inevitably concerned with the fate of other people as well.[6]

Jonah's message to Nineveh becomes Wiesel's message to the contemporary world: "If you do not change, if Nineveh does not stop hating Jerusalem, its hate will spread beyond its borders and the world of Nineveh will lie in ruins."[7] Jonah learns that one must love other people through one's own and never outside one's own—in *Wiesel*'s variant, which seems curiously at odds with the biblical story in which Jonah is reluctant to go to Nineveh precisely because he does not want to concern himself with any other people than his own!

Wiesel sees Hasidism, like biblical Judaism, in the context of Jewish identity. Having defined Hasidism as a movement against despair, he defines Judaism and the Jew the same way: "A Jew is he—or she—whose song cannot be muted, nor can his or her joy be killed by the enemy . . . ever."[8] For Hasidism, as for

Wiesel, Jewish identity includes concern for all the rest of mankind. The Maggid of Kozhenitz's favorite prayer is Wiesel's favorite, too: "Master of the Universe, know that the children of Israel are suffering too much; they deserve redemption, they need it. But if, for reasons unknown to me, You are not willing, not yet, then redeem all the other nations, but do it soon!"[9]

When Wiesel was a boy, the rebbe said to his mother: "I want you to know that one day your son will grow up to be a great man in Israel, but neither you nor I will be alive to see it." In conversation with Harry James Cargas, Wiesel said that he assumed the entire destiny of his people from beginning to now, *and* that to be Jewish is to speak on behalf of everybody. Every person becomes metaphorically Jewish the moment he becomes authentic, and every Jew is universal the moment he is genuine. "I would never accept a view that would oppose Jewishness to universalism," Wiesel said. In accepting his own condition and identity, the Jew gives himself to his people and through it to the entire world, to mankind. He reaches the universal precisely through the particular. The secularists who wanted to have a nation like all the others were wrong because Israel *cannot* be a nation like all others. The old dream that one can attain universalism by abolishing one's Jewishness is a lost, a false dream. Wiesel defines his own position, in contrast, as a witness within the Jewish community and a defender from without. "Through speaking of Jews, we illustrate the human condition. We never made a distinction between Jew and man." "The Jewish experience may become universal only through an intensification of its Jewishness. . . . No one is more universal than Isaiah and no one is more Jewish than Isaiah." In a world hostile to Jews, the Jew must become more and more Jewish—not only for his own benefit but for that of the world as well. "Mankind has betrayed us, but we have never betrayed mankind. Nor have we betrayed ourselves."[10]

In 1966 Wiesel complained that what was lacking in modern literature by or about Jews was any intensity or even awareness of the Holocaust and the creation of the State of Israel, without which these books could not be called Jewish. Each Jew represents all Jews and all Jewish history, from the vision of Sinai to the flames of the *Khourban*. Even when Wiesel lost all faith in men during the war, he did not lose faith in the Jew, because the Jew during those times stood up better than the others. Of the Jews who died inside the concentration camps the number who collaborated with the Germans was so small that it is unbelievable. The cardinal principle of the Jews is "Do not remove yourself from the community." "In other religions one must cease to exist as an individual before creating his link with the community. In Judaism it is just the opposite." To Wiesel this identification of the Jew with the whole of the Jewish community past and present is almost archetypal in Jung's sense. When the Jew comes to the Wall, the Wailing Wall in the old city of Jerusalem, made accessible to Jews only after the 1967 war, some ancestor in him succeeds in getting through him to that wall, and the tears that the Jew cries are his and that ancestor's, for he is more than his self. "We are all part of a great memory and we are responsible for that memory . . . if we choose not to end three thousand years of Jewish history."[11]

Wiesel's sense of Jewish identity carries over to the Diaspora. Those like Ben-Gurion who would say a Jew can be a Jew only in Israel are wrong. "A Jew can be a Jew everywhere provided he links his fate to the fate of his people." Whoever opposes Israel to the Diaspora will end by annihilating both, for one is an extension of the other. "Despite the unconditional love that I bear for Israel, I am not ready to sacrifice to it the Diaspora." There was a time when Wiesel dreamed of living in the land of his ancestors. Before 1948 he wanted to emigrate to Palestine but could not; after, he could but did not want to. Now he feels that he belongs to both communities.[12]

Wiesel's Jewish identity is by no means a secular one. Without God the Holocaust ceases to be a mystery and becomes merely history. A Jew can be Jewish with God and against God but not without God. To be totally without God would be to be outside the Jewish community and outside Jewish history. The Jews kept the Torah alive for four thousand years, and it kept them alive, for one is justified by the other. The Jews are "living links in an endless chain suggesting eternity, for God's voice reverberates in it forever." To choose life means, to Wiesel, to seek Creation through Torah; for then all things will come to life and acquire meaning, intensity. Judaism is a heritage offered by the living to the living. The Torah is an answer to suffering, cruelty, indifference, destruction, and self-destruction. "The Torah is ultimately and primarily a human document destined to humanize fate, and its truth is also human, not divine or sacred." Given by God, the Torah is interpreted by man and by man alone, and once man gives the interpretation, God must obey. The Jewish ideal of education is not only to take knowledge but to live it. The Greeks and Hellenists believed in abstraction and conceptualization. The Jewish spirit taught that everything must be turned into a living example. "In our tradition we must live . . . the truth, however, burdensome, painful, or beautiful."[13]

Even when Wiesel doubted the eternity of man and the eternity of the Eternal, he never doubted the eternity of the Jewish people. A part of that eternity for him is that the Jewish people have never appealed to hatred, even when it was a question of fighting to survive. When President François Mitterand of France came to visit Elie in New York, Elie persuaded him to sponsor in Paris in December 1985 an international conference devoted solely to the understanding of hatred. That applies within the Jewish community as well as in relation to what is without. Wiesel could not remain friends with an old friend who joined the Satmar Hasidim and the Neturei Karta, which regard all Jews outside of those within that movement as non-Jews.[14]

It is not surprising that an important element in Wiesel's Jewish identity is a strong feeling about the part Christianity played, directly and indirectly, in the Holocaust. In conversation with the Catholic scholar Harry James Cargas, Wiesel characterized

Pope John XXIII as one of the most humanistic men he ever met. Even though he personally tried to help more than anyone else in his Church, he felt guilty because he understood that Auschwitz represented a failure, a defeat for two thousand years of Christian civilization. It marked an end to Orthodox Christianity. For this reason he opened the doors and liberalized the Church through Vatican II and the ecumenical movement.[15] Wiesel goes further and says that there would have been no Auschwitz had it not been for one thousand years of Christian teachings which prepared the ground for the dehumanization and atrocities of the Holocaust.

> Christianity killed itself when it killed Jews in Treblinka. After all, twenty-two percent of the SS killers, of those who killed, were good and devout Christians. Hitler was never excommunicated. . . . There would have been no massacre, there would have been no dehumanization on that scale had it not been for what they—*they, the Christians*—have done to *us* for so many centuries.[16]

The final solution was rooted in the centuries-old Christian hatred of the Jews. "Protestant leaders applauded Hitler—as did their Catholic counterparts. Those who killed . . . felt no tension, no conflict between their Christian faith and their criminal deeds." "Today's pope," said Wiesel in 1978, "walks in the footsteps of Pius XII, not in those of John."[17]

> For a believing Christian there can be no question more distressing than this: How is it that Christianity, which originated in a call to love and peace, has inflicted so much suffering? How is it possible that once Christianity attained power it used that power to dominate and conquer amid fire and slaughter? How can we explain the fact that while those who died in the accursed world of Treblinka and Auschwitz were not all Jews, those who killed them were all Christians?[18]

In 1973 I took my class in "Judaism and Literature" at Temple University to hear Elie lecture at a Reform temple in Philadelphia. Among the students was a mature Catholic woman in the forefront of those who are shaping a new Catholicism in our day. This woman reacted so strongly to a comment of Elie about Jesus that henceforth she could not read his works or write about him without extreme, belligerent antipathy. What Elie said was that Jesus must bear some responsibility for what has been done in his name in the two millennia since he lived. My own first thought was that Elie spoke out of discomfort with the liberal and in many ways assimilated temple in which he spoke. My then wife, Eugenia, said that it clearly arose out of his identification with the European Jews and his consequent antagonism to that traditional Christian anti-Semitism that had supplied the structures (the yellow badge and the ghetto) to the Nazis and that had expressed itself in the willing cooperation of the non-Jewish populations of Eastern Europe in the Nazi extermination of the Jews.

When I asked Elie about it, he explained it as a reaction against the growing Christian campaign to convert young Jews to Christianity. It was not an antipathy to Christianity as such but to its presumption in trying to capture the Jewish youth that angered Elie, even as his gratitude for François Mauriac's preface to *Night* was tempered by the latter's statement: "Did I speak of . . . the Crucified, whose Cross has conquered the world? Did I affirm that the stumbling block to his faith was the cornerstone of mine, and that the conformity between the Cross and the suffering of men was in my eyes the key to that imperishable mystery whereon the faith of his childhood had perished?"

In the light of Wiesel's conversations with Cargas, it is clear that both my former wife's explanation and Elie's are necessary to understand the statement which he also repeats there: "Whether he was the Christ is for Christians to decide. As far as the Jews are concerned, he may be retroactively guilty for all the murders and massacres that were done in his name. I believe that the Christians betrayed the Christ more than the Jews did." "The Christ" is not the historical man Jesus first of all, but the symbol, and it is this which may make sense of Wiesel's retroactive attribution of guilt. His real accusation, in any case, is neither against Jesus nor against Christ, but against Christianity and Christians.

His first accusation concerns the Christian responsibility for the Holocaust:

> Auschwitz would not have been possible without Christianity. John XXIII understood this. The fact that Hitler was never excommunicated; the fact that, I think, over twenty percent of the SS killers were practicing Christians; the fact that Pius XII never spoke up means that Christianity's role, or the Christian Church's role—both Protestant and Catholic—was so dominant in the fact that so many Jews could have been killed.

His second accusation concerns the Christian desire to convert the Jew:

> If the Christians give up their dream to convert Israel (Israel never tried to convert the Church) then I'm sure we can find some common ground. . . . For many centuries the Christian defined himelf by the suffering he imposed on the Jew. The more the Jew suffered, the better a Christian was. Theologically, the Christian saw that he was *the* Jew, the true Jew; the true Israel was the Church. The others had to suffer for not becoming part of the new concept of Judaism.[19]

In 1981 Wiesel confessed himself worried about the movement of conversion—the "crusades," a word which has a terrible meaning for the Jews. He called upon the Christian leadership to make an open statement for a pluralistic society in which they can become better Christians without it being at the expense of the Jews. "I resent their effort to proselytize. As a Jew I can respect the Christian faith in Christians, the Moslem faith in Moslems—that is the beauty of it."[20]

After the birth of his son, Wiesel linked his willingness to continue life with his Jewishness:

> I'm convinced that if I had not been Jewish I would not have accepted the awesome responsibilities of bringing life into this world. It is really the Jew in me that says that we must go

on, we must build endurance, no matter what. We must show that although there is no hope, we must invent hope.[21]

Wiesel wanted his son to learn what he learned: "*ahavat Yisrael*, love of the Jews, which is the principal commandment in Judaism," a commandment which includes the command to love all Jews, those who died as well as those who are alive.[22]

In Wiesel's first novel, *Dawn*, Elisha responds to Gad's description of the Movement as the first story he had ever heard in which the Jews were not the ones to be afraid. "Until this moment I believed that the mission of the Jews was to represent the trembling of history rather than the wind which made it tremble." Gad justifies the terrorist activities of the Movement in terms of this reversal of Jewish history. The desire to be more pure in heart than those who persecuted them, the choice of being victim rather than executioner, led to Hitler and the silence of all the other nations in the face of Hitler. When Elisha has to kill the English hostage Captain John Dawson, he thinks to himself that he has to try to hate him because his people has never known how to hate. "Their tragedy, throughout the centuries, has stemmed from their inability to hate those who have humiliated and from time to time exterminated them."[23]

Wiesel came back from his visit to the Soviet Union with a glowing report of the longing of the Soviet Jews for some link to their Jewish identity. "For the Jews of Russia, Israel is not simply a geographical location but an abstract messianic principle, a part of their own inner spiritual life," Wiesel wrote in *The Jews of Silence*.[24]

> Their isolation is so total and absolute that they will do anything to break out, even for a minute. If they fall upon you, begging for a prayer book, a Jewish calendar, a *talith*, it is not simply because they are religious; they want something to link them to the rest of their people, something to remind them that somewhere Jewish history continues to be written. Frequently I was approached by young people who wanted anything I could give them, anything at all, so long as it was Jewish. . . .

> The Jews who throng the synagogues do not all come to pray. They come to see Jews, to be in Jewish company, and, if luck is with them, to be near a Jew from abroad. . . .
>
> The true source of their comfort . . . lies . . . in the knowledge that there are other Jews in the world, whether near or far, who live in freedom, faithful Jews who are not haunted by the shadows of fear but proudly evidence their Jewishness for all to see.[25]

"If I should be remembered," said Wiesel in 1970, "I would hope it would be as a messenger of the young Jews of the Soviet Union."[26]

It is the plight and the longing for Jewish identity of these Jews that Wiesel dramatized in his play *Zalmen, or The Madness of God*. In the Soviet Union it was the Jews who were the first to brave their jailers and defy the regime, Wiesel informs us in the introduction to *Zalmen*:

> On the eve of Simchath Torah, I saw them dance and sing in front of synagogues, shouting their faith and their pride in Jewish history, celebrating with joy and exultation their inner liberation and loyalty in their past. Before Solzhenitsyn, before Sakharov, they dared proclaim a non-violent rebellion against their oppressors. Well before any other dissidents, they demonstrated their courage by writing letters, signing petitions, calling hunger strikes, occupying government offices. . . . They were the ones who allowed hope to ring out across the world.[27]

When the old rabbi finally does give his sermon of protest in the synagogue in the presence of American Jewish visitors, he proclaims to any and all who will listen that the Torah in the Soviet Union is in peril and the spirit of a whole people is being crushed and warns that if this continues, they will be "the last witnesses, the last of the Jews who in silence bury the Jew within them." Every Jewish child is full of dreams of peace and messianic victory of man over what makes him inhuman, the rabbi later says to the inspector who has come to take him to task for his sermon. When the rabbi weeps, it is the Jew in him that is grieving, the chairman says to the inspector; when he keeps silent, it is the Jew in him despairing of language. Although the inspector derides the concern of the Jews abroad for Jewish suffering in the Holocaust or in the Soviet Union, Wiesel gives the doctor the word that is his own: "What counts is not to forget."[28]

On Wiesel's second visit to the Soviet Union in 1979, he went again to Kiev and looked for the site of Babi Yar, the place where so many Jews were murdered by the Nazis. This time the site boasted a large and grandiose monument with nowhere the word "Jew" to show that they and they alone were the victims. In an impassioned and angry speech from the depths of his heart, Wiesel asked by what right they deprived of their identity these men, who lived, worked, dreamed, and died as Jews. "Why don't you grant them the posthumous justice of returning to them the place that, when alive, they claimed in Jewish history." During that same visit Wiesel arranged to meet the leaders of the refusenik movement and spent a whole night with them. When he asked what he could do for them, they said, "Work. Continue to protest." When he asked them what he could send them, they did not ask for money, medication, or clothes, but for books. They wanted to learn Judaism and Jewish philosophy. This commitment to learning and the schools that facilitate it is essential to the survival of the entire Jewish community, Wiesel concluded.[29]

Wiesel's identification with the State of Israel does not entail a hatred for Israel's enemies. The victorious Jew "is no longer a victim, but he will never become a torturer" or seek to break the will of the vanquished. That Wiesel *does* identify himself with the State of Israel he leaves in no doubt. Although he says that only those whom Eichmann killed could decide what to do with him, he tells Cargas, "What Israel does—maybe I'm too weak and too inhibited and also too Jewish to criticize or to say one way or another—what Israel does, Israel does. And does it for me." At the same time he makes clear that Israel is not for him a matter of nationalism in the modern sense: "I think that the secularists were wrong when they wanted to have a nation like all the others.

They were wrong because Israel *cannot* be a nation like all others. It is impossible. It's a counter-sense, it's a nonsense, really, a contradiction in terms." The State of Israel in no way cancels out the extermination of six million Jews. It may nonetheless be permitted to the Job of Auschwitz—the survivor who trusts *and* contends and holds fast to the integrity of the human in so doing—to see in Israel a "victory over the absurd and the inhuman." "I belong to a generation," writes Wiesel, "that has not known many such victories."

When the General Assembly of the United Nations voted to label Zionism "racist," Elie, who was in Paris at the time, wrote an article entitled "The Honor of Being a Zionist," which was published on the front page of *Paris-Soir*. "I had not strongly identified myself as a Zionist before," Elie said to me, "but in the face of this I had to." Wiesel also identifies with Israel in its isolation: "Like the Jewish people throughout the centuries, the Jewish state today stands alone and must continually justify its existence":

> Not a day goes by without its "case" being examined and tried. By the right and the left. And by professional neutrals and pacifists of every stripe. Israel is criticized for its stubbornness; its enemies are not. It is reproached for its victories, and what preceded and provoked them is forgotten. Under the pretext of anti-Zionism, young German anarchists engage in active anti-Semitism. Chinese, Russians and Algerians train and equip Arab terrorists to kill and be killed. Then come the "revolutionaries" among Western intellectuals, who create an aura of romance around air-piracy and air-killings, thereby succeeding in conducting "guerilla" warfare by remote control. A saddening and grotesque phenomenon surpassed only by the one we witness in Poland: an anti-Semitism without Jews.[30]

This judgment after the 1948 war was repeated by Wiesel after 1967. Again he saw Israel isolated with no friends or protectors. The Arabs wanted to drive the Jews back into the sea, and the shadow of Auschwitz enveloped Jerusalem. But the hardened Jewish soldiers who wept on reaching the Wall in the Old City of Jerusalem testified to a harrowing immediacy of the past that transcended any search for power or material superiority. What made Wiesel as proud of them as of their victory was their moving humility in the face of it—no celebration or ceremony, military parades, or public rejoicing. "Humanity has never known victors less arrogant, heroes more sober and eager for peace and purity." In a letter to a concerned friend, Wiesel claimed that what the world cannot forgive Israel is its "determination, both daring and irritating, to remain human in a situation which is not." Israelis are resented because they commit no sacrilege and profane no mosques. In words that he could hardly have used after the 1982 war in Lebanon, Wiesel suggested that the Beirut raid was condemned *because* it had caused no bloodshed. Wiesel pictured Israel's victory as a moral one, contrasting the way Arab prisoners are treated in Israel with the way Jewish prisoners are treated in Iraq, Egypt, and Syria. Israel must wait for some recognition, some first contact, so that she will no longer be reduced to an object. "For the duration of its torment, the Jewish soul has remained Jewish—that is, vibrant to everything human—and Jewish it will remain now that we can see a glimmer of light."[31]

As a person who identifies with both Israel and the Diaspora, Wiesel does not allow himself to criticize Israel from without. But on at least one occasion, when addressing the Jewish Agency Assembly in Jerusalem in June 1974, he did allow himself a criticism from within—not of the citizens and soldiers, but of some of its leaders, advisers, and bureaucrats:

> At times we wish we could say to them: You are too self-centered, too authoritarian. In your eyes, we are second-class Jews. Worse: second-rate Jews. Our concerns, our aspirations, our setbacks and triumphs are of no interest to you. A mediocre film star is better known here than A. J. Heschel. André Néher is widely respected and admired all over Europe—is his voice being heard here? You have leaders, and we are ready to listen . . . if only your emissaries were of some intellectual stature.
>
> . . . We wanted statesmen, and you gave us experts. We wanted poets and philosophers, and you sent us public relations men. You offered us politicians instead of messengers.[32]

In 1981 Wiesel reaffirmed that, in spite of pressure and threats, Israel became the "most humane new independent nation in our time" and claimed that no other nation showed such humanity in times of war. At the same time he expressed anger at the criticisms of Israel in the United Nations by nations such as Uganda and the Soviet Union: "An ancient nation of 3,500 years is being judged by dictators." The next year, however, Wiesel disclosed that at the prompting of a Palestinian poet who told him terrible stories about some of his friends in Israel, he went to Israel, spoke to the chief-of-staff and Golda Meir, and arranged the release of the Palestinian's friends. "Sometimes the writer can succeed."[33]

On the other hand, his first reaction to the Israeli invasion of Lebanon was shock at the antagonism that it aroused in Europe toward the Jews. Day after day the television and press in France used such phrases as "Final Solution," "Nazi barbarity," "Holocaust." Not since the fall of the Third Reich had Jews encountered such hostility. People were unconsciously exploiting the situation to make the Jewish people pay for its upright conscience and dignity during the Nazi era. Contrary to my expectation that he would now have to modify what he said earlier about Israel's "bloodless" raid on Beirut, Wiesel stressed how wrong it was to judge an ancient people by the actions of a month or a year:

> Was it necessary to criticize the Israeli government, notwithstanding the spate of lies disseminated in the press? Or would it not have been better to have offered Israel unreserved support, regardless of the suffering endured by the population of Beirut?
>
> In the face of hatred, our love for Israel ought to have deepened, become more wholehearted, and our faith in Israel more compelling, more true.[34]

This does not mean that Wiesel felt no concern for the Lebanese civilian population. On the contrary, he called for some kind of Marshall Plan to aid them and asserted that, as Jews and human beings, this should be our first priority—something we can do with and for Israel. After the massacre of Palestinians by the Lebanese Christian militia in the refugee camps, Wiesel published a statement in *The New York Times* proclaiming that the darkest time for him since the end of World War II:

> It is not that I accuse or indict anyone, and surely not the people of Israel, but I felt sadness, incommensurate sadness, almost disarmed. In a strange way, I felt responsible. Perhaps if we had told the story more convincingly, if we had prevented the trivialization and cheapening of what was and remains a unique catastrophe, things would not have happened this way.
>
> I believe now that a gesture is needed on our part. Perhaps we ought to proclaim a day of fasting, surely a day of taking stock.[35]

In his letter "To a Young Jew Today," Wiesel identifies the Jew and his questioning:

> Rooted both in the contemporary and the timeless, he invites hesitation and doubt. He sows disquiet in the heart of the victor and undermines the good conscience of the vanquished. Two thousand years of exile have taught him to wait for the Messiah and to suspect him once he has arrived. Push interrogation to its limits and beyond, and you will do what the Jew has been doing for centuries.[36]

"I leave you the task of working out your own relationship with God," Wiesel says to the young Jew. "What matters to me is the relationship between the individual and the community." "To be a Jew is to work for the survival of a people—your own—whose legacy to you is its collective memory in its entirety." Like Martin Buber in his early "Speeches on Judaism," Wiesel links the "I" of the individual Jew to the doubts, turmoils, and victories of his earliest forebears. By working for his own people the Jew makes his most valuable contribution to mankind.

> By struggling on behalf of Russian, Arab or Polish Jews, I fight for human rights everywhere. By calling for peace in the Middle East, I take a stand against every aggression, every war. By protesting the fanatical exhortations to "holy wars" against

my people, I protest against the stifling of freedom in Prague. By striving to keep alive the memory of the Holocaust, I denounce the massacres in Biafra and the nuclear menace. Only by drawing on his unique Jewish experience can the Jew help others. A Jew fulfills his role as man only from inside his Jewishness.

That is why, in my writings, the Jewish theme predominates. It helps me approach and probe the theme of man.[37]

Wiesel sees Judaism as the only possible way to humanism for the Jew; for Judaism stresses human relations even more than God-man relations. "Whoever betrays humanity, whoever torments one's fellow man, denies the existence of God." Wiesel finds it a source of astonishment and pride that the Jewish people, in spite of twenty centuries of persecution, have not become dominated by bitterness, vengeance, violence, and resentment. At the same time, as we have seen, he continually insists on the uniqueness of the Jewish experience of the Holocaust. Speaking to the Main Commission for the Investigation of Hitlerite Crimes in Poland in 1979, Wiesel said, as he said at Babi Yar, that he was deeply pained by the failure of the Polish government to give the three million Polish Jews who died under the Nazis their identity as Jews. To remember them as they were, as human beings and as Jews, would be an act of justice.[38]

In the days of the Holocaust, more than ever, to be Jewish signified *refusal*, writes Wiesel in *A Jew Today*. "Above all, it was a refusal to see reality and life through the enemy's eyes—a refusal to resemble him, to grant him that victory, too." "In Auschwitz all the Jews were victims, all the killers were Christian," Wiesel points out. How was it that Pius XII never condemned Auschwitz and Treblinka and that a large proportion of the SS killers were faithful Christians who went to Confession between massacres? The few brave Christians who came to the aid of the Jews do not explain away the passivity of the populations and the cruelty of the killers who were not impeded by their Christianity. This is, Wiesel suggests, a problem for the Christians. For the survivor the question was whether or not to remain a Jew, and most survivors answered this question by strengthening their Jewish ties. Auschwitz has resulted in a renascence of Jewish consciousness and a flourishing of Jewish history.[39]

> Whatever he chooses to do, the Jew becomes a spokesman for all Jews, dead and yet to be born, for all the beings who live through him and inside him.
> His mission was never to make the world Jewish but, rather, to make it more human.[40]

As vivid testimony to this last statement, *A Jew Today* contains essays on the suffering in Biafra, Paraguay, South Africa. Wiesel asks Israel to be a model and expects of it the impossible in the name of the unity of Jews everywhere. Wars may be forced upon Israel, but its warriors are sad. The essence of being Jewish is never to yield to despair, to face the human condition—and to do so as a Jew. The Jews began their adventure in the world as realists as far as war was concerned and evolved over the centuries into humanists. "Other religions and traditions did the reverse: they began by preaching love, but with the passage of time, perpetrated unconscionable massacres in the name of that very love."[41] In the three classic volumes of Jewish martyrology there are episodes of Jews resisting the invaders, fighting them valiantly to the end, yet remaining faithful to a certain concept of Israel and mankind:

> There were never any religious persecutions instigated, organized or implemented by Jews. None of the notorious killers in history . . . was of our people. The Jewish people never answered hate with hate; yes, they sometimes had to take radical measures to protect themselves, but the enemy never succeeded in bringing his Jewish victims down to his level. Both Israel's ancient and modern wars prove it.[42]

Jewish identity stands at the center of Wiesel's novel *The Testament*. Paltiel Kossover writes his testament for his son, Grisha, to tell him not to make the mistake *he* did of leaving his Jewish

roots to espouse a universal cause. As a young man Paltiel abandoned the Hasidism of his father to become a Communist and
wandered through Berlin, Paris, civil-war Spain, and the Soviet
Union until he was imprisoned and awaiting execution as one
of the Jewish poets that Stalin has determined to eliminate. *This*
novel is not continuous with *Night*, as so many of the others
seem to be. Neither Paltiel nor Grisha is recognizably the Eliezer
of *Night*, who reappears in *Dawn*, *The Accident*, *The Town Beyond
the Wall*, and *The Gates of the Forest*, and even in David in *A
Beggar in Jerusalem*. What is there instead is a complex double
plot weaving back and forth between the life of Paltiel Kossover
stretching from before the First World War to his execution in
1952 and the life of his son, Grisha, in the twenty years since
then. It is a tour de force of evocation of life and events that
Wiesel himself did not live through, and it is a successful one.

"Don't follow the path I took, it doesn't lead to truth," Paltiel
tells Grisha at the beginning of his Testament. "Truth for a Jew
is to dwell among his brothers."[43] To the examining magistrate
who is trying to trip him up through his Testament, Paltiel writes:
"I plead guilty to having nurtured . . . an exaggerated, boundless
love for an obstinate people, my own, whom you and your people
have endlessly denigrated and oppressed." Declaring his solidarity
with the Jewish people everywhere and always, he breaks his links
with the world of Soviet Communism, "a world protected and
represented by this prison." "Jews remain Jews wherever they
are: united, charitable, hospitable," he later declares to the magistrate:

> You condemn Jewish nationalism for its internationalist
> character, and in a way you're right: between a Jewish busi-
> nessman from Morocco and a Jewish chemist from Chicago,
> a Jewish ragpicker from Lodz and a Jewish industrialist from
> Lyons, a Jewish mystic from Safed and a Jewish intellectual
> from Minsk, there is a deeper and more substantive kinship,
> because it is far older, than between two gentile citizens of the
> same country, the same city and the same profession. A Jew

may be alone but never solitary, for he remains integrated within a timeless community, however invisible or without geographic or political reality. The Jew does not define himself within geographical categories, Citizen Magistrate; he expresses and identifies himself in historic terms. Jews help one another in order to prolong their common history, to explore and enrich their common destiny, to enlarge the domain of their collective memory.[44]

Before Paltiel leaves home, his father asks him to remember always that he is a Jew first and foremost and that it is as a Jew that he will be helping mankind. "If you care for others to the detriment of your brothers, you will eventually deny everyone." Later Paltiel himself proclaims to the magistrate that the Spanish civil war is linked to Jewish history. Just as the destruction of the Jewish community in *The Oath* led to the destruction of Kolvillàg in general and as the Holocaust has prepared the way for nuclear war, so the burning of Jews at the stake in 1492 and the expulsion of the rest led to Spaniards massacring one another. "You begin by hating and persecuting others and you wind up hating and annihilating your own." Later in the novel it is David Aboulesia, the mysterious messianic figure whom Paltiel repeatedly encounters, who says to Paltiel that the place a Jew occupies in universal history is determined by his place in Jewish history. "If you believe you must forsake your brothers in order to save mankind, you will save nobody, you will not even save yourself."[45] It is significant that the novel which ends with Zupanev's account of the execution of Paltiel begins with Grisha's arriving in Israel.

"The Jews are God's memory and the heart of mankind," Wiesel has written, and he means just that—not as any form of superiority but in terms of the never-ending messianic task of making the human world genuinely human. After pointing out, as we have already seen, that the essays in *A Jew Today* express "moral concern about human indignities in Biafra, South Africa, Bangladesh, the Sahel, Vietnam, and even reach out to initiate a dialogue with Palestinian Arabs," Robert McAfee Brown relates an episode from Wiesel's own life which "speaks volumes about how particularistic Jewish concerns reach out to encompass universal human concerns":

> His first public action as chairman of the President's Commission on the Holocaust was not to stress the special needs or concerns of Jewish people, but to call public attention, through an open letter to the American people, to the plight of the Vietnamese "boat people," refugees being denied access to their own land and refused entrance to all other lands. This contemporary concern grew out of a specific Jewish memory—the experience in 1938 of Jewish "boat people," who left Hamburg in search of asylum in any other country than Germany, were denied entrance by all countries in the North Atlantic, and finally had to return to Germany, where most of them were sent to Theresienstadt. . . .
>
> To begin with the particular is to be moved to a concern for all.[46]

Elie Wiesel as the Job of Auschwitz and Elie Wiesel as the spokesman for Jewish identity flow together and culminate in Wiesel's messianism—the messianism of the unredeemed.

Messianism: Biblical, Kabbalistic, and Hasidic

Messianism—the concern not only for individual salvation but for the completion of God's creation, the redemption of God's world—has a long history in Judaism. In Wiesel's writings, correspondingly, we can distinguish successive layers of messianism and messianic concern—biblical, talmudic, kabbalistic, and Hasidic—all of which set the stage for the messianism of the unredeemed which emerges from the Holocaust world.

Wiesel's biblical messianism does not center on the exact prescriptions for the coming of the Messiah—no biblical text, not even Isaiah, does that—but on the concern for life, the covenant between one human being and another. "Since the world was created for one human being," comments Wiesel in his portrait of Adam, "whoever kills one human being, kills all mankind; and whoever saves one human being, saves all mankind." Why should messianism be concerned with man and not simply God? Because "God needs man to make Himself known." After Adam and Eve are expelled from paradise, they decide to fight by giving life, by conferring a meaning on life. Adam had the courage to get up and begin anew. Adam shows the secret God gave man in creating him—how to begin again. Man begins again every time he chooses to defy death and to side with the living.[1] Wiesel's biblical mes-

221

sianism, as we would expect, is still the messianism of the Job of Auschwitz.

> We believe in defiance. We Jews believe that no matter how strong the enemy, no matter how serious the danger, man is capable of defying both. Man should defy what tries to destroy him. If it is done with dignity and humanity, in the name of friendship, then the defiance may become redemption.[2]

Wiesel offers a new twist on the old story of Cain and Abel. Each was responsible for the other; neither was entirely guilty or innocent; each was indifferent to the other. Each is responsible for his fellow man, himself, and God. "Whoever kills, kills his brother; and when one has killed, one no longer is anyone's brother." The story of Jacob wrestling with the angel also becomes for Wiesel a story of responsibility: Jacob knew that whosoever kills man kills God in man. But there is a connection, too, between divine and human solitude: "Man must be alone to listen, to feel and even to fight God, for God engages only those who, paradoxically, are both threatened and protected by solitude." In suffering, misfortune, even in evil, God is in man, accompanying man through the exile. God is the road, God is the exile.[3]

Jeremiah the prophet is paradigmatic for Wiesel. Like the sufferer in Wiesel's novel *The Accident*, Jeremiah is alone with God, at times against God, and wherever he goes, he breathes misfortune and shatters serenity. Constantly in opposition, like all prophets before him, he emphasizes the fragility of the present and the uncertainty of the future, robbing his listeners of their desire to live. Yet though he is alone, Jeremiah defines himself in relation to his fellow men, who reject him. "Living in a disorganized, dehumanized world, he forces himself to pick up the broken pieces and dreams of man's possibilities to create harmony." He fights so as not to be overwhelmed by history and so that he can act on it concretely, simply, humanly. Jonah, too, the reluctant prophet, Wiesel turns into a paradigm of the way to humanity rather than to abstract absolutes. God teaches Jonah to be humble in the face of suffering, and to fight for a justice, truth, and compassion that is human. "The way to God leads through man, however alien, however sinful he may be."[4]

As a child Wiesel was deeply immersed in the Kabbala, the esoteric tradition of Jewish mysticism, and overtones of kabbalistic messianism and the search for the Messiah run through all Wiesel's works. Since, according to the Kabbala, one can bring the Messiah to the earth if one's soul is sufficiently pure and one's love deep enough, Wiesel and his close friend decided to try, even though they were aware that one cannot force God's hand with impunity.[5] The Zohar, the kabbalistic Book of Splendor, pictures God as saying to man after He created him on the sixth day, "I have worked heretofore, now you shall continue." But the work of man toward redemption, like the coming of the Messiah, remains shrouded in mystery. "The Talmud tells us that the Messiah sits waiting to be called, at the gates of Rome, amid beggars and cripples and other outcasts," Gavriel tells Gregor in *The Gates of the Forest*. But the Kabbala says that the Messiah conceals himself near God and far from men where, in the most holy and inaccessible of sanctuaries, he sees time unfold, filled with pity and distress. It is pity that prevented the Messiah from coming when the famous medieval kabbalist Joseph di-la-Reina overcame Satan and prepared for the coming of the Messiah. The sage took pity on his captive and succumbed to his tears, as a result of which Satan broke his chains, "and the Messiah, already on the threshold, was forced to return to his prison, somewhere infinitely far away, in the chaos of time and man's hope!"[6]

A glimpse of what Wiesel's youthful kabbalistic messianism meant to him is offered to us in Wiesel's portrait of the thirteen-year-old Michael in *The Town Beyond the Wall*:

> The year that he spent beside the master was for Michael the most wondrous of his life. The most profound, the fullest. Suddenly all actions had meaning, occupied a definite place in that immense mosaic of which even the outlines escape our

understanding. God was *presence*. He manifested Himself in every thing, behind every act. An aspect of God was concealed even in evil, and the theory of the *Nitzotzot* said so poetically: every man possesses a divine spark. The Shekina is the sum of the sparks. Let the Shekina—the divine emanation—be reunited with God, and the world will have achieved its final liberation.[7]

Wiesel's father, on the other hand, urged his son not to lose sight of his fellow man. In *A Beggar in Jerusalem*, these sentiments are ascribed to the mother, who says to the Hasidic rebbe that she wants her son to love God but only through man, but that she does not want him to fear God through man.[8]

In *Souls on Fire* Wiesel tells a story of the Baal Shem's longing to bring the Messiah, which tale, Wiesel holds, contains most of the basic elements of Hasidism:

> The fervent waiting, the longing for redemption; the erratic wanderings over untraveled roads; the link between man and his Creator, between the individual act and its repercussions in the celestial spheres; the importance of ordinary words; the accent on fervor and on friendship too; the concept of miracles performed by man for man.[9]

To be a Hasidic Jew is to know how to listen and to receive. Though the Torah was given only once, each one of us must receive it every day. A Hasid is also one who shares solidarity with other Hasidim and feels responsible for their fate. God, too, is ally of man inside creation and needs man's love. But if one is not to reduce God to an abstraction, one must love Him in and through man. Through his concrete actions man can gather in the dispersed sparks and uplift them to their divine source. "Man's role is to mitigate solitude." Every encounter, every meeting, between one human being and another quickens the steps of the Redeemer. In imposing meaning on creation through accepting one another, two human creatures give meaning to creation. The new idea introduced by Hasidism is that it is within the power of every person to modify the very laws which imprison us. We can accept our contradictions, discovering humility within pride, simplicity within generosity, charity within justice. "One must impose meaning on what perhaps has none and draw ecstasy from nameless, faceless pain."[10]

For Hasidism the redemption of the Messiah must mean the redemption of all. The next generation will be far worse than this one, Rabbi Israel protested to God in asking him why he had not sent his Messiah. Rabbi Nachman of Bratzlav kept "bad company" because he knew that to pull a person out of the mud, the Just Man must set foot into that mud.

> To bring back lost souls, he must leave the comfort of his home and seek them wherever they might be. "In every man, there is something of the Messiah." In every man, in every place. The Kabbala says it, the mystics repeat it. To free mankind one must gather the sparks, all the sparks, and integrate them into the sacred flame. A Messiah who would seek to save only the Just, would not be the Messiah. The others must be considered too—they must be prepared. Miscreants need redemption more than saints.[11]

By putting the accent on friendship and love, rather than on erudition and strict observance of the law, "Hasidism brought back to the fold large numbers of Jews who, faltering under the weight of their burdens, came close to conceding defeat." Once again the road to God goes through men. The essence of Hasidic legend is that it is an attempt to humanize fate: "In Hasidism, everything is possible, everything becomes possible by the mere presence of someone who knows how to listen, to love and give of himself."[12] "A good story in Hasidism is not about miracles, but about friendship and hope—the greatest miracles of all."[13]

The significance of *Tikkun*, the reparation and restoration of the fallen world and the uplifting of the sparks, is to be concerned not only with oneself but with everything and everyone around one. Start to serve God by serving God's children. The fact that God's ways are not always understandable or bearable is no reason to leave a disciple exposed to solitude, danger, and death. Faith is not opposed to anguish but part of it.[14]

> God waits for Israel while Israel is waiting for God, who is looking for His Shekhina, who is following Israel, who suffers with God, and at times for God, and always because of God.
> And yet—beyond sadness, beyond despair, there *is* love, and there always will be. Without such love, which forever calls for its own transcendence, man's life would not be less tragic but less lofty and therefore empty and pointless.[15]

Hasidism in its origins is a protest against solitude. "To follow a certain Rebbe means to relate to his pupils." The Hasidic master, oppressed by the sufferings and trials of his people, by the exile of the Shekinah and the failure of the Messiah to come, "creates happiness so as not to yield to unhappiness. He tells stories so as to escape the temptation of silence." Michael, who in *The Town Beyond the Wall* sets out to cure his mad cellmate so as not to succumb to madness himself, is following in the footsteps of the Hasidic masters.[16]

In Hasidism even anger is a part of messianic concern. Rabbi Barukh "was angry because he cared, because he was concerned, because he was present to anyone in need of human presence." To the desperate young student, he said that there are reasons enough for man to explode with rage at the injustice of God's creation. "Fine, let us be angry. Together." Rabbi Moshe Leib of Sassov used as his touchstone of whether something was right whether it brought one closer to his fellow man. If it does not, then you are moving away from God; for even the love of God must be measured in human terms. "One must love God *and* man and never act against man or without man." Learn to listen, to care, to be concerned, to be involved. "The opposite of love is not hate but indifference; the opposite of life is not death but insensitivity." Like the other great Hasidic masters, Moshe Leib, too, transcended his own fear and pain and put them in the service of others. Hasidism was nothing other than an attempt to tear down everything that separated one man from another.

Because God is everywhere, in the Hasidic kingdom men were not one another's prisoners but their companions. "One man was not another man's boundary but, on the contrary, an opening unto other men." The Messiah can wait: "First priority goes to the sick child who needs medicine; or to the desperate mother who needs to be consoled; or surely to the father who loses his mind when he is unable to feed, to preserve, his family." Fervor, study, ecstasy can wait until the hungry stomach is fed, the sick child healed. To diminish and despise your body is to sneer at God's creation. The love of God when it is not linked to the love of man leads to idolatry and inhumanity. To mutilate life and choose suffering is to offend the source of life and reject a gift both rare and irreplaceable. "God is in His creation—God is present, God is presence. It is up to man to be present, too—present to God, to himself, and to his fellow man." "When you love your friend as you love yourself, God is the third partner."[17]

Love of Israel, love of Torah, love of God are all three one single love. "Who loves, loves God. Who loves God, loves man." It is not even permitted to hate oneself, for then, as the Besht said, you will ultimately hate others even more. Love is the ultimate purpose in man's existence, and its true opposite is not hate but indifference, neutrality, passivity, and resignation, all of which lead to decadence. The tradition of Hasidism was an open one which tolerated diversity—what I call the "community of otherness." When the Satmar rebbe says that he is the only Hasid and publishes vicious attacks on Israel, this "community of affinity," again to use my phrase, is not, according to Wiesel, within the tradition of Hasidism. "A Hasid does everything a good Jew does but with one difference—passion."[18] It is this passion that strove to bring the Messiah.

Although Wiesel points out, in his portrait of Hasidic masters, that it is not sufficient to call upon the Messiah for the Messiah to come, nonetheless his emphasis, as Michael Berenbaum points out, is on Hasidism as a way of combating despair by sharing it, finding hope by living in hope, overcoming mourning by demanding joy. "The Hasid is one whose rebellion is found in his fidelity. He is a man who cries with song and mourns with joy and who disobeys by remaining obedient." Hasidism, and Judaism too, for Wiesel, is a movement out of despair, away from despair, against despair. The reason that many Jews were attracted to Communism originally is that they wanted to save mankind, to search for the redemption of man. The suffering of the Jews in Eastern Europe was so powerful that every Jewish child wanted to stop not only their own but all suffering. "They wanted to bring the Messiah."[19]

EIGHTEEN

The Messianism of
the Unredeemed

*"Standing, bound and shackled, in the
pillory of mankind, we demonstrate
with the bloody body of our people
the unredeemedness of the world."*
MARTIN BUBER

Wiesel's modern messianism is continuous with his understanding of biblical, kabbalistic, and Hasidic messianism. In *Dawn*, before Elisha kills John Dawson, he comes to understand that an act as absolute as killing involves all those who formed him and makes them, too, into murderers. When he tries unsuccessfully to hate John Dawson, he sees God incarnate in the liking with which John Dawson inspired him. "The lack of hate between executioner and victim, perhaps this is God."[1] In *The Accident* the hero's kabbalistic teacher teaches him that "the Messiah, called to liberate man, can only be liberated by him. . . . Man—who is nothing but a handful of earth—is capable of reuniting time and its source, and of giving back to God his own image." When he is a grown man after the Holocaust, his friend Gyula says to him, "Maybe God is dead, but man is alive. The proof: he is capable of friendship. Suffering is given to the living, not to the dead. . . . It is man's duty to make it cease, not to increase it. One hour of suffering less is already a victory over fate."[2]

As if in continuation of this conversation, Pedro says to Michael in *The Town Beyond the Wall* that God is the weakness of strong men and the strength of weak men, and that man is God's strength and also His weakness. When man is imprisoned and under torture, God is imprisoned, and it is up to man to free Him, Pedro tells Michael. Earlier Michael's father tells him that to remove the possibility of union between one human being and another by killing the body is as grave as destroying life. "Who does not live for man—for the man of today, for him who walks beside you and whom you can see, touch, love and hate—creates for himself a false image of God." In almost the same words, Pedro says to Michael, "He who thinks about God, forgetting man, runs the risk of mistaking his goal: God may be your next-door neighbor." When Pedro shows up in the "City of Luck," Michael thinks: "Together, we'll win. When two solitudes unite . . . they are stronger than the world." Michael renews his strength in finding himself responsible for his cellmate—"a life that was an inseparable part of the life of mankind." He makes the boy aware of his presence, establishes a rapport, and pushes back the night with his bare hands. He dances, laughs, claps his hands, makes faces, tells stories, sings, weeps, until he brings him to the point when he speaks and sketches arabesques in the air.[3]

"I wouldn't have the coming of the Messiah depend upon our lack of generosity and pity, even toward Satan," Gregor says to Gavriel in *The Gates of the Forest* after the latter tells him the story of the medieval kabbalist Joseph di-la-Reina. "I don't want salvation to come through fire, through cruelty, and through the sacrifices of others." But Gavriel relates to Gregor a conversation which he has with the prophet Elijah in which the Messiah's not coming is seen in far bitterer terms. Madmen have begun to kill our people in cold blood, Gavriel says to Elijah:

> "If the Messiah doesn't hurry, he may be too late; there will be no one left to save. I spoke to him of Jewish children, with dreams in their eyes, massacred in front of their speechless parents, who went to join them in the grave. . . . Elijah smiled at me. . . . 'I know,' he said, nodding his head, 'I know. I walk across this land . . . condemned to live, to watch, to observe, and to witness the unfolding of the Holocaust!' I was sorry

for him, and in return he told me a secret. 'The Messiah is not coming. He's not coming because he has already come. . . . He's neither at the gates of Rome nor in heaven. . . . Ever present, he gives each passing moment its taste of drunkenness, desolation, and ashes.' "

When Gavriel says that God can afford to wait but he can't, Elijah tells him that God's final victory lies in man's inability to reject Him:

> You think you're cursing Him, but your curse is praise; you think you're fighting Him, but all you do is open yourself to Him; you think you're crying out your hatred and rebellion, but all you're doing is telling Him how much you need His support and forgiveness. No, you mustn't blaspheme against someone who shares your suffering.[4]

Gregor does not respond, but he thinks of his father, to whom the Messiah was something not someone. "The Messiah," Gregor's father used to say, "is that which makes man more human, which takes the element of pride out of generosity, which stretches his soul towards others."

When the Hungarian soldiers come with dogs, Gavriel gives himself up to prevent their discovering Gregor. Before going, he tells Gregor of how he discovered the Messiah in a simple beadle who at night wept for the destruction of the Temple, for the exile of Israel and that of the Shekinah. When the Nazis came, Gavriel went to Moshe the Silent and demanded that he do his duty and disobey God for the sake of saving from annihilation the people of the witness, the martyr people, the people of the covenant. But the "Messiah" laid down his arms without resisting and let himself be taken prisoner and executed. "I tell you, Gregor," says Gavriel, "that hope is no longer possible nor permitted . . . The Messiah has come and the world has remained what it was: a vast slaughterhouse."[5]

In autumn when Gregor tells Leib the secret of the extermination of the Jews that Gavriel discovered, he joins himself to Gavriel's lament over the Messiah:

> The Messiah is not coming; he got lost along the way, and from now on the clouds will obscure his sight. There are no more men, Leib, I tell you. Here and there, a few, but they are hiding in caves, like frightened animals, while the others mistake themselves for gods because they are thirsty for blood. If this goes on, we shall witness a new deluge: a sea of blood will envelop the earth, and the ark will be engulfed.[6]

Later, when Haimi, one of the younger Jewish partisans, tells Gregor of the death of his father, Gregor's bitterness deepens to an accusation of God as unjust and life a farce. "God doesn't love man or deserve his love. . . . God created man in order to kill him; he created him because he has no pity." Still later, Gregor understands that he is responsible, that the injustice perpetrated in an unknown land concerns him. "He who is not among the victims is with the executioners. This was the meaning of the holocaust: it implicated not only Abraham or his son, but their God as well."[7]

When another partisan, Yehuda, tries to get Gregor to admit that he is in love with Clara, Leib's girlfriend, Gregor refuses to respond to what he sees as out of place in wartime. "This is the time to love. This is the time to choose," Yehuda says to Gregor. "An act of love may tip the balance." In an inhuman world like this one, love is the greatest of victories, Yehuda says to Gregor, and reproaches him with his cruelty in insisting upon suffering alone, thus shrinking and diminishing himself:

> It's inhuman to wall yourself up in pain and memories as if in a prison. Suffering must open us to others. It must not cause us to reject them. The Talmud tells us that God suffers with man. Why? In order to strengthen the bonds between creation and the creator. God chooses to suffer in order to better understand man and be better understood by him.[8]

In winter, in his duel-conversation with the Hasidic rebbe, Gregor asks him how he can believe in God after what has happened to the Jewish people. "With an understanding smile on his lips the Rebbe answered, 'How can you *not* believe in God after what has happened?' " When the rebbe asks Gregor what he expects of himself, Gregor replies that his only purpose now is not to cause others to suffer: "I'm no longer intent upon measuring myself against fate and saving humanity . . . to help a single human being is enough for me." It does not matter whether or not the Messiah comes, Gregor realizes in the end, or the fact that he comes too late. If we are sincere, humble, and strong, the Messiah will come—every day, a thousand times a day—for he is not a single man but all men. When Clara learns to sing again and Gregor to weep, it will be he that sings and weeps in them.[9]

In 1968 Wiesel suggested that existentially the world has turned Jewish. For two thousand years the Jewish people lived on the edge of extinction. Now the whole world lives in the shadow of the atomic bomb. As the death of Jesus in Jerusalem involved every Jew everywhere and in every generation for two millennia, so today one person may push a button and involve the lives of everyone. The challenge for everyone, as a result, is now identical with what Wiesel defines as the substance of Judaism—"to remain human in a world that is inhuman."[10] This is the messianism of the unredeemed.

The names of the three major characters of *A Beggar in Jerusalem* carry messianic overtones in themselves. David is named after the king who was the first prototype of the true leader who would bring the people of Israel to the messianic completion of the kingship of God. Katriel is a shortened version of Kether Elyon, the throne of God—the first of the Sefiroth, or emanations of God, in the Zohar. Malka is the Queen, Shabbat, the Shekinah, the indwelling Glory of God that wanders in exile in the world and that must be reunited with the Ein Sof, the infinite, transcendent God, as bride with her bridegroom, for the messianic redemption to take place. As such, she is also identified with the last of the Sefiroth in the *Etz Hayyim*, the kabbalistic tree of life.

When Katriel confesses to his rabbi father that he is afraid of

being killed in the war, his father tells him that he still has a lot
to learn.

> "What you should fear is to inflict evil, to cause death. To
> die for God and His commandments is nothing: our ancestors,
> the saints and the martyrs, did just that. But to kill for God,
> to cause blood to flow in His name, is serious and difficult. It
> is alien to us; it goes against our nature and tradition: that is
> what should frighten you."[11]

At the end of *A Beggar in Jerusalem* a child asks his grandfather
whether there is not a contradiction in the fact that "it is written
that the Shekinah, the divine presence, never leaves Jerusalem;
but it is also written that it follows the Jews, all the Jews, into
exile," to which the grandfather responds: "That proves the Shekinah is present even within contradictions." And a father in a
Nazi photograph, pointing to the sky a moment before he and
his son reach the ditch where they are to be shot, says: "Whoever
kills, becomes God. Whoever kills, kills God. Each murder is a
suicide, with the Eternal eternally the victim."[12] David must un-
learn being jealous of Katriel's past and his innocence, must go
home to the woman who will welcome him even though he still
does not know who she is:

> A victor, he? Victory does not prevent suffering from having
> existed, nor death from having taken its toll. How can one
> work for the living without by that very act betraying those
> who are absent? The question remains open, and no new fact
> can change it. Of course, the mystery of good is no less dis-
> turbing than the mystery of evil. But one does not cancel the
> other. Man alone is capable of uniting them by remembering.[13]

The Messiah does not dwell above in glory, but below in the
suffering and exposure of human beings: "The Word is the history of man; and man is the history of God."

In *One Generation After* Wiesel tells the story of a Just Man
who comes to Sodom, determined to save its inhabitants from
sin and punishment, only to be met by totally deaf ears. When

a child takes compassion on him and asks him whether he does not see that it is hopeless, the Just Man responds: "In the beginning, I thought I could change man. Today, I know I cannot. If I still shout today, if I still scream, it is to prevent man from ultimately changing me." We can well imagine that Elie Wiesel identifies himself with the Just Man of that story! He also tells the story of a Hasidic rebbe who went up to heaven and knocked at the Messiah's gate, asking the Messiah why he is taking so long when mankind is expecting him. When the Messiah responds that it is not he they are expecting but good health, riches, serenity, knowledge, peace, or happiness, the rebbe loses patience and cries that if he cannot help men resolve even the most insignificant of their problems, then he should indeed remain in shadow. If he does not understand that he is bread for the hungry, a voice for the old man without heirs, sleep for those who dread the night, then indeed it is not he that mankind is waiting for. Upon which the rebbe returns to earth, gathers his disciples, forbids them to despair, and says: "Now the true waiting begins."[14]

Speaking of Jewish tales of survival in 1970, Wiesel recognized that they may seem absurd—"Why survive in a world that denies us the right to survive?"—only to add immediately that we must always remember that "a tale of absurdity ultimately means a tale against absurdity." Again and again Wiesel affirms that it is possible to remain human in an inhuman society. Even with the best reasons in the world to send the entire human race to hell, one may choose not to destroy but to go on working, speaking, and rebelling in its behalf. "As a child I dreamed of bringing the Messiah," Wiesel said in 1971. "I don't believe in a world redemption anymore. I'm satisfied with small daily blessings and with helping one person, if I can."[15]

The pathos of the messianism of the unredeemed, the inverted messianism of a cursed century, is perhaps nowhere expressed more clearly than when Elie recalls his grandfather's blessing "May you see the Messiah put an end to exile and the reign of evil":

A blessing that almost came true. It was night. I found myself transported into a strange and distant kingdom. In the shadow of the flames, the exiled were gathered. They came from everywhere, they spoke every language and all told the same story. Seeing them together under the fiery sky, the child in me had thought: This is it; this is the end of time, the end of everything. Any moment the Messiah will appear out of the night, the Messiah of fear, the Messiah of death. I thought of my grandfather and I trembled for him, for myself. And for his blessing.[16]

At the beginning of *The Gates of the Forest* Wiesel retells the story of how when the Baal Shem saw misfortune threatening the Jews, he went to a certain place in the forest, lit a fire, and said a special prayer, and the misfortune was averted. In the next generation the Maggid of Mezeritch went to the place and said the prayer and in the one after that Moshe Leib of Sassov knew only the place in the forest, and still later Israel of Rizhin did not even know that but could tell the story. And that, too, was sufficient. In *Souls on Fire* Wiesel repeats this story, but now he concludes, it no longer is sufficient: "The proof is that the threat has not been averted. Perhaps we are no longer able to tell the story. Could all of us be guilty? Even the survivors? Especially the survivors." The Hasidim who knew trust, giving and receiving, sharing and taking part, warmth and generosity "could not survive in a society ruled by cold cruelty, a cruelty both impersonal and absurd."[17]

In 1972, musing on the fact that the majority of the Jewish victims, more than three million, came from Hasidic communities, Wiesel suggested that the Holocaust was a psychological contest between Nazi paganism and Hasidism, between Hitler and the Besht. The Nazi goal of depriving their victims of all human dignity and turning them into objects could not coexist with the Hasidic goal of glorifying humanity and man's role in Creation. Five years later, Wiesel declared that the Holocaust made no sense to him at all, even in messianic terms, which would be for him simply blasphemy.[18]

Of all Wiesel's novels, *The Oath* best expresses this inverted messianism. "Alternately savage and attentive, radiant and hideous, sovereign and cunning," the apocalyptic beast crushed all the inhabitants of Kolvillàg into a single one, twisting and torturing him "until in the end he had a hundred eyes and a thousand mouths, and all were spitting terror." But in *The Oath*, too, appears that modern messianism that leads Wiesel to reaffirm the human in spite of and because of the Holocaust. The old Azriel warns the boy who is contemplating suicide against opposing despair to despair and committing one more injustice, and advises him to stay and face night. "I am not telling you not to despair of man," he says to him. "I only ask you not to offer death one more victim, one more victory. . . . Every death is absurd. Useless. And ugly." Like Emil Fackenheim, Wiesel adds a new commandment: not to give Hitler any posthumous victories, not to swell the ranks of death. To triumph over death, Azriel says, you must begin by helping your fellow man.[19]

Later Azriel expresses his messianism in more somber tones: "Fool that I was, I was convinced that at the end of night there lay redemption." Man waits and clamors for the Messiah, yet it is Satan that he follows and death that fascinates him. And now he says that the thought of the boy's death does not frighten him, it makes him feel ashamed. The Christians imagine their Saviour expiring on the cross and thus situate him outside the circle of shame. He dies before the others, instead of the others.

> The Messiah, as seen by the Jews, shows greater courage; he survives all the generations, watches them disappear one after the other—and if he is late in coming, it is perhaps because he is ashamed to reveal himself.
> For us, the living—therefore the survivors—the great shame is that we claim to be brothers when we are nothing but wild, solitary beasts.[20]

"Every truth that shuts you in, that does not lead to others, is inhuman," Azriel's friend Abrahsa says to him. The self is linked to infinity only through the intermediary of another self, it is written in the *Book of Kolvillàg*. And Moshe the Madman says, What is the Messiah if not man transcending his solitude in order to make his fellow man less solitary? If man speaks to God through man, that is good; if he speaks to man through God, it is not. God needs man to manifest Himself, to affirm His power or His mercy. We are all messengers.[21]

The Messiah likes to disguise himself as a child, says Mad Moshe, and everyone's childhood is messianic. But today it has become a game to kill childhood. If the Messiah were at our gates, would man let him enter? Men imagine mistakenly that the mission of the Messiah is to save them from death. Actually "he would save them from boredom, from mediocrity, the commonplaces of routine!"[22] Moshe knew that nothing justifies the pain man causes another.

> Any messiah in whose name men are tortured can only be a false messiah. It is by diminishing evil, present and real evil, experienced evil, that one builds the city of the sun. It is by helping the person who looks at you with tears in his eyes, needing help, needing you or at least your presence, that you may attain perfection.[23]

When Moshe wants to make himself a martyr to save the rest of the community, the rebbe says to him that man sanctifies life by celebrating it, by rejecting that which makes it poorer. "Whoever renounces his life, rejects life, rejects Him who gives life."[24]

Neither Moshe's readiness to martyr himself nor anything else can save the Jewish community or Kolvillàg itself. When night finally comes to Kolvillàg, it is a night of supreme ultimate stupidity: "Caught up in the frenzy, the killers were killing each other, senselessly, with swords, hatchets and clubs. Brothers and sisters were striking one another, friends and accomplices strangling one another." This vision of horror is a glimpse of the future, Azriel realizes, the story that remains a secret thanks to "the will of my mad friend named Moshe, last prophet and first messiah of a mankind that is no more."[25]

The most sublime and impassioned expression of Wiesel's messianism of the unredeemed is neither novel, play, nor essay but his cantata *Ani Ma'amin*, which in November 1973 was performed at Carnegie Hall to music composed for it by the great French composer Darius Milhaud in honor of the hundredth anniversary of the Hebrew Union College–Jewish Institute of Religion. It is the haunting and powerful plaint of Abraham, Isaac, and Jacob, the traditional intercessors for Israel, who, in the face of the Holocaust, turn to God and then away from God to Israel to share the fate of the exterminated millions and the tormented survivors. Maimonides's statement of perfect faith that, though the Messiah tarry, he will come is not here the affirmation of those pious Jews who went to their deaths in the gas chambers singing these words as a hymn. It is an affirmation *despite* God and *despite* man, an affirmation of trust and contending voiced by the man who, more than any other living human being, has become in his own person the Job of Auschwitz:

> The Messiah.
> You will send him,
> Ani ma'amin.
> He will come,
> Ani ma'amin.
> In spite of us,
> In spite of himself,
> He will come,
> Ani ma'amin.
> Defying
> The dawn of the doomed,
> Defying
> The gloom of cemeteries,
> Defying
> The gravediggers, so numerous,
> He will come.
> Ani ma'amin.
> That is our faith, O God. . . .
> A faith fraught with danger—yes,
> And often murderous—yes,

But necessary.
Be worthy of it, O Lord.
Be worthy of us, O Savior.
Ani ma'amin, ani ma'amin.
For you, O Lord.
With you.
In you.
Against you.[26]

"Never before have there been such flames," says the Narrator. "And in every one of them it is the vision of the Redeemer that is dying." The witnesses testify, but the celestial tribunal listens in silence while an entire people enter night, plunge into the divine abyss—an abyss inhabited by God alone. "What kind of a messiah is a messiah who demands six million dead before he reveals himself?" Abraham protests to God. The Messiah will come but not for us, says the Chorus. "Auschwitz has killed Jews but not their expectations," and it calls on mankind to pray to, against, and for God.[27]

Stressing that for the Jews the theme is always waiting for the Messiah, who is also waiting, Wiesel defined the Messiah in 1973 as "prayer inside darkness, a memory of a dream, the dream of a dream . . . ageless, timeless, a name heralding Creation, the song that carries the world, the silence within tales, for dreamers a dream, for marchers a light." In that same year Wiesel characterized the human condition as living on the edge of the mountain where you see the abyss but also very far. "Because never in human history have people had more reasons to despair, and to give up on man, and God, and themselves, hope now is stronger than before." This may be the way of achieving a small measure of victory—not bringing the Messiah, as he hoped when he was a child, or saving mankind, but achieving "a daily miracle—the small wonder of giving a human being a reason to take one step forward in his life, perhaps in mine." It is not enough to live through dramatic events. We have to share them and transform them into acts of conscience. "I must believe in the coming of the Messiah," said Wiesel in the same year. Even though man suffers and ultimately death is the victor, as long as man is alive, he must claim victory with every breath and say, "*Ani Ma'amin.*" The fact that the Jews on their liberation from the extermination camps did not set Europe aflame in a revolt unprecedented in scope and brutality, but in spite of everything chose to have faith, to build instead of destroy, to affirm man instead of denying him, was an act of faith. "We Jews believe profoundly that man is not a stumbling block in God's Creation. We believe that man *is* ultimately sacred, even when he betrays the image in which he was created."[28]

God requires of man not that he live but that he choose to live—at the risk of being defeated, says the rabbi in *Zalmen, or The Madness of God*. But Wiesel's modern messianism goes even further. Thanks to Job, Wiesel tells us at the end of *Messengers of God*, "We know that it is given to man to transform divine injustice into human justice and compassion."[29] What this means in practice Wiesel illustrates in his "Letter to a Young Arab" in *A Jew Today*. At the end of the Second World War adolescents who could have set fire to cities and entered into violence and crime helped one another to rebuild. In an inhuman society, they remained human. From them, Wiesel suggests, we can learn that suffering confers neither privileges nor rights. "If you use it to increase the anguish of others, you are degrading, even betraying it." We evoked our trials only to remind others of the need to be human. "Suffering is often unjust, but it never justifies murder." Wiesel concludes with what is indeed a messianic vision:

> And yet the day will come—I hope soon—when we shall all understand that suffering can elevate man as well as diminish him. Neither end nor means, it can bring him closer to his truth and his humanity. In the final analysis, it is not given to us to bring suffering to an end—that frequently is beyond us— but we can humanize it. To turn it into dialogue rather than sword depends only on us, on you. . . . Help us not to despair

of you. Or of mankind. And then perhaps, out of our reconciliation, a great hope will be born.[30]

Communism appealed to many Jews in the beginning as a sort
of messianism without God, with all the prophetic ideas of justice,
equality, and truth. But messianism without God cannot work.
Communism degenerated into a movement of murder and deceit.
The Jew in me seeks redemption for the whole world, for mankind and in history, said Wiesel in 1977, the year after this
statement about Communism. But even in encouraging others
to fight for justice and against injustice, Wiesel said, "I do not
believe in violence, not even in violence for justice." Instead, he
pointed to the survivors and their children as an example for the
world of how to deal with evil and its memory, how to remain
generous, compassionate, and committed to humanity in a cold,
cruel, cynical society. Using the Kotzker rebbe's image of the
world as a house on fire, Wiesel stressed the necessity of remembering, writing, and teaching—"not so much to extinguish the
fire but to limit it, perhaps even to purify it, and hopefully to
save the house."[31]

In 1978 Wiesel pointed to a beautiful legend in the Midrash
that says that ever since he ascended into heaven, the prophet
Elijah has gone around the world as a chronicler, collecting tales
of Jewish suffering (much what Elie does himself!). When the
Messiah comes, Elijah will give him his book of Jewish suffering,
and it will become the New Torah. Commenting on the poi-
gnancy of this legend, Wiesel added: "Not one tear should be
wasted. Not one sigh should go astray. Nothing should be lost."
In the same year Wiesel said, "If Elijah were to come today, I
think he would speak not of the coming of the Messiah but of
the necessities of today. He would ask for small gestures." Acknowledging two years later that the character of the Messiah
has been present in all his writings, Wiesel defined the Messiah
as "the embodiment of eternity in the present, the embodiment
of eternity in the future. He is waiting for us as long as we are

waiting for him." We are responsible for one another, for the past and for the future, for seeing that our words are turned into prayers not swords, for teaching coming generations of the origins and consequences of violence, for seeking answers that grow out of compassion and the quest for justice and memory, even in a society of bigotry and indifference. All this sets Wiesel in unrelenting opposition to Communism or any experiment that sacrifices living people for the sake of an abstraction. "The end does *not* justify the means. When it comes to human life, every person is an end, not a means."[32]

In *The Testament* Reb Mendel the Taciturn tells the young Paltiel Kossover that "only man, for whose sake the Messiah is expected, is capable and worthy of making his advent possible." Any human being can seize the keys that open the gates of the celestial power and liberate the prisoner. "The Messiah, you see, is a mystery between man and himself." Later Paltiel meets a strange, almost legendary figure, David Aboulesia, who goes from one country to another in quest of the Messiah.[33] Later still, when Paltiel visits Maidanek, one of the extermination camps, he accuses God of being a gravedigger and asks God whether he at least wept for the death of his people. At this an internal dialogue ensues between Paltiel and the voice of a companion from his past:

> "You exaggerate, my friend; you go too far. God is resurrection, not gravedigger; God keeps alive the bond that links Him and you to your people; is that not enough for me!" "What do you want? Tell me what you want." "Redemption," I said. And I hastened to add, "In this place I have the right to demand and receive everything; and what I demand is redemption." "So do I," said my companion sadly. "So do I. And so does He."[34]

One of the most intriguing motifs in Wiesel's modern messianism is the relationship of father and son. This motif stands at the center of *Night*, and it recurs in one fashion or another in most of his novels. Ellen Fine links this theme to that of re-

demption through witness and through memory. Speaking of
the guilt-ridden, numbed, and nearly lifeless son who is condemned to survive after his father's death, she writes:

> The "surviving" self emerges as witness and counteracts the
> "dead" self, an important theme in Wiesel's works, linked to
> the theme of father-son. In order to continue the succession,
> the son must take his father's place. An imperative reaching far
> beyond himself compels him to complete the story his father
> was in the midst of telling the night in the ghetto before news
> of the deportation interrupted his words. The son himself must
> become a storyteller, for the story is a mode of transcendence,
> and the power of the word a protest against the nihilism of
> the Holocaust. As heir to the aborted tale, the son's task is to
> bring the destroyed Jewish communities and their inhabitants
> back to life. The need to remember transcends the particular
> to include an entire tradition that has vanished in the night.
> Before all else, the author-narrator seeks to resurrect his father
> and to prolong his voice: *the father's unfinished story becomes the
> story of the father.*[35]

The son of whom Fine writes is, of course, Elie Wiesel himself,
and the task of completing the father's story is one that Wiesel
has carried out not only in *Night* but in all the books that follow
it. The father-son relation itself is central in *The Gates of the Forest,
A Beggar in Jerusalem*, and above all in *The Testament*. The hero
has internalized the voice of his father and finds therein an ad-
monition toward a messianism that affirms the human and the
friendship and mutual support that one human being can offer
another. In *The Testament*, as we have seen, the father's voice
speaks above all of serving mankind through remaining Jewish.
For Wiesel Jewish identity is inseparable from his modern messianism. The Jew can contribute to redemption in an unredeemed
world only through making real his existence as a Jew. But to
make real his existence as a Jew he must contribute to the redemption of an unredeemed world. "Taciturn guardian of the
living book that he carries within," Ellen Fine says of Grisha in
The Testament, "the son bears witness to his father's unfinished

life through history's silent and invisible dimension—the language of memory." Thus the passive spectator becomes the active witness who tells future generations of the outer and inner reality of the murder of fathers and sons, "thereby creating a new reality that combats 'the finality of the event.' "[36]

Wiesel's latest novel, *Le Cinquième Fils (The Fifth Son)* is as centered on the father-son relationship as is *The Testament*. It, too, goes back and forth between the youth of the father and the youth of the son, only in this case the father has survived and is living with his son in Brooklyn, New York, in the 1960s and 1970s. The father, Reuven Tamiroff, so far from leaving a written testament for his son to read, is extremely reluctant to tell him anything of what happened in the days of the Holocaust. It is left to the son to find out from friends of his father's the story of the ghetto of Davarowsk and of his father's activities as president of the Jewish council that the "Angel," the Nazi executioner-actor-commandant Richard Landers, has established there. The plot of *The Fifth Son*, insofar as it has one, is the gradual revelation of the history of those past times plus the son's attempt to finish the father's story by carrying out the assassination of the Angel that his father and his friend Simha imagined they had accomplished.

Simha the Gloomy passes his free nights in calculating the time that separates us from the messianic deliverance. But the Hasidic rabbi whom they all visit urges them not to saintliness or perfection but to fervor, and he quotes Rabbi Israel of Rizhin: "When two persons love each other, God becomes their associate." Reuven's son is the son of a survivor. His patrimony includes neither the one way to redemption nor the other. "The children of the survivors are almost as traumatized as the survivors themselves," he comments. "I suffer from an event that I have not even lived." In the College of the City of New York, Wiesel found that many of his students were children of survivors and became acutely aware of their plight. It is as if "survivor guilt" were hereditary, and the child of the survivor finds as little justification for his or her existence as the survivors themselves.[37]

On his way to confront the Angel, who is now head of a great industrial organization in Germany, Reuven's son reflects on the paradox of his obsession with Richard Landers and with the impossible task of transforming his natural nonviolence and inability to hate into the will to hate and the will to murder:

> I want to hate him, I hate him for having killed and for having escaped death. With all my being, I demand of my hate that it grow from day to day, from memory to memory, from page to page. It is because I cannot hate any person that I am intent on hating him. It is because I am against violence that I wish his defeat, his agony. It is because I cannot injure any person that I wish to imagine him dead, to know him dead in order to perfect the work of my father, in order to savor the taste of vengeance.[38]

But after Reuven's son has traveled all the way to Germany and meets the Angel face to face, he makes no attempt to kill him or even to threaten to expose him. In a powerful confrontation in which he transcends himself and proves himself to be indeed the completor of his father's life and his father's story, he unmasks him, indicts him, and leaves him with the knowledge that he is known for what he is.

> *The Angel* no longer inspired in me either hatred or thirst for vengeance: I have disturbed his existence, refreshed his memory, spoiled his future joys, that suffices for me. He will no longer be able to act or live or laugh as if the ghetto of Davarowsk had not served him as scene and as magnifying glass.[39]

The fact that he has not killed Richard Landers should not cause shame or embarrassment to his father. "Justice can only be human. . . . It is in life that just words transform themselves into acts of justice; never in death." "You will feel yourself everywhere as an intrusion purchased by death," he says to the Angel. "People will think of you with repugnance; they will curse you as they curse the plague and war; they will curse you in cursing death."[40]

Looking back from 1983 on what he had written twenty and ten years before, Reuven's son compares himself to Simha, who sees shadows arise on the horizon. Thinking of George Orwell's *Nineteen Eighty-four* and of the year 2000, he perceives "an immense shadow, resembling a mushroom, monstrously large and high, which links heaven to earth in order to condemn and destroy it." This prevision of the nuclear holocaust, which more and more concerns Elie Wiesel, as it must us all, leads to a somber reflection on Simha's kabbalistic messianism, which anticipated that the chastisement would be followed by deliverance. The Hasidic master foresaw more correctly when he said that the Messiah risks arriving too late: he will come when there will be no one left to save. "So much the worse; I shall await all the same." He had waited to meet his brother Ariel, the angelic six-year-old whom Landers had killed when his parents were deported. He had tried to live the lives of his parents and brother by taking them on and saying "I" in their place. In turns he took himself for the one and then for the other. All the differences, quarrels, and conflicts have only issued in renewed ties. Now at thirty-four his love for his father is whole, as if his father had been his son, as if he had been his father's son Ariel, whom he lost there, far away.

> A sad balance: I have moved heaven and earth, I have risked downfall and madness in interrogating the souvenirs of the living and the dreams of the dead in order to live the life of beings, near and far, who continue to haunt me: but when, yes, when, shall I finally begin to live my own life?[41]

A sad balance, indeed! And so perhaps is Wiesel's modern messianism, his messianism of the unredeemed. Not so sad that we can go along with Michael Berenbaum, whose theological reflections on the works of Elie Wiesel lead him to conclude that what Wiesel really offers us, beneath all the religious trappings, is "A Vision of the Void." He is not wrong in noting the progressive humanization of Wiesel's messianism or the fact that in

Wiesel's later writings the Messiah loses some of his grandeur in favor of moments of sanctification. Nor is he wrong in stressing Wiesel's own statements that "in a world of absurdity, we must invent reason, we must create beauty out of nothingness . . . we have to fight murder and absurdity and give meaning to the battle, if not to our hope."[42] This 1967 statement reads, out of context, like Sartre's call to invent values in the face of the absence of any objective meaning or the early Camus's call to make a subjective affirmation of life despite the absurd. In the context of Wiesel's work as a whole and, in particular, in the context of Wiesel's modern messianism that we have set forth in this chapter, Berenbaum's conclusion cannot hold: "Perhaps, for Wiesel, to be a Jew after Auschwitz is to hope for a Messiah and to work for a Messiah while knowing full well that the hope is for naught."[43]

Robert McAfee Brown has offered us a more just appraisal of Wiesel's modern messianism in his *Elie Wiesel: Messenger to All Humanity*. As we have done in this chapter, Brown notes the pervasive emphasis in Wiesel's novels of what Martin Buber calls "dialogue," or the "I-Thou" relationship:

> One thing that happens in the progression of the writings is that individuals, cut off from each other and unable to make the most elemental acts of trust in other human beings, gradually become empowered to leave the shell of self-imposed isolation, participate in the destiny of others, realize how risky it is, and nevertheless embrace the risk. . . . Wiesel tells us that personhood is never achieved in isolation; it is always a matter of relationship. For there to be an "I" there must also be an "Other," a "Thou."[44]

Wiesel's modern messianism is not limited to human relationships, as Berenbaum would hold. It is also, as Brown points out, a continuous call to overcome despair with hope. "To despair now would be a blasphemy—a profanation," Wiesel concludes in his essay "Against Despair," in *A Jew Today*. "We must show our children that in spite of everything, we keep our faith—in ourselves and even in mankind, though mankind may not be worthy of such faith."[45]

Everybody's suffering involves me and, if I do not speak up, indicts me, said Wiesel in 1978, with specific reference to the Palestinian Arab and the suffering in Cambodia and Vietnam. He is responsible for their suffering but not for what they do with their suffering, for suffering confers no privileges. In using his suffering to murder Jews, the PLO is betraying the Palestinian Arab. In a strong plea for the "boat people" in the following year, Wiesel insisted that the victims of injustice must be cared for—these homeless, helpless, voiceless, anonymous uprooted men and women with their emaciated, forlorn children who can barely walk or even breathe, their enormous eyes mute with terror and devoured by hunger. In the same year, as chairman of the President's Commission on the Holocaust, and on behalf of the commission, Wiesel implored all countries to open their borders and extend rights of refuge and asylum to the boat people so that the world might not once again be divided into perpetrators, victims, and bystanders. A month later Wiesel told of how he served as a member of the American delegation to the Conference on the Boat People in Geneva. In his report it became clear that Vice President Mondale, the chairman of the American delegation, had followed Wiesel's lead. Mondale spoke of the tragedy of the boat people in the light of the Holocaust and compared their situation to that of the refugees discussed at the Evian Conference in 1938. Then tens of thousands of Jewish people might have been saved but were not.[46]

What such hope against despair means in our contemporary world Wiesel has shown in the way in which he points to the danger of the nuclear holocaust that may destroy mankind, yet does not despair in face of it. Hope in this case means memory. "Let us remember for their sakes, and ours: memory may perhaps be our only answer, our only hope to save the world from the ultimate punishment, a nuclear holocaust," Brown quotes Wiesel from his speech at the Day of Remembrance ceremony in the rotunda of the United States Capitol on April 24, 1979. Brown also points to how Wiesel fought to recover the past and redeem the present when in February 1980 (in company with Bayard

Rustin, Marc Tannenbaum, Liv Ullmann, and members of the French parliament), he went to the Thai border of Cambodia, seeking to deliver twenty truckloads of food and medical supplies to starving Cambodians. Denied access, Wiesel spoke by loud-speaker across the border: "One thing that is worse for the victim than hunger, fear, torture, even humiliation, is the feeling of abandonment, the feeling that nobody cares, the feeling that you don't count." "I came here," Wiesel said over the loudspeaker, "because nobody came when I was there." It was the thirty-sixth anniversary of his father's death![47]

When Wiesel returned from Thailand he wrote for *The New York Times* a remarkable essay entitled "The Death of a People?", an essay he reprinted in *Paroles d'étranger* (*Words of a Stranger*). "Everything in me rises up in protest against the idea that, today, thirty-six years after the cruelest war in history, a people with age-old traditions and memories can be swallowed up in death and oblivion." At the same time, Wiesel remembers that he had thought the same thing at the time of "night" and that everything is possible for his generation. "That is why," Wiesel concludes, "I have come to the Thailandese frontier. To see, to listen, and to bear witness."[48]

He is aware, of course, of the differences. Here the injustice is not racist. Here the victims and the executioners are brothers: the Cambodian people have suffered more from their own sons gone mad than from American or Vietnamese bombers. Nor is it proper to employ the terms "Auschwitz" or "holocaust" here. Every tragedy deserves its own vocabulary. Nonetheless, having lived through one nocturnal and tenebrous experience, and hav-ing written what he had attempted to write for three decades, it was impossible for him not to confront this massive suffering that defies us and at times accuses us. He could not know the repercussions of his actions, but he did not know that, before what is happening on both sides of the frontier between Cam-bodia and Thailand, a man like him with a memory such as his ought to be present. What he suggests is not an analogy with

Auschwitz but rather Auschwitz as a benchmark, a reference
point, an anguishing warning.

> I do not regret having come. I do not regret having spent
> fifty hours on airplanes—circling the globe—to fail here, at the
> frontier which remains, like Kafka's Castle, inaccessible. I do
> not regret having made this voyage for nothing. To my activist
> friends I would say: We have not succeeded in changing society,
> let us try at least to act in such a way that it does not change
> us.[49]

In 1980 Wiesel said that he would never have imagined that
he should one day feel compelled to vent his rage against the
present as he had against the past. The images of starving men
and women and shriveled children that reached him from Uganda
led him to cry out that even if we cannot evade our own suffering
we can give it meaning through combating the suffering of others. "If I struggle for today's victims, it is because yesterday's
were forgotten, abandoned, handed over to the enemy without
protest." While talking with General Petrenko, whose Red Army
troops had liberated Auschwitz, Wiesel suddenly had the idea of
bringing together liberators from *all* the Allied forces—to listen
to them, thank them, and solicit their help in silencing the voices
of morally deranged Nazis and Nazi lovers who are disputing
the testimony that the Holocaust ever took place. This is exactly
what Wiesel called for in his welcoming address to the International Liberators Conference, which, following his initiative,
the United States Department of State convened in Washington
on October 26, 1981.[50]

Another conference that Wiesel played a key role in organizing
was the World Gathering of Jewish Holocaust Survivors in Jerusalem. In an interview with Samuel Dresner, Wiesel said of
that gathering that every day was special, every minute a high
point, every meeting profound. What struck him as particularly
eerie was speaking at the Wall to 15,000 people, 10,000 of them
survivors, and meeting with Antek Zuckerman, a member of the
High Command of the Warsaw Ghetto, just before his death. In

1983 Wiesel protested against the imprisonment and execution of members of the Bahai religious group in Iran, where once again religious hatred was taking a terrible toll. "We all vowed after the Nazi outrages—Never Again! Now is the time to act on that vow."[51]

In 1984 Wiesel gave the keynote address at the First International Conference of Children of Holocaust Survivors in New York. Much in that address was a beautiful recapitulation of Wiesel's messianism of the unredeemed. As the survivors have shown what they can do with their suffering, so their children have shown what they can do with their observation of suffering.

> In deciding to get married, to have children, to build on ruins, your parents sought to teach history a lesson: that we are not to give up on life, not to give in to despair. And deep down you have felt the need to justify your parents' absurd and persistent faith in life, in faith itself, in history, in society, in humankind.

We have learned in our adult lives that human experiences, whatever their nature, must be shared, that suffering is a vehicle, not a prison, invoked not to create more suffering, but to limit, curtail, and eliminate it. An entire generation of Jews has risen from the ashes determined to build on and with those ashes. The *Akedah*, the temptation of Abraham to sacrifice Isaac, was not consummated. "The testimony of our life and death will not vanish."[52]

Wiesel's poignant story "Etruscan Eternity" ends with an affirmative note when the Etruscan scholar tells his lover, after total silence on the subject, that in the universe of cold horror and total and abject humiliation that he knew in the extermination camps, human solidarity, compassion, goodness, and self-abnegation remained possible. A similar note recurs in Wiesel's essay "Celebration of Friendship." In *The Gates of the Forest*, Wiesel himself recollects, Gavriel defines a friend as one who for the first time makes you conscious of your solitude and his and enables you to emerge from it as you in turn enable him. The Messiah that Wiesel had expected as a boy did not arrive. In his place came the enemy of the Messiah: the killer, the assassin, the exterminator of peoples. Those in the extermination camps who lived for themselves, to nourish themselves alone, ended by giving in to the law of death, whereas those who lived for a parent, a brother, a friend succeeded in obeying the law of life. Elie lived for and through his father. They needed each other to live one day more, one hour more. "I see him again and in the depths of my being I experience a nameless laceration: nothing has replaced that friendship." Now more than ever friendship is necessary, Wiesel concludes. A Hasid crushed by his memories, broken by his powerlessness to affirm life, while at the same time weeping for those who are dead, cannot open himself to joy and ecstasy alone. With friends the Hasid who has survived the long *nuit concentrationnaire* can remain faithful, love, laugh, sing, resist, communicate to others the salt of his life and his secret, too. "The unhappy Hasid is obliged to choose happiness in order not to influence his friends, to prevent them from following him into the abyss."[53]

In a short chronicle addressed to his Christian friends, Wiesel sets forth the possibilities and limits of the confirmation of otherness in the post-Holocaust world. Having overcome the suspicions and inhibitions of his childhood, he feels himself from now on capable of talking to Christians about his Jewish life, and he knows that certain of them are capable of understanding. "Between a Jew and a Christian, if they are authentic and open, dialogue remains possible. And even inevitable." If we have learned that history is one and indivisible after the event of Night, then we know that what happens to one of us as Jew also affects the other as Christian. "We are responsible for one another, and that on the scale of humanity." Rather than divide, separate, and oppose us to one another, Auschwitz should bring us closer. "That is our sole possibility of salvation, or at least of survival."

In another chronicle entitled "A Cry for the Victims of Today and Tomorrow" Wiesel looks at the fate of victims in Argentina, the Congo, Cambodia, Uganda, and the Gulag Archipelago (Solzhenitsyn's name for the slave camps of the Soviet Union). "It is impossible to evade our own suffering," Wiesel concludes, "but it behooves us to give it a meaning through combating the suffering of others."

> If we fight for today's victims, it is because yesterday's were forgotten, abandoned, delivered to the enemy. It is in thinking of the past that we desire to save our common future.
> The future is in danger. My traumatized generation has realized that. Too much hate has accumulated in too many places. Too many fingers risk pushing the nuclear button. Do not tell me that it is impossible, unthinkable. Today more than yesterday, because of yesterday, the impossible becomes possible.
> Have we survived just to see our witness fall into the dust and the cinders?[54]

In a final chronicle, "The Nuclear Peril," Wiesel points out that today we know with certainty that had the great free powers acted more quickly and with greater firmness, the Hitlerian regime would have collapsed after its first aggression and history would have been spared Auschwitz and Treblinka. Today we know that evil lies in indifference, that indifference to evil allows it to grow, expand, take root. In periods of crisis, neutrality only aids the aggressor, never his victim. "If the nuclear war breaks out one day, it will be because of our apathy." The atomic arsenal doubles from day to day, the nuclear proliferation extends over several continents, but we act as if we were still secure. To evoke Auschwitz is to combat future Hiroshimas. The next holocaust cannot help but be nuclear, worldwide. Unilateral disarmament only aids the dictators, but universal disarmament remains a possibility if the youth and the people of the two sides (the Communist and ours) cry out their disgust with atomic death, if they denounce together, and for the same reasons, the nuclear peril, if they oppose together, and for the same mortal and human motives, the destruction of the earth. This is improbable, Wiesel admits, but not impossible. "The young dissidents, the political prisoners, the militant humanists who defy the police in the totalitarian countries are there to witness that, after the death of Stalin, the communist empire is no longer the same: give them our confidence; they deserve it."[55]

In his remarkable essay "The Stranger in the Bible," Wiesel goes much further in setting down the possibility and limits of "the confirmation of otherness" (to use the title of one of my books). Crueler than the barbarians of antiquity, the Nazis tried to dehumanize their victims before killing them: they reduced the stranger to an object. But it is possible and even necessary for human beings to relate to the stranger as a Thou and not an It. Conscious of his limits and, at the same time, of his desire to transcend them, the human being sees in the stranger a calling in question not only of his own being but of the relations between beings. Faced with the unknown, he realizes that he is a stranger to someone else. This means that there exists in the human being a zone that remains unknown. In confronting the stranger, he hopes, thanks to the stranger, to know himself better. "For the human being cannot attain truth—or God—without passing through the other, just as God cannot accomplish his work except through the medium of the human being."

In *I and Thou* Martin Buber says that the moments of the Thou teach us to meet the other and to hold our ground when we meet her. Wiesel, in similar fashion, insists that the interaction with the stranger should exclude all elements of submission or defeat. "To submit myself to the stranger in order to approach him leads inevitably to dissolution of being." This is a danger which we should not underestimate because there exists in human beings a desire that pushes them to break with their surroundings, their community, their past, and lose themselves in the mass, to solve the problem of existence and identify by effacing it, by becoming and living the life of an other. In order to forget suffering, shame, sin, some persons wish to disappear without a trace. Seeing themselves with the eyes of the stranger and feeling their inferiority to the stranger, they wish to founder in unconsciousness.

> We should love the stranger as long as he fulfills his role as stranger, i.e. as long as he overturns our certainties and forces us to reevaluate our positions, as long as he represents the question. But we must oppose and combat him as soon as he imposes himself on us as the possessor of truth, as the sole possessor of the unique truth. Not to resist him then is to become his caricature.[56]

Friendship transformed into hatred is preferable to indifference, forgetfulness. I look at a human being and know that he belongs to the same universe, that we share the same secrets, are linked by the same memories, dreams, plans. I am a stranger to him, too. I recognize the stranger in and through him. It is possible that the stranger in him is me. But it is much more serious if I discover the stranger in myself, someone who speaks, lives, and dies in my place, incites in me a disgust in myself, and wishes that I cease to be altogether. We must refuse that comportment in all circumstances and situations. That you should love the stranger means that you should act so that the stranger at your side loves himself. During the centuries of exile and persecution, and above all during the Nazi reign, the enemy has done everything to inculcate in us the fear and shame of ourselves: he has deprived us of our goods, our homes, our social attachments, our names, and reduced us to the state of an object or a number. He wanted the Jew to regard himself with contempt and disgust, to become his own enemy, his own executioner. He wanted the stranger in us, the enemy in us, to eliminate us from history. We shall never act as he did.

To live without contact with a stranger would mean to draw an impoverished image from life; to live without having, in face of the stranger, the constant duty to interrogate ourselves on the meaning and goal of existence or of coexistence, would be to diminish ourselves. Certainly, we cannot choose between total uprooting and ultimately taking root: we oscillate between the two. We are finally strangers on the earth, but it is given us to try not to be, to remain faithful to what we are, living our experience while sharing it, assuming our existence while communicating it to our neighbor, who proclaims his with equal fervor and faith. One day we shall greet in our midst a being who has not yet come, but who will come because we await him. "And one day he will not appear as a stranger because he will be one no longer; for the Messiah in each of us will have given Abraham's dream its ultimate fulfillment."[57]

When, at the time he received the Congressional Medal of Honor, Elie Wiesel told President Reagan that Bitburg was no place for him, Wiesel stood before the world as the Job of Auschwitz. He embodied the Job of Auschwitz too, as we have seen, when he refused to accompany Reagan to Bitburg. But the Bitburg affair led to a visit to Germany in which Wiesel deepened the meaning of the messianism of the unredeemed. Joining an informal committee of American Jews and Germans established by Chancellor Helmut Kohl, Wiesel met with young German students in West Berlin and found the depth of their own painful search for an understanding of the German Nazi past extremely moving. Wiesel urged reconciliation between young Germans and Jews on the basis of unflinching recognition of the Nazi crimes.

The symbolic highpoint of Wiesel's messianism of the unredeemed was the award to him of the Nobel Peace Prize on December 10, 1986, in Oslo, Norway. When the award was announced on October 14, Egil Aarvik, chairman of the Norwegian Nobel Committee and a former president of the Norwegian Parliament, made a statement that clearly recognized how the concern that started with the Holocaust reached out from there to all mankind:

> Elie Wiesel has emerged as one of the most important spiritual leaders and guides in an age when violence, repression and racism continue to characterize the world. Wiesel is a messenger to mankind. His message is one of peace, atonement

and human dignity. His belief that the forces fighting evil in
the world can be victorious is a hard-won belief. His message
is based on his own personal experience of total humiliation
and of the utter contempt for humanity shown in Hitler's death
camps. The message is in the form of a testimony, repeated
and deepened through the works of a great author. Wiesel's
commitment, which originated in the sufferings of the Jewish
people, has been widened to embrace all oppressed peoples and
races.[58]

Wiesel, who had been in second or third place for this prize
several times in the past, was supported in his candidacy by,
among others, American lawmakers, the West German government, and Lech Walesa, the Polish union leader who won the
award in 1983.

The first thing Wiesel did on learning that he had been named
the Nobel Peace laureate for 1986 was to make a public appeal
to the Soviet leader, Mikhail S. Gorbachev, to permit the emi-
gration of "his hero," the well-known physicist and dissident
Andrei D. Sakharov, who is not Jewish, and five Jews—Vladimir
Slepak, Iosif Begun, Ida Nudel, Viktor Brailovsky, and Zakhar
Zonshein. When I reached Elie by phone the following week, I
asked him if he had seen Gorbachev. "No, that will be in two
weeks," he answered. "I imagine your life has been totally
changed," I remarked. "No, it has not changed," Elie replied,
confirming the statement he made to a questioner: "If the war
did not change me, do you think anything else will change me?"[59]
It is precisely Elie Wiesel, the Job of Auschwitz, who has pointed
the way to the messianism of the unredeemed!

CONCLUSION

"You Are My Witnesses"

Thirty years ago, after the publication of Abraham Heschel's philosophy of religion *Man Is Not Alone*, I received a call from the president of the American Jewish Congress asking me to write an article for *Congress Weekly* defending Heschel from a growing number of attacks from the right and from the left. Trude Weiss-Rosmarin, Orthodox editor of the *Jewish Spectator*, had criticized Heschel for his alleged irrationality. "Hermann Cohen has proved that Judaism is a religion of reason," she wrote, referring the reader to her own translation of Cohen's posthumous book, *Religion der Vernunft aus Quellen des Judentums*. At the other end of the spectrum, the eminent Reform rabbi Levi Olan contemptuously dismissed *Man Is Not Alone* as "another back-to-God book." Olan himself put forward "logic and the laboratory" as the self-evident touchstone of reality for the contemporary religious Jew. The more recent criticisms of Heschel— by Eugene Borowitz, Jacob Petuchowski, and Arthur Cohen— have been on a more sophisticated level. Yet they all seem to me to fall far short of understanding Heschel from within in the way such Jewish thinkers as Samuel H. Dresner, Fritz Rothschild, Edward Kaplan, and Harold Kassimow, such Protestant thinkers as Franklin Sherman and Edmond LaB. Cherbonnier and, most

259

impressively of all, the Catholic thinker John C. Merkle have done.

In his book *The Natural and the Supernatural Jew*, Arthur A. Cohen subsumes Heschel under the double category of "rhetoric" and "prophecy," while reserving philosophy and theology for his own. There can be no objection to Cohen's pointing out that Heschel has revived the ancient art of rhetoric for the sake of persuading in an age when argument is no longer taken seriously or in good faith. But nothing justifies his deducing from Heschel's concern with rhetoric that he is unconcerned with philosophy or theology. He is concerned with them in precisely that existential, time-bound and history-responding sense that Cohen has pointed to as desirable for Jewish theology. Heschel never says philosophy is a "dead end," but only what Cohen himself has said, that it articulates the assumptions of faith. In my own writings on Heschel I have pointed to problems and inconsistencies that I have found in his philosophy, but this does make him any the less one of the profound and original religious philosophers of our time. It is not true, as Cohen says, that Heschel's distinctions "possess rhetorical power but are not intellectually resilient." They are both to a remarkable degree and fall down only when, as does indeed happen, Heschel falls into the trap of sharpening a contrast without sufficient consideration of whether he really means the logical opposite of the position he is attacking. Cohen quotes with approval Jacob Petuchowski's statement that Heschel "shuns conceptual thought altogether"—an assertion so palpably false as to illuminate the antagonism between philosophies which is the central issue here. As Paul Tillich has remarked, the definition of philosophy is itself a philosophical question.

What is good in Cohen's treatment of Heschel is his insistence that disbelief is not dishonesty but is something real and tragic. But his conclusion that in Heschel "the faithless are confirmed in disbelief and the faithful become arrogant" does not follow. It is true that Heschel belabors the arrogance of the naturalists in a way that is likely to antagonize them, but it is not true that his thought reaches only those already faithful. It has far more power to awaken stirrings and insights in the unaware than any amount of medievally cogent theology. Heschel's "depth theology" and "situational thinking" speak more to the person of our age than the narrower conceptions of traditional philosophy, however much one may desire for greater consistency in Heschel's thought. Neither the philosopher nor the theologian in our age is likely to "begin the pilgrimage of prophecy," as Cohen thinks. It is, in fact, a naïve misreading of our age to equate the person whom Heschel does not move with the person who *will* be moved by the philosophy permeated by wonder which Cohen, quite rightly, recommends.[1] A person who is open to a philosophy permeated by wonder will be open to much that Heschel has to say, while the dominant philosophies of our age, at least in England and America, are founded upon a systematic shutting out of wonder in favor of the "certainties" of logical empiricism and linguistic analysis.

Eugene Borowitz offers an appreciative understanding of Heschel's power of imagery and his religious thinking in *A New Jewish Theology in the Making*. Heschel's religious epistemology of doing the commandment is "very impressive," says Borowitz, who offers us insight into what Heschel means by his "leap of action."

> In the fullness of a decision confirmed as it can be only in a deed, man more than becomes himself. He meets God. He knows himself to be responding not merely to his own desires but to God's. The final stage of human religiosity is learning to make God's needs man's own, to want to the point of continually doing what God wants.[2]

Yet Borowitz feels that Heschel falls short in understanding and meeting points of view of those less religiously committed than he.

> Heschel regularly fails to see the validity of the questions that come from the other side, and he cannot appreciate even

> the possibility of alternative positions to his own. Again and again he begins with the discussion of a modern problem, shows its assumptions or its implications, and just as one expects that he will respond to these directly, he says, instead, that from the standpoint of faith that is not the real question at all. . . . No one likes to have his questions ultimately dismissed as meaningless if not downright wrong, particularly when they are not individual whim but a product of the major intellects of the day. That unease increases to downright irritation when dismissal of the questions gives way to the rejection of alternate positions to the author's as simply "arrogant," "absurd," "insane," "incredible." They are not even considered, only anathematized.[3]

We can see here a decided mismeeting between Heschel's philosophy of wonder and Borowitz's more rational and liberal stance. In my own relationship to Heschel's thought I have tried to witness for what speaks to my condition and that of the modern person even while saying, in a manner not unlike Borowitz, that Heschel fails to understand *from within* the plight of those like myself who were born outside the Jewish law (Halakhah) and do not know the order of Jewish doing from within. On the other hand, I cannot say, as Borowitz does, that "Heschel often makes no contact" or that he is unsympathetic to those whose belief is less than his own. That is perhaps why I have marked "unfair" in the margin of Borowitz's book by this passage:

> He regularly offends men who do not have as firm a belief in God's revelation to the Jewish people as he has. And when they want to be believing Jews, when they are searching for some greater Jewish faith than that which they now have, to thrust them back so rudely with the left hand without seeking a way to draw them more closely to himself with the right seems to betray a faulty sympathy for their earnest if limited belief.[4]

In almost thirty years I never encountered in Heschel any "faulty sympathy" for what must have been, to Heschel, *my* "earnest if limited belief." I shall never forget an afternoon in his office at the Jewish Theological Seminary in 1956 when Heschel approached me with a passion I had never before witnessed in him, urging me to begin an observant way of life. This took place in connection with the possibility of his supporting me for a position in the Department of Religion at Columbia University, and I, being something of a moral prig, registered shock in my heart at what seemed to me a less than intrinsic reason for adopting the "way of deeds." Only later did I adequately glimpse what was in Heschel's heart: his deep and passionate longing that I should be able to follow him into Judaism as he understood and practiced it—not all at once and entirely, but a little at a time. My refusal to accede to his passionate plea in no way estranged him or made him any less concerned about my spiritual and intellectual progress in the years to come!

More important for our purposes than either Cohen or Borowitz, and also far more inclusive and up to date, is John C. Merkle's book *The Genesis of Faith: The Depth Theology of Abraham Joshua Heschel*. Because of the thoroughness of Merkle's scholarship, the precision and depth of his critical questions, and the scope of what he has covered, *The Genesis of Faith* is likely to be recognized for decades to come as the definitive study of Heschel's theology. The only qualification I must express here is that Merkle's book is so precise that one feels Heschel is in danger of being swallowed up in a scholasticism of which Heschel himself would hardly have approved. Occasionally Merkle corrects Heschel in the name of the "Heschelian." Yet he never quite faces up to Heschel's inconsistency and his lack of system. Still, it must be said that Merkle has tried to distinguish and systematize Heschel's treatment of the sources and antecedents of faith and has succeeded beyond Heschel himself.

Merkle gives us an excellent presentation of the presence of the transcendent in Heschel and an excellent critique of Heschel's assertion that the oneness of God is immediately given with the awareness of the ineffable. To repair this problem, Merkle adds to Heschel "a sense of the ultimate," but this is not Heschel and it is not in itself convincing. Neither does it seem to me to answer my criticisms of Heschel that Merkle himself cites. More impressive is his recognition that for Heschel God is both "a dimensional Person, a Person in whom we dwell" and a Person whom we meet. I was thinking of both Buber and Heschel when I characterized mysticism in my book *To Deny Our Nothingness*:

> It is customary, and not inaccurate, to say that the mystic realizes the paradox of God's being both immanent and transcendent. We may put this more concretely by saying that mysticism is immediacy and presentness *plus* presence—a strong sense of the immanence of God not as doctrine but as immersion in a directly experienced reality of divine presence. Mysticism includes not only person-to-person contact with God but also the presence of the spirit of God . . . the testimony of Saint Paul that in God "we live and move and have our being." To the mystic, our existence is not only God's address and our answering response, but also discovering ourselves in the presence of God, knowing ourselves as known by him.[5]

I was thinking of *both* Buber and Heschel, as I said, Buber as the dialogue with God, Heschel as knowing ourselves as known by God. Merkle's contribution is pointing out that Heschel includes both his own emphasis and that with which we are more familiar from Buber—the meeting with God in address and response.

> God is all-embracing, but not all-inclusive. Those who dwell within the Spirit of God are not a part of God but are surrounded by God's glory. If . . . we were all parts of God's being, perhaps it would make sense to speak of our "dwelling within" God, but it would make no sense to speak of "encountering" God. And if God were a person among persons it would perhaps make sense to speak of "encountering" God, but it would make no sense to speak of "dwelling within" God. But since God is a transcendent, divine Person, it makes sense to speak of encountering the God in whom we dwell.[6]

Merkle takes both Harold Kassimow and myself to task for suggesting that deed before devotion implies action without integrity. Only those who think the action may be valuable or who seek to attain faith through action will take Heschel's leap, says Merkle. This raises in my mind the question of whether the "value" one finds in keeping the law prior to belief that the law is of God is an instrumental one. Merkle is right in saying that Heschel "is calling upon those who long for faith to do things faithful in order to give faith a chance to flower." But that leaves us with the question of what it means "to do things faithful." Merkle himself, for example, as a Catholic, could hardly accept the Jewish law as "things faithful." Nor can we accept Merkle's statement that "performing mitsvot in the hope of attaining faith is like studying the Bible in the hope of finding God. Neither need lacks integrity." This is very similar to Franz Rosenzweig's attempt in "The Builders" to convince Martin Buber that one could be open to the law in the same way that one is open to the teachings. This is not to deny Merkle's further suggestion that "when Heschel speaks of taking a leap of action to attain faith he perhaps means that the leap itself is the beginning of faith which may lead to a life of faith" or Heschel's own statement, quoted by Merkle, that "the way *to* faith is the way *of* faith." Both make sense in terms of Heschel's claim that only in the doing can we know the holy dimension. Yet neither touch on what is the major issue for Buber and for me: that this doing is a command to me, to us by God. Still, however strange it may seem to us for a Catholic to be explaining to a believing Jew why the latter should accept the Halakhah as divine, we cannot deny that Merkle has quite accurately reflected and understood Heschel's own position.

Actions, whereby we realize that "*the wonder of doing* is no less amazing than the marvel of being," (*Search*, p. 28) may prompt us to discover "*the divinity of deeds*" (Ibid., p. 288). In other words, in doing sacred deeds we may begin to realize that there is more in our doing than ourselves, that in our doing there is something—nay, someone—divine. And this realization may provoke the dawn of faith. . . . Heschel himself says that "through the ecstasy of deeds"—halachic deeds—we learn "to be certain of the hereness of God" (*Search*, p. 283) and that, speaking personally, "the foremost sources of my own religious insight lie in reverence for halacha" (*Freedom*, p. 219).[7]

If Elie Wiesel has not been subjected to the same criticism as Abraham Heschel, it is because the intellectual climate in which Wiesel wrote was a more receptive one, partly due to Heschel's own influence, because Wiesel is primarily a novelist and only by implication a philosopher and theologian, and also, I suspect, because Wiesel is so much a symbol of the Holocaust and of the growing unification and identity of the Jewish people after the Holocaust that few would have the courage to attack him even if they were so inclined.

The two best studies of Wiesel to date, in my opinion, are Ellen Fine's *Legacy of Night: The Literary Universe of Elie Wiesel* and Robert McAfee Brown's *Elie Wiesel: Messenger to All Humanity*. There are many references to both of these books, as we have seen, in the Wiesel section of *You Are My Witnesses*. Here, however, we shall turn to other studies for the sake of the different perspective they throw on Wiesel's achievement. In his paper "A Narrative Jewish Theology," Steven D. Kepnes of Southern Methodist University sets Wiesel within the context of what he holds to be true Jewish theology, namely that Jewish Haggada which unfolds the concealment and disclosure of God in the Bible by telling tales about those tales. "Story is more than a reflection," Kepnes quotes Martin Buber from the introduction to *Tales of the Hasidim: The Early Masters*; "the holy essence it testifies to lives on in it. The miracle that is told acquires new force; power that was active is propagated in the living word and continues to be active—even after generations." This is because, as Buber also says, the retelling of an event is an event itself. A story is an evocation, a re-creation of an original religious experience. These "narrative interpretations of narrative" offer what Emil Fackenheim has called "the profoundest and most authentic theology ever produced in Judaism." They mediate the tradition of the past to the present, responding to the challenge of the contemporary Jewish situation and teaching the principles of the tradition to contemporary Jews.

From this standpoint Martin Buber is to be understood neither as religious existentialist nor as philosopher of religion but as narrative theologian: "Buber retold personal, biblical, and hasidic tales for theological purposes. He told tales to open a dialogue between God and humanity, between God and the contemporary situation and between the Jew and his tradition." That contemporary situation in our day is above all the confrontation with the Holocaust. "Only an Haggadic theology can express the deep contradictions and the radical challenge caused by the mysterious and terrible absence of God at Auschwitz." The primary example of that Haggadic Holocaust theology that Fackenheim terms "mad Midrash," Kepnes continues, is Elie Wiesel's work.

> Wiesel weaves into his novels midrashic and biblical references to the exile, the suffering servant, and Job, to seek a response from the tradition to the situation. Wiesel's mad-midrash may challenge and even distort traditional aggadot, but in the challenge and radical reinterpretation, the tradition is often further developed. An aggadic response to the Holocaust, a response that tells the tales of survivors and executioners, a response that seeks wisdom from the past by retelling and interpreting traditional tales, is an honest response that both serves as a warning—"Never again, never another holocaust"—and as a statement of courageous faith—"Ani-Maamin," I believe.[8]

We have already noted—and rejected—Michael Berenbaum's central position in his book *The Vision of the Void: Theological Reflections on the Works of Elie Wiesel*. Nonetheless, Berenbaum offers us an interesting and challenging perspective on Wiesel—a set of variations, as it were, on Wiesel's own statement that at Auschwitz the Covenant was broken. Berenbaum makes an intriguing comparison and contrast between Wiesel and Rabbi Nachman of Bratzlav, to whom Wiesel is much indebted:

Both are tortured souls yearning for renewed innocence and both approach the world with a great deal of skepticism. Both share a fascination with the Messiah and the ability of man to force God's hand. However, Rabbi Nachman's questions point toward their resolution in the leap of faith, while Wiesel's questions remain forever questions.[9]

Auschwitz forced Wiesel to take history with utmost seriousness, says Berenbaum, and precluded his accepting messianism as an alternative to facing the Holocaust or accepting the Messiah, who refused to appear at the time when he was so crucially needed. As a result, the image of God has been replaced for Wiesel by the human image, "the image of a people who have routed defeat and survived, in community, in celebration, and in relationship with a past that is being transmitted. The void has been bridged, in solidarity, in hope, in despair, in pain, and in violence."[10]

Wiesel has suggested an additional covenant forged at Auschwitz, says Berenbaum. "This covenant is no longer between humanity and God or God and Israel, but rather between Israel and its memories of pain and death, God and meaning." Since God has proved an unreliable partner, the Jewish people must base their self-affirmation on their choice to remain Jews and to assume the past of Jewish history as their own. The threefold elements of this additional covenant are: solidarity, witness, and the sanctification of life. "In the beginning there was the Holocaust," says Wiesel, and everything must begin anew with it. "Even the images of God must be altered," interprets Berenbaum, "if such images lead to powerlessness or acquiescence to oppression." "Sanctification no longer leads to the messianic event of redemption but is rather a solidarity act of an individual and/or community designed to momentarily rout the void."[11]

Although we cannot accept Berenbaum's dismissal of Wiesel's modern messianism, we *can* accept the "vision of the void" as one of the poles with which Wiesel has throughout stayed in tension. "My being Jewish is to me more important than my thinking about God," said Wiesel in 1977. "God can take care of himself."[12] Only through this tension has Wiesel been able—

honestly and convincingly—to make such affirmations as he has been able to make on the other pole. It is in this spirit, too, that we must look at André Neher's theological approach to the Holocaust in his little essay "*Shaddai*: The God of the Broken Arch." This essay does not even mention Wiesel, yet it was included by Alvin Rosenfeld and Irving Greenberg in their anthology *Confronting the Holocaust: The Impact of Elie Wiesel*. Neher introduces us to the terrifying, self-sufficient God of Silence, who nonetheless is the God who demands of us that we enter into dialogue with Him.

> The God who is sufficient unto himself—*Shaddai*—is the God who has no need of men, no more than he needs any being other than his own. He is the God of the farther slope, of the inaccessible, of the unfathomable, the God who eludes creation, revelation, communication. This God who is sufficient unto himself is likewise self-sufficient in his Word: He is the *God beyond dialogue*. He requires no partner, neither to whom to address the Word, nor from whom to receive a reply. He is the God without an echo, without yesterday and without tomorrow, the God of absolute Silence.
>
> The grave theological point with which we are now confronted is that this God of absolute Silence persists in speaking even across this Silence; that this God beyond dialogue provokes man and dares him to take up the challenge of dialogue; that this God without echo, without yesterday and without tomorrow, imposes his intolerable presence on the very instant, on the *hic et nunc*.[13]

Neher sees *Shaddai* as at the heart both of the Book of Ruth and the Book of Job, "ever-present, not suspended on the wings of the promise but deep at the heart of an irremediable failure." The silence of God is as repellent as it is absolute in Chapters 3 to 37 of the Book of Job, "as if God wished to bring to the point of rupture the impossible yet inexorable dialogue between man and God." No assurance is provided as to the outcome of the test to which God puts us: "an Omega is as little certain of appearing as man is of attaining it." From this Neher concludes that "the God of the false test—

Shaddai—is the *God of the broken arch*." At the beginning and the end of the Bible is not the Word but silence, the silence before speech and the silence "beyond the Bible, in the zone where the prophetic dialogue was abruptly broken off, and whose night envelops us still." This is the silence of Isaiah's hidden God (Isaiah 45:15). Underlying his questions, says Neher, is "the shock-effect of a brutal, experienced reality, the throbbing trace of an *event* . . . the *event of Auschwitz*," "whose very name is the most tragic invitation to an encounter with *Shaddai*." "*Shaddai* is God in the 'test' of the Holocaust," "this new extremity of the history of the covenant."[14] Thus Neher leaves us where Wiesel himself leaves us: not with a theology of the void, but with an unanswerable question, a question, nonetheless, that remains within the dialogue between God and the human, God and Israel, as it also remains within the Dialogue with the Absurd!

We have taken Heschel and Wiesel separately. Now let us try to take them together. Heschel, as we have seen, is a poetic philosopher and theologian, Wiesel a philosophical novelist, playwright, and essayist. That in itself represents a convergence of the two—not an identity but a meeting. There are other important ways in which Heschel and Wiesel meet. Both are contemporary Jews who began in Europe and moved to America.[15] The lives of both were stamped by the Holocaust—Wiesel as one who lived through it, Heschel as one whose whole family, community, and culture were destroyed by it and who only narrowly escaped being destroyed by it himself. In 1965–66 Heschel was the Harry Emerson Fosdick Visiting Professor at Union Theological Seminary in New York City. The opening words of the lecture he gave upon assuming this professorship were:

> I speak as a person who was able to leave Warsaw, the city in which I was born, just six weeks before the disaster began. My destination was New York, it would have been Auschwitz or Treblinka. I am a brand plucked from the fire of an altar of Satan on which millions of human lives were exterminated to evil's greater glory, and on which so much else was consumed:

> the divine image of so many human beings, many people's faith
> in the God of justice and compassion, and much of the secret
> and power of attachment to the Bible bred and cherished in
> the hearts of men for nearly two thousand years.[16]

Even though Heschel did not himself experience the Holocaust,
it was a negative touchstone of reality for him even as it is for
Wiesel. One cannot appreciate the lifelong tension in which Heschel stood between the mines of meaning of the Baal Shem and
the mountains of absurdity of the Kotzker rebbe without im-
aginatively understanding the ever-present specter of the Holocaust in Heschel's life. Heschel's testimony of his vain efforts to
arouse American Jewry to concern for the Jews in Nazi Europe
is deeply touching *and* deeply shocking.[17]

The meeting of Heschel and Wiesel does not end here. They
lived in New York; they were close personal friends; Wiesel read
one of Heschel's early Yiddish poems at his funeral. Both were
Hasidim in their childhood, and both carried the world of Hasidism with them into their writings, their life attitudes, and their
confrontation with the modern world. Both were deeply attached
to the Hebrew Bible and witnessed for it as a bearer of the
covenant and a messenger of life. Both stood and stand in an
especially close relation to the Hebrew prophets, and both have
become in their own persons prophets for contemporary hu-
mankind. Both were and are rooted in the whole range of Jewish
experience and Jewish thought, and were and are, above all,
grounded in their identity as Jews. Yet both precisely through
this grounding transcended the worldwide Jewish community to
which they continue to speak and are, in the words of Robert
McAfee Brown, "messengers to all humanity."

We could say more about what Heschel and Wiesel have in
common and where they meet. Both are, in a highly meaningful
sense of the term, "Jewish existentialists." Along with Martin
Buber they are the two Jewish thinkers whose witness in our
time is so striking that I find myself compelled to witness to
them. Both have had a powerful impact on Christian thought

and witness in our time. All of these are reasons enough for our looking at them together in this book. Yet we must go beyond that and ask whether they converge in such a way as to form something of a common witness, and if so where.

The answer to the first question is clearly yes. It is astonishing the extent to which their witnesses converge, or it would be if we had not just brought to mind the many important ways in which they have common ground and meet as thinkers and as persons. The answer as to where they converge is more complex. They both witness for Jewish identity, as we have seen, and for the whole range of Jewish experience and thought from the earliest stories in the Hebrew Bible to the present. They both ask us to keep alive the wonder of being human and the wonder of Jewish living. They both make their witness because and in spite of the Holocaust—affirming life through faithfully facing the Holocaust and remaining in tension with it. "There has never been so much guilt and distress, agony and terror," wrote Heschel in *Man's Quest for God*. "At no time has the earth been so soaked with blood. Fellow men turned out to be evil ghosts, monstrous and weird." And again: "Our world seems not unlike a pit of snakes. . . . In our everyday life we worshipped force, despised compassion, and obeyed no law but our unappeasable appetite. The vision of the sacred has all but died in the soul of man."[18]

Both Heschel and Wiesel began in self-enclosed Hasidic communities, ventured into the Western world, and became Western men who could not go back to those self-contained communities. Yet both witness for the enormous significance of Hasidism for our contemporary life—that very world which the modern Hasidic community tends to shut out. Like Martin Buber, they had to bring Hasidism to the Western world *against its will* for the need of the hour. Like Buber, too, both Heschel and Wiesel have found in their dialogue with the Hasidic rebbes, or zaddikim, a direction-giving image of the human for an age which is notably lacking in just such an image. When Wiesel emphasizes the concern of the Hasidim for overcoming solitude and for friendship, he is speaking from Hasidism to us contemporaries who are sorely lacking both in friendship and in community. But as we have seen from Wiesel's latest essay on Hasidism, a distinction must be made between one type of community and another. The Baal Shem and the generations that followed him established what was essentially a "community of otherness," to use the language of my book *The Confirmation of Otherness*; whereas the modern Hasidic community for the most part is a "community of affinity," or like-mindedness. The openness that characterized the Baal Shem characterizes Buber, Heschel, and Wiesel in their sense for Hasidic awareness of the ineffable, joy, friendship, solidarity, care for the unique, reverence for all life, and "hallowing the everyday."

Both Heschel and Wiesel witness for the deep Jewish truth that God needs us as we need God, that we are partners of existence together, that the God who is unutterably transcendent is also the God who dwells with us in the midst of our uncleanness, the God whose Shekinah, or indwelling Glory, suffers in our suffering and is exiled in our exile. Heschel and Wiesel alike struggle for redemption in the midst of suffering and exile and point us toward what we have called the "messianism of the unredeemed."

Such common witness as we may discern here, and we could multiply it many times, in no way deprives either man of his unique voice. One cannot simply add them together and get a sum total. Yet their voices can sing in harmony and even in unison. Their double witness can be for us a touchstone of reality that we may touch and enter into dialogue with so that it becomes for us a dialogue of touchstones. The Hasidic master Pinhas of Koretz said that if one person who tries to sing but cannot lift his voice is joined by another who can lift his voice, then both can sing together. Heschel and Wiesel were each able to sing by himself. Yet something ineffable is achieved if we can hear them singing together. For that, as Rabbi Pinhas said, "is the secret of the bond between spirit and spirit"!

If we say no more about Heschel and Wiesel's common witness here, it is precisely to avoid that analytic-synthetic approach that is common to contemporary philosophy and theology. Such an approach would attain a commonality only by reduction and abstraction, losing the poetic fullness of each one's voice and word. The reader who has entered into a dialogue with each in turn will not find it difficult to warm his or her self in their common fire.

In witnessing to these witnesses to God, I must also witness for what they witness to. My concern ultimately is to point not to them but through and beyond them to what they witness for. This whole book is such a witness; for I have made their witness my own. Yet there are two questions more that I must address here, however briefly and inadequately. Why does God need witnesses and what sort of witnesses does God need?

I am no theologian. I cannot make statements about God in God's self or his or her "nature" and "attributes." Neither am I a metaphysician. I cannot put forward a metaphysic showing God in interaction with the world, as Alfred North Whitehead has done in our time. I always find myself stumped by the naïve question: How did Whitehead get outside the dialectic between God and world so that he could tell us about it? The question *is* naïve, because I know that Whitehead has developed his metaphysics from an analysis of what is given in our experience. Nonetheless, he ends up making pronouncements about God and the world *as if from the outside*, and that I cannot do. I have not even been able to join my friends in a call for a "Jewish theology," because I cannot hold with a Judaism based upon certain theological assumptions that one must accept on faith and on which one may then confidently build a system in which God is included.

Nonetheless, I must witness for creation as I understand it— not from a standpoint before or above creation but in the midst of it. Once I wrote Martin Buber and asked him if God had an I-Thou relationship with man in creating him. "Now you are

talking like the theologians," Buber replied. "How do we know
what relationship God had to us before creation?" If I speak of
creation, it is rather to say that, in contrast to what I held when
I affirmed with the Hindu Vedantist that Brahman is Atman, I
believe that human existence as we know it is not maya, or
illusion, but genuine historical destiny. This destiny is not a divine
plan or blueprint that we merely act out. On the contrary, we
are given a real ground on which to stand, real freedom with
which to act, real resources to praise, bless, thank, but also to
contend with God, to bring him, her, or it to trial as does the
Job of Auschwitz whom Wiesel portrays and embodies.

It is because we have a real ground of created uniqueness, if
a fragile and a mortal one, that God needs us. We are the partners
of God in existence, the co-creators who work together in completing creation, in bringing it within our dialogue with God
and, as we can, helping it toward redemption. "Does God need
man?" writes Buber in *I and Thou*. "He *wills* to need him for the
very purpose for which He created him." That "purpose," again,
is not some divine scheme. "Do not show me the secret of your
ways? I could not bear it," cries the great Hasidic rebbe Levi
Yitzhak of Berditchev. "Rather show me what what is happening
at this moment means to me, what it demands of me, what you,
Lord of the world, are asking me by way of it." "It is not *why* I
suffer but that I suffer for your sake that I want to know," Levi
Yitzhak concludes. "Why" would mean an explanation, a theology, a metaphysic. "For thy sake" means that our suffering,
without in any way being denied or explained away, can take on
meaning through being brought into the dialogue with God, the
Dialogue with the Absurd.

How do I "know" this—I who am no theologian or metaphysician but a philosopher—a philosopher of religion, but still
more a philosophical anthropologist, concerned with the wholeness and uniqueness of the human. Not from above but from
below. Not because I have schematized the mysteries, as the
Kabbala attempts to do, but because I know no other way to

point to authentic human existence as I have experienced it. The creation of the Hebrew Bible is paradoxical; for it means that we are simultaneously at a distance from and in relation to God, even as we are simultaneously at a distance from and in relation to the world and to our fellow animals and our fellow human beings within the world. This paradox was carried forward with great subtlety and brilliance in the Lurian Kabbala's idea of *tsimtsum*, in which God, who is the whole, withdraws from it to a point in order to leave room for the world and for man. The flavor of God remains in the world as the flavor of wine remains in the empty bottle.

Our task is to take part in the *tikkun*, the restoration that helps uplift to their divine source the sparks that have fallen after the shattering of the vessels of light that were so full that they could not withstand the grace. This restoration is itself part of the messianic redemption; for it helps lead to the *yihud*—reunification of God and his exiled Shekinah. We have a part in this messianic redemption insofar as we help in this *tikkun*.

This brings us to our second question. What sort of witnesses does God need? One of the most powerful religious movements in the twentieth century is that of the Jehovah's Witnesses. I knew many Jehovah's Witnesses in the Civilian Public Service camps for conscientious objectors in which I served during the Second World War. I can witness to them as hard workers, as believing persons, as fine human beings. But I cannot witness to what they witness. Though they derive their name from the identical verse in Deutero-Isaiah that gives the title to this book, their notion of witness, as I have encountered it, is that of the printed pamphlet, the *written* Bible, the memorized speech, the contents of belief rather than the way of life per se. I have no brief against doctrine if we remember that it comes from teaching. But when doctrine becomes objectified and crystallized as something that can be handed over in pamphlet form, I can no longer witness for it. Once a young Jehovah's Witness woman came to my door and asked me to listen to a set speech on the Bible. "I

am interested in the Bible, too," I said. "Let us discuss it." She
showed every sign of visible frustration until I gave up and let
her recite her set speech, at which point she left fully satisfied.
"What does she imagine she has accomplished?" I asked myself.
She seemed to have no concern with *my* side of the dialogue,
with how I related to, understood, or made my own what she
said, only that she said it.[19]

Let us go back to the Lurian Kabbala. One thing that is common to the classical Kabbala of the Zohar, to the Lurian Kabbala,
and to Hasidism which grew out of both is the emphasis upon
devekut, cleaving to God. All three would agree that our *devekut*
helps in the reunification of the *Ein Sof*, the unutterably transcendent God, and the exiled Shekinah, the indwelling Glory of
God that suffers with us as we with it. Yet the Lurian Kabbala
also developed a concept of *kavanot*, special magical and mystical
intentions that can be brought to prayer, study, and life, through
which we can bind ourselves to one or another of the Sefiroth,
or divine emanations, and thus help in achieving *tikkun*, or restoration.

Hasidism took over this notion of *kavanot* from the Lurian
Kabbala. But Hasidism also emphasizes *kavana*, the dedication
of one's whole being. This spontaneous, unwilled, and unwillful
relation to life also is seen as capable of freeing the imprisoned
sparks from the shells of darkness and raising them to their divine
source. "What are all *kavanot* compared to one really heartfelt
grief?" exclaimed the Baal Shem. It is possible, of course, to
bring *kavana* to our more conscious and intentional *kavanot*. But
when I am told by a Lubavitcher Hasid that, according to Shneur
Zalman's great work, the *Tania*, a Jew does not need to have
kavana because a Jew has a special Jewish soul that makes his
action effective even without it, then here my shared witness
ceases. At the risk of offending my mother's father and her sainted
grandfather, I can accept no service that is less than wholehearted,
no devotion to God that can be performed by external actions
plus being a Jew without the *kavana* that must go with it. "A

little with *kavana* is better than much without," says Abraham Heschel, and I, as he well knew, add my assent and affirmation to that statement.

What sort of witnesses does God need? Witnesses like Buber, Heschel, and Wiesel, who withstand the cruel demands of the hour and of the century. Witnesses who contend even as they affirm, witnesses who point the way to renewed wonder and reverence, who hallow this life and sanctify the everyday; who witness for the uniqueness of Judaism, the uniqueness of the biblical covenant in every aspect of personal, familial, communal, and social life, the particularity of the Jewish people in their long and fateful struggle to persevere in existence as the people of the covenant, the people of the witness.

Does that mean that God needs only Jews or only the Jewish people? God forbid! "All nations shall come to Zion to learn the Torah." Torah here is not law but teaching, instruction in the way, and the way of every people as of each person is unique. What is more, it is unique situation by situation and historical hour by historical hour. "The soul teaches incessantly," Rabbi Pinhas of Koretz used to say. "If that is so why don't people obey the soul?" asked a disciple. "Because it never repeats itself," replied the rebbe. God brings each people up from its own exile to its own land.

If Israel wishes to claim to be Israel and not "Lo ami"—"not my people"—as Hosea names one of his children after the Israel that has turned away—it must shoulder anew the task of the covenant. The task of the covenant is not individual morality or even individual spirituality. It is the call to become a kingdom of priests and a holy nation, to make real the kingship of God in actual lived community and in relation to other communities— with righteousness, justice, loving kindness, and holiness. What that means in *our* time, as opposed to the times when Amos, Hosea, and Isaiah brought the demand of the covenant to the people of Israel, we can only discover by our commitment, our hearkening, our responding. *"Na-aseh v'nishmah"*—"we shall do and we shall hear," the people of Israel respond when Moses brings down the Ten Commandments from Mount Sinai. We shall hear out of our doing. But we shall also respond out of hearing. "For if you are not my witnesses, then I, as it were, am not the Lord."

"God needs men" is the title of a classic French film that Martin Buber particularly liked. When Buber was five years old, an older man told him of the Messiah who waits at the gates of Rome. "What is he waiting for?" asked the five-year-old Martin. "He is waiting for you," the man replied. Isaiah does not tell us of a *hidden* God, as Neher suggests, but of a *hiding* God, the God of the eclipse who waits for us to turn back to him, to seek him.

> Rabbi Barukh's grandson Yehiel was once playing hide-and-seek with another boy. He hid himself well and waited for his playmate to find him. When he had waited for a long time, he came out of his hiding-place, but the other was nowhere to be seen. Now Yehiel realized that he had not looked for him from the very beginning. This made him cry, and crying he ran to his grandfather and complained of his faithless friend. Then tears brimmed in Rabbi Barukh's eyes and he said: "God says the same thing: 'I hide, but no one wants to seek me.' "[20]

Sources and Notes

INTRODUCTION: BIBLICAL COVENANT, HASIDIC
FERVOR, AND AMERICAN JUDAISM

1. New York: E. P. Dutton, 1982, 1983.
2. Chicago: University of Chicago Press, Phoenix Books, 1973.
3. Maurice Friedman, "Liberal Judaism and Contemporary Jewish
Thought," *Midstream* (Autumn 1959).
4. Chambersburg, Pa.: Anima Publications, 1982.
5. Martin Buber, *Tales of the Hasidim: The Later Masters,* trans. by
Olga Marx (New York: Schocken Books, 1961), p. 214.

1. MY FRIENDSHIP WITH ABRAHAM JOSHUA HESCHEL

1. Maurice Friedman, *Touchstones of Reality: Existential Trust and
the Community of Peace* (New York: E. P. Dutton, 1972), pp. 43 f.
2. *Conservative Judaism,* Vol. XXII, No. 3 (Spring 1968).
3. Heschel's poem "God Follows Me Everywhere." Translated from
the Yiddish by Samuel Rosenbaum. Quoted with the permission of
Sylvia Heschel.
4. *Against Silence: The Voice and Vision of Elie Wiesel,* selected and
edited by Irving Abrahamson (New York: Holocaust Library, 1985),
3 vols., Vol. II, "My Teacher's Desk" (1983), p. 43.

2. THE SCION OF HASIDISM

1. Samuel H. Dresner, "The Contribution of Abraham Joshua Heschel," *Judaism,* Vol. XXXII, No. 1 (Winter 1983), pp. 61–63. This
essay is based on the introduction referred to in the text.

2. Abraham Joshua Heschel, *Man's Quest for God* (New York: Charles Scribner's Sons, 1954), pp. 94–98; Heschel, "Toward an Understanding of Halakha," *Yearbook of the Central Conference of American Rabbis* 63 (1953): 386–391.

3. Abraham Joshua Heschel, *The Circle of the Baal Shem Tov*, ed. with an introduction, "Heschel as a Hasidic Scholar," by Samuel H. Dresner (Chicago: The University of Chicago Press, 1985), pp. xxxiv f.

4. Ibid.

5. Ibid., p. xxvii.

6. Ibid., pp. xiii, xxi.

7. Ibid., pp. xxi–xxiii, xxx.

8. Ibid., p. xxiv.

9. Ibid., p. xlii.

10. Ibid., pp. 19–30.

11. Ibid., pp. 9 f., 14, 33 f.

12. Ibid., pp. 136 f., 140, 143.

13. Ibid., pp. 145 f.

14. Ibid., pp. 147 f.

3. A PASSION FOR TRUTH

1. Published in Israel and New York.

2. Abraham Joshua Heschel, *A Passion for Truth* (New York: Farrar, Straus and Giroux, 1973), p. xv.

4. THE AWARENESS OF THE INEFFABLE

1. Abraham J. Heschel, "Hope through Renewal of the Self," *Tempo*, Vol. I, No. 25 (October 15, 1969), p. 2.

5. "TO BE IS TO STAND FOR"

1. Abraham J. Heschel, *Israel: An Echo of Eternity* (New York: Farrar, Straus and Giroux, Noonday Books, 1969), Chap. 4, "Israel and Meaning in History."

2. Edward J. Kaplan, "Language and Reality in Abraham J. Heschel's Philosophy of Religion," *Journal of the American Academy of Re-*

ligion, Vol. XLI, No. 1 (March 1973), p. 111. Professor Kaplan's essay (pp. 94–133) is a particularly fine and sensitive appreciation of Heschel both as poet and prophet and of the role of religio-poetic language in evoking profound and mutual trans-subjective understanding and response.

3. From five pages of notes taken during a visit to Heschel at his office in the Jewish Theological Seminary in New York in the fall or early winter of 1971–72. Heschel's comments were in response to the original version of this chapter, which has since been published as part of a longer monograph in Hebrew translation in Israel in Volume II of *Spiritual Contributions of American Jewry* (Jerusalem: Brit Ivrit Olamit, 1973).

6. PHILOSOPHY OF JUDAISM

1. Lou H. Silberman, "Philosophy of Abraham Heschel," *Jewish Heritage*, Vol. II, No. 1 (Spring 1959), p. 26. Professor Silberman, who is commenting on an address given by me at an Alumni Convocation at Hebrew Union College, Cincinnati, in which the above criticism of Heschel was substantially embodied, rightly characterizes me as a "friendly critic."

7. SYMBOLISM, PATHOS, AND PROPHECY

1. Heschel, *Man's Quest for God*, p. 130.
2. Abraham J. Heschel, *The Prophets* (Philadelphia: The Jewish Publication Society of America, 1962), p. 221.

8. EXISTENTIALISM OF DIALOGUE AND SOCIAL ACTION

1. Abraham J. Heschel, *Who Is Man?* (Stanford, California: Stanford University Press, 1965), p. 8.
2. Abraham Joshua Heschel, "Reflections on Death," *Conservative Judaism*, Vol. XXVIII, No. 1 (Fall 1973), pp. 6 f.
3. Ibid., p. 9.
4. Franklin Sherman, *The Promise of Heschel* in *The Promise of Theology* series, ed. by Martin E. Marty (Philadelphia and New York: J. B. Lippincott Co., 1970), p. 32.

5. Donald Grayston and Michael W. Higgins, eds., *Thomas Merton: Pilgrim in Process* (Toronto: Griffin House, 1983), pp. 100 f.

6. Abraham J. Heschel, *The Insecurity of Freedom: Essays on Human Existence* (New York: Farrar, Straus and Giroux, 1966), pp. 260 f.

9. THE HOLOCAUST AS TOUCHSTONE OF REALITY

1. Ellen S. Fine, *Legacy of Night: The Literary Universe of Elie Wiesel* (Albany: State University of New York Press, 1982), pp. xi f.

2. Ibid., pp. xii f., xv.

3. Ibid., pp. 8 f., 53, 56.

4. Michael Berenbaum, *The Vision of the Void: Theological Reflections on the Works of Elie Wiesel* (Middletown, Connecticut: Wesleyan University Press, 1979), p. 9.

5. Robert McAfee Brown, *Elie Wiesel: Messenger to All Humanity* (Notre Dame: Notre Dame University Press, 1973), p. 208.

6. *Harry James Cargas in Conversation with Elie Wiesel* (New York: Paulist Press, 1976), p. 91.

7. Alvin H. Rosenfeld, "The Problematics of Holocaust Literature" in Alvin H. Rosenfeld and Irving Greenberg, eds., *Confronting the Holocaust: The Impact of Elie Wiesel* (Bloomington, Indiana: Indiana University Press, 1978), pp. 2, 26.

8. Elie Wiesel, *Legends of Our Time* (New York: Holt, Rinehart and Winston, 1968), pp. 9, 180, 190.

9. *Against Silence*, Vol. II, "Facing the Questions" (1961), p. 47; "The Burden on Jewish Youth" (1966), p. 133; Vol. I, "The Fiery Shadow—Jewish Existence out of the Holocaust" (1968), pp. 251 f.; Vol. II, "The Writer and His Universe" (1971), p. 62; "On Revolutions in Culture and the Arts" (1973), p. 71; Vol. I, "Are We Worthy of the Story?" (1973), p. 280; Vol. III, "The Holocaust" (1974), p. 311, (1975), p. 312; Vol. II, "The Writer and His Obsessions" (1977), p. 106; Vol. III, "Autobiographical" (1977), p. 278; "The Victims of Injustice Must Be Cared For" (1979), p. 145.

10. Ibid., Vol. III, "The Holocaust: Beginning or End?" (1979), p. 153; "The Focus Is Memory" (letter to President Jimmy Carter, September 27, 1979), p. 162; "This Is History" (1980), p. 193; "The Mystery and the Fear" (1982), p. 386.

11. Ibid., Vol. III, "We Must Remember" (1984), p. 146.

12. Elie Wiesel, *Signes d'exode: Essais, histoires, dialogues* (Paris: Bernard Grasset, 1985), pp. 187, 193, 198, 221 f., 225 f. My translations.

13. Elie Wiesel, *Paroles d'étranger: Textes, Contes, Dialogues* (Paris: Éditions Seuils, 1982), pp. 156 f. My translation.

14. Ibid., p. 165. My translation.

15. Ibid., p. 169. My translation.

16. Ibid., pp. 176 f. My translation.

17. Ibid., p. 187. My translation.

18. Ibid., p. 188. My translation.

19. Ibid. My translation.

20. *Against Silence*, Vol. I, "The Jewish Tradition" (1982), pp. 223 f.

21. Ibid., Vol. III, "Golda at 75" (1973), p. 206.

22. Ibid., Vol. I, "The New Anti-Semitism" (1981), pp. 379 f.

23. *Los Angeles Times*, April 20, 1985, pp. 1, 23.

10. "PEDDLER OF NIGHT AND AGONY"

1. *Against Silence*, Vol. II, "The Storyteller's Prayer" (1970), p. 57.

2. Brown, *Elie Wiesel*, p. 46.

3. Alvin Rosenfeld, *A Double Dying: Reflections on Holocaust Literature* (Bloomington, Indiana: University of Indiana Press, 1978), p. 22. See also pp. 27 and 70 f.

4. Sidra Ezrahi, "The Holocaust Writer and the Lamentation Tradition: Responses to Catastrophe in Jewish Literature," in Rosenfeld and Greenberg, *Confronting the Holocaust*, p. 143.

5. *Cargas, in Conversation with Wiesel*, p. 6.

6. Fine, *Legacy of Night*, p. 9.

7. *Cargas in Conversation with Wiesel*, p. 108.

8. Robert Alter, *After the Tradition* (New York: E. P. Dutton, 1969), pp. 154 f.

9. *Cargas in Conversation with Wiesel*, pp. 65 f.

10. Fine, *Legacy of Night*, pp. 6 f.

11. *Against Silence*, Vol. II, "A Body of Work" (1972), p. 64; "How Does One Write?" (1972), p. 65.

12. Ibid., "How and Why I Write" (1980), pp. 117–20.

13. Elie Wiesel, *Night*, Foreword by Francois Mauriac, trans. from the French by Stella Rodway (New York: Avon Books, 1969), pp. 43 f.

11. TO WITNESS OR KEEP SILENT: THE UNRESOLVED TENSION

1. *Against Silence*, Vol. I, "The Memorial for Sighet," p. 129.

2. Wiesel, *Legends of Our Time*, p. 10.

3. Elie Wiesel, *One Generation After*, trans. from the French by Lily Edelman and Elie Wiesel (New York: Random House, 1970), pp. 8–11, 85.

4. Elie Wiesel, *The Oath*, trans. from the French by Marion Wiesel (New York: Random House, 1973), p. 9.

5. Ibid., pp. 238–41.

6. *Against Silence*, Vol. III, "The Call to Life" (1970), p. 61.

7. Ibid., Vol. II, "The Holocaust and the Anguish of the Writer" (1973), pp. 66 f.

8. Ibid., "On Revolutions in Culture and the Arts" (1973), p. 71; Vol. I, "Let Us Remember, Let Us Remember" (1973), p. 107; Vol. II, "In Search of Integrity" (1974), p. 87; Vol. I, "Where Is Hope?" (1975), p. 137; "The Crisis of Hope" (1975), p. 143; Vol. III, "The Creative Act: Subject" (1973), p. 287; Vol. I, "Then and Now: The Experiences of a Teacher" (1977), pp. 149, 152; "Trivializing the Holocaust: Semi-Fact and Semi-Fiction" (1978), p. 158.

9. Elie Wiesel, *Messengers of God: Biblical Portraits and Legends*, trans. by Marion Wiesel (New York: Random House, 1976), pp. 95–97.

10. Elie Wiesel, *A Jew Today*, trans. by Marion Wiesel (New York: Random House, 1978), pp. 15, 45.

11. Ibid., p. 198.

12. Ibid., pp. 199 f.

13. Elie Wiesel, *Five Biblical Portraits* (Notre Dame: University of Notre Dame Press, 1981), pp. 126 f.

14. *Against Silence*, Vol. I, "The Call to Remember" (1981), p. 114.

15. Ibid., Vol. II, "Does the Holocaust Lie Beyond the Reach of

Art?" (1983), p. 126; Vol. I, "Answer to a Young Boy" (1983), p. 198.

16. *Cargas in Conversation with Wiesel*, p. 7.

17. Lily Edelman, "A Conversation with Elie Wiesel" in Harry James Cargas, ed., *Responses to Elie Wiesel* (New York: Persea Books, 1978), p. 19.

18. Elie Wiesel, "Why I Write" in Rosenfeld and Greenberg, *Confronting the Holocaust*, pp. 202–6.

19. For an excellent discussion of the unresolved tension between witness and silence that says much that is not touched on in this chapter, see Brown, *Elie Wiesel*, pp. 24–32, 36 f.

12. SILENCE

1. Elie Wiesel, *Dawn*, trans. by Frances Frenaye (New York: Hill and Wang, 1961), pp. 68 f.

2. Elie Wiesel, *The Town Beyond the Wall*, trans. by Stephen Becker (New York: Atheneum, 1964), p. 96.

3. Elie Wiesel, *The Gates of the Forest*, trans. by Frances Frenaye (New York: Holt, Rinehart and Winston, 1966), p. 63.

4. Elie Wiesel, *The Jews of Silence*, trans. from the Hebrew with an Historical Afterword by Neal Kozody (New York: Holt, Rinehart and Winston, 1966), p. 127.

5. Elie Wiesel, *A Beggar in Jerusalem*, trans. from the French by Lily Edelman and Elie Wiesel (New York: Random House, 1970), p. 108.

6. Wiesel, *One Generation After*, p. 198.

7. Elie Wiesel, *Souls on Fire: Portraits and Legends of Hasidic Masters*, trans. by Marion Wiesel (New York: Random House, 1972), pp. 201, 237, 240, 248, 253.

8. *Against Silence*, Vol. II, "Tales Change People" (1970), p. 60; Vol. III, "The Creative Act: Subject" (1973), p. 286; Vol. I, "The Silence of Man and God" (1977), p. 110.

9. Elie Wiesel, *Four Hasidic Masters: And Their Struggle Against Melancholy*, Foreword by Theodore M. Hesburgh (Notre Dame: University of Notre Dame Press, 1978), pp. 118, 120.

10. *Against Silence*, Vol. II, "In the Shadow of Flames" (1979), pp.

112 f.; "How and Why I Write" (1980), p. 119; "On Silence, Words, and Salvation" (1980), p. 121; Vol. I, "The Trial of Man" (1980), p. 176; Vol. III, "Before the End of History—And After" (1981), p. 267. Cf. Wiesel, *Signes d'exode*, pp. 46, 128.

11. Elie Wiesel, *Somewhere a Master: Further Hasidic Portraits and Legends*, trans. by Marion Wiesel (New York: Summit Books, 1982), pp. 200 f.

12. Ibid., pp. 197–201.

13. Wiesel, *The Oath*, pp. 15, 187, 143.

14. Elie Wiesel, *The Testament*, trans. by Marion Wiesel (New York: Summit Books, 1981), pp. 30, 207–10.

15. *Cargas in Conversation with Wiesel*, pp. 90, 94.

16. Cargas, *Responses to Elie Wiesel*, pp. 19 f.

17. André Neher, "*Shaddai*: The God of the Broken Arch (A Theological Approach to the Holocaust)," in Rosenfeld and Greenberg, eds., *Confronting the Holocaust*, pp. 152, 155–58.

18. Brown, *Elie Wiesel*, pp. 30–32.

19. Ellen Fine, "The Journey Homeward: The Theme of the Town in the Works of Elie Wiesel" in Cargas, *Responses to Elie Wiesel*, p. 250.

20. Fine, *Legacy of Night*, p. 144.

21. Ibid., pp. 120 f.

13. MADNESS AND LAUGHTER

1. *Against Silence*, Vol. III, "The Holocaust" (1974), pp. 311 f.

2. Ibid., "Bringing the Messiah" (1974), p. 44; Vol. I, "Blessed Be the Madmen—And Their Friends" (1974), p. 305; Vol. III, "Questions and Answers: At the University of Oregon, 1975," pp. 229 f.

3. *Cargas in Conversation with Wiesel*, p. 110.

4. Wiesel, *Messengers of God*, p. 211.

5. Wiesel, *Five Biblical Portraits*, p. 109.

6. Brown, *Elie Wiesel*, p. 216.

7. *Against Silence*, Vol. II, "Hasidism and Man's Love of Man" (1972), p. 255.

8. Wiesel, *Souls on Fire*, pp. 13 f., 105, 198, 170, 202.

9. *Against Silence*, Vol. III, "Out of the Night" (1976), p. 242; *Cargas in Conversation with Wiesel*, pp. 2 f.

10. Cargas, *Responses to Elie Wiesel*, p. 15.

11. *Against Silence*, Vol. III, "Questions and Answers: At Washington University, 1978," p. 253.

12. Brown, *Elie Wiesel*, p. 211.

13. Emil L. Fackenheim, "Midrashic Existence after the Holocaust: Reflections Occasioned by the Work of Elie Wiesel," in Rosenfeld and Greenberg, *Confronting the Holocaust*, p. 114.

14. Brown, *Elie Wiesel*, p. 211.

15. Wiesel, *Legends of Our Time*, p. 76.

16. Wiesel, *One Generation After*, pp. 19–21.

17. Wiesel, *Night*, pp. 16, 24, 34–38, 46.

18. Berenbaum, *The Vision of the Void*, p. 103.

19. Wiesel, *The Town Beyond the Wall*, pp. 14, 16, 19.

20. Ibid., p. 47.

21. Ibid., pp. 92–94.

22. Ibid., pp. 118, 134.

23. Ibid., p. 169.

24. Wiesel, *The Gates of the Forest*, pp. 14, 20, 40, 120.

25. Wiesel, *A Beggar in Jerusalem*, p. 25.

26. Ibid., pp. 42 f.

27. Ibid., pp. 192 f.

28. Wiesel, *The Oath*, p. 13.

29. Fine, *Legacy of Night*, p. 123.

30. Elie Wiesel, *Zalmen, or the Madness of God*, adapted for the stage by Marion Wiesel (New York: Random House, 1974), p. 79.

31. Brown, *Elie Wiesel*, p. 213.

32. *Against Silence*, Vol. III, "A Tale of Defiance" (1975), p. 96. Cf. Wiesel, *Signes d'exode*, p. 19.

33. Wiesel, *Dawn*, pp. 42 f., 61.

34. Elie Wiesel, *The Accident*, trans. by Anne Borchardt (New York: Hill and Wang, 1962), p. 42.

35. Wiesel, *The Town Beyond the Wall*, pp. 85, 137.

36. Wiesel, *The Gates of the Forest*, p. 3.

37. Ibid., pp. 7, 50, 58.

38. Wiesel, *Messengers of God*, p. 97.

39. Elie Wiesel, *Ani Ma'amin: A Song Lost and Found Again*, music for the cantata composed by Darius Milhaud, trans. by Marion Wiesel (New York: Random House, 1973), p. 107.

40. Wiesel, *Souls on Fire*, p. 174.

41. Ibid., pp. 198–200.

42. Ibid., p. 202.

43. Wiesel, *Somewhere a Master*, pp. 101, 115.

44. Wiesel, *The Oath*, p. 76.

45. Ibid., p. 212.

46. Wiesel, *The Testament*, pp. 28 f., 63, 345.

47. *Against Silence*, Vol. III, "The Watchman and the Poet" (1981), p. 124.

48. Brown, *Elie Wiesel*, p. 223.

49. Harry James Cargas, "What Is a Jew? Interview of Elie Wiesel" in Cargas, *Responses to Elie Wiesel*, pp. 155 f.

14. THE JOB OF AUSCHWITZ I

1. Martin Buber, *On Judaism*, ed. by Nahum N. Glatzer (New York: Schocken Books), pp. 224 f.

2. Martin Buber, "Replies to My Critics," trans. by Maurice Friedman, Chap. VI. "Theology, Mysticism, Metaphysics," in Paul Arthur Schilpp and Maurice Friedman, eds., *The Philosophy of Martin Buber* (LaSalle, Illinois: Open Court Publishing Co., 1967), p. 713.

3. Maurice Friedman, *Problematic Rebel: Melville, Dostoevsky, Kafka, Camus*, 2nd rev., enlarged, and radically reorganized ed. (Chicago: The University of Chicago Press and Phoenix Books, 1970), pp. 17 f.

4. Wiesel, *Messengers of God*, pp. 129, 201 f.

5. *Against Silence*, Vol. II, "The Question of God" (1966), pp. 140 f.

6. Wiesel, *Messengers of God*, p. 221.

7. Ibid., p. 224.

8. Ibid., pp. 226, 229.

9. Ibid., pp. 223–35.

10. Brown, *Elie Wiesel*, pp. 12–18.

11. See Friedman, *Problematic Rebel*, pp. 12–22, for a full-scale interpretation of the Book of Job.

12. Wiesel, *Signes d'exode*, p. 34.

13. Wiesel, *Souls on Fire*, p. 91.

14. Ibid., pp. 107, 109, 111 f.

15. Wiesel, *Four Hasidic Masters*, p. 57.

16. Wiesel, *Somewhere a Master*, p. 11.

17. Weisel, *Souls on Fire*, p. 254.

18. *Against Silence*, Vol. II, "Hasidism and Man's Love of Man" (1972), p. 253.

19. Ibid., Vol. III, "God" (1968), p. 309; Vol. II, "My Teachers During the Tempest" (1973), p. 19; Vol. III, "God" (1975 & 1978), p. 310.

20. Ibid., Vol. III, "The Deportation" (1956), p. 57; "The End and the Beginning" (1956), p. 59.

21. Ibid., "Questions and Answers: At the University of Oregon, 1975," pp. 229 f.; "Jewish Identity" (1976), p. 307; "Questions and Answers at Brandeis-Bardin, 1978), p. 246.

22. Wiesel, *The Accident*, pp. 105 f.

23. Ibid., pp. 21, 91, 93.

24. Ibid., pp. 110 f.

25. Ibid., p. 120.

26. Wiesel, *The Town Beyond the Wall*, pp. 95 f.

27. Ibid., pp. 114 f.

28. Ibid., p. 127.

29. Ibid., p. 183.

30. Wiesel, *The Gates of the Forest*, p. 161.

31. Ibid., p. 196.

32. *Against Silence*, Vol. III, "A Simple Dialogue" (1980), p. 63.

15. THE JOB OF AUSCHWITZ II

1. *Against Silence*, Vol. I, "Jewish Atheist: A Quarrel with God" (1965), pp. 243 f.; "On Being a Jew" (1967), pp. 246 f.; Vol. II, "The Storyteller's Prayer" (1970), p. 58.

2. Wiesel, *Legends of Our Time*, p. 2.

3. Ibid., p. 6.

4. Ibid., p. 37.

5. Ibid., p. 173.

6. Ibid., p. 194.

7. Wiesel, *A Beggar in Jerusalem*, pp. 116 f.

8. Ibid., pp. 132 f.

9. Wiesel, *One Generation After*, p. 157.

10. Ibid., p. 170.

11. Ibid., p. 172.

12. Wiesel, *The Oath*, pp. 54, 78, 189, 191.

13. *Against Silence*, Vol. III, "Question and Quest" (1974), p. 93; "Questions and Answers: At the University of Oregon, 1975," p. 230; Vol. I, "The Crisis of Hope" (1975), pp. 144–46; "Freedom of Conscience—A Jewish Commentary" (1976), p. 208.

14. Wiesel, *The Gates of the Forest*, p. 197.

15. Elie Wiesel, *The Trial of God (as it was held on February 25, 1649 in Shamgorod)*, A Play in Three Acts, trans. by Marion Wiesel (New York: Random House, 1979), pp. 54, 133.

16. Ibid., pp. 133, 156.

17. *Cargas in Conversation with Wiesel*, pp. 56 f.

18. Wiesel, *Paroles d'étranger*, pp. 179 f. My translation.

16. JEWISH IDENTITY

1. "It is the failure to recognize the centrality of Jewishness in Wiesel's stories that mars Maurice Friedman's analysis. The argument that Wiesel's hero is the 'Job of Auschwitz' who 'trusts and contends' with God has point, but it is overstated when Friedman interprets this motif according to the existentialist doctrine of moral responsibility before evil as expressed by Camus. The rebellion against the Absurd waged by Dr. Rieux, the hero of Camus's *The Plague*, is not parallel with Wiesel's struggles to learn to live with the memories of all those whom he knew and loved in the Jewish community in Sighet. Wiesel's 'contention' with God occurs within an acutely Jewish sensibility where one can be angry with, pity, and even pray for God, but never reject God in favor of an ethical, universal, rebellion against the absurd, as Rieux did. Maurice Friedman, 'Elie Wiesel: The Job of Auschwitz,' unpublished paper delivered at the national meeting of the American Academy of Religion, New York, October, 1970." Thomas Idinopolous, "The Holocaust in the Stories of Elie Wiesel" in Harry James Cargas, ed., *Responses to Elie Wiesel* (New York: Persea Books, 1978), p. 131, n. 19. Perhaps it is because Idinopolous read (or heard) my unpublished paper and did not read my treatment of Camus in *Problematic Rebel: Melville, Dostoevsky, Kafka, Camus* and the Wiesel essay

in the context of *The Hidden Human Image* that he so misreads me as to imagine that I saw either Camus or Wiesel in the terms of "the existentialist doctrine of moral responsibility before evil" or "an ethical, universal, rebellion against the absurd." Undoubtedly, these are *his* interpretations of Camus; they are not mine, and any reader of my chapter "Elie Wiesel: The Job of Auschwitz" in *The Hidden Human Image* will acknowledge that it is fully set within the context of Wiesel's Jewishness. In fact, when *Commentary* rejected this essay, Elie commented to me, "It was probably too Jewish for them."

2. *Against Silence*, Vol. I, "The Passionate Tradition" (1977), pp. 349 f.

3. Wiesel, *Messengers of God*, pp. xii f. Cf. Brown, *Elie Wiesel*, p. 29.

4. Wiesel, *Messengers of God*, p. 69.

5. Wiesel, *Ani Ma'amin*, p. 17.

6. Wiesel, *Five Biblical Portraits*, pp. 151 f.

7. Ibid., p. 152.

8. Wiesel, *Four Hasidic Masters*, p. 95.

9. Wiesel, *Souls on Fire*, p. 133.

10. *Cargas in Conversation with Wiesel*, pp. 75, 8, 14 f., 32–35; *Against Silence*, Vol. III, "The Jew and the Human Condition" (1977), p. 104; Vol. II, "Let Us Celebrate" (1978), p. 203; Vol. I, "Our Jewish Solitude" (1975), p. 314; Vol. III, "The Creative Act: Author" (1975), p. 283.

11. *Against Silence*, Vol. III, "Jewish Identity" (1966, 1971), pp. 306 f.; Vol. I, "On Being a Jew" (1967), p. 246; "The Fiery Shadow— Jewish Existence out of the Holocaust" (1968), p. 252; "The Wall" (1972), p. 277; "On Teaching Jewish Identity" (1974), p. 293; Wiesel, *Signes d'exode*, pp. 10 f., 40 f.

12. *Against Silence*, Vol. I, "The Tradition of Dayenu" (1973), p. 285; *Signes d'exode*, pp. 177–79.

13. *Against Silence*, Vol. III, "The Great Adventure" (1978), p. 255; Vol. I, "The Endless Chain" (1975), pp. 307–9; "The Jewish Tradition of Learning: A Personal View" (1977), p. 344.

14. Ibid., Vol. III, "Judaism" (1978), p. 304; *Signes d'exode*, pp. 42 f.; Vol. II, "Friendship" (undated), pp. 38, 40.

15. Ibid., Vol. I, "What Is a Jew?" (1971), p. 272.

16. Ibid., "The Meaning of Munich" (1972), p. 134.

17. Ibid., Vol. III (1974, 1975, 1978), p. 299.

18. Ibid., Vol. II, "A Word of Gratitude" (1977), p. 374.

19. *Cargas in Conversation with Wiesel*, pp. 134 f.

20. *Against Silence*, Vol. III, "Christianity" (1981), p. 299.

21. *Cargas in Conversation with Wiesel*, p. 111.

22. Edelman, "A Conversation with Elie Wiesel," in Cargas, *Responses to Wiesel*, pp. 21 f.

23. Wiesel, *Dawn*, p. 86.

24. Wiesel, *The Jews of Silence*, p. 101.

25. Ibid., pp. 93–95.

26. *Against Silence*, Vol. III, "Soviet Jewry" (1970), p. 316.

27. Wiesel, *Zalmen*, p. 3.

28. Ibid., pp. 82 f., 92, 118, 169, 171.

29. *Against Silence*, Vol. II, "Forty Years After: Remembering Babi Yar" (1981), pp. 242 f.; Vol. I, "The School and Survival" (1983), p. 390.

30. Wiesel, *One Generation After*, pp. 130 f.

31. Ibid., pp. 135–37, 149–51, 153–55.

32. *Against Silence*, Vol. I, "Two Images, One Destiny" (1974), pp. 300 f.

33. Ibid., Vol. II, "Israel's Dilemmas" (1982), p. 214.

34. Ibid., "Voice of Hate" (1982), pp. 216 f.

35. Ibid., "The Massacre in Lebanon" (1982), p. 218.

36. Wiesel, *One Generation After*, p. 165.

37. Ibid., p. 173.

38. *Against Silence*, Vol. I, "Memory—And Building a Moral Society" (1978), p. 371; Vol. III, "For the Sake of History and Justice" (1979), p. 160.

39. Wiesel, *A Jew Today*, pp. 9, 11–13.

40. Ibid., p. 13.

41. Ibid., p. 175.

42. Ibid., p. 178.

43. Wiesel, *The Testament*, p. 20.

44. Ibid., p. 68.

45. Ibid., pp. 97, 224, 237.

46. Brown, *Elie Wiesel*, pp. 195 f.

17. MESSIANISM: BIBLICAL, KABBALISTIC, AND HASIDIC

1. Wiesel, *Messengers of God*, pp. 10, 13, 31 f.

2. Elie Wiesel, "A Tale of Defiance," Transcript, *The Eternal Light*, Chapter 1192, March 9, 1975, quoted by Irving Abrahamson in introduction to *Against Silence*, Vol. I, p. 50.

3. Wiesel, *Messengers of God*, pp. 59, 125, 132.

4. Wiesel, *Five Biblical Portraits*, pp. 109, 121, 148.

5. Wiesel, *Dawn*, p. 67.

6. Wiesel, *The Gates of the Forest*, pp. 18, 30 f.

7. Wiesel, *The Town Beyond the Wall*, p. 41.

8. Wiesel, *A Beggar in Jerusalem*, p. 68.

9. Wiesel, *Souls on Fire*, p. 5.

10. Ibid., pp. 6, 19 f., 31, 33, 35 f.

11. Ibid., p. 189.

12. Ibid., pp. 208, 257.

13. Wiesel, *Four Hasidic Masters*, p. 3.

14. Ibid., pp. 16, 59.

15. Ibid., p. 58.

16. Ibid., pp. 122–24.

17. Wiesel, *Somewhere a Master*, pp. 94, 105, 108, 113, 128, 147 f., 151, 167, 191; *Against Silence*, Vol. II, "The Relevance of Hasidism Today" (1977), p. 262.

18. *Against Silence*, Vol. II, "Hasidism and Man's Love of Man" (1972), pp. 252 f., 256; Vol. III, "Judaism" (1979), p. 305.

19. Berenbaum, *The Vision of the Void*, p. 57; *Against Silence*, Vol. I, "Paltiel Kossover's Search" (1981), p. 122.

18. THE MESSIANISM OF THE UNREDEEMED

1. Wiesel, *Dawn*, pp. 55, 76.

2. Wiesel, *The Accident*, pp. 41, 117 f.

3. Wiesel, *The Town Beyond the Wall*, pp. 9 f., 43, 115, 118, 124 f., 172–79.

4. Wiesel, *The Gates of the Forest.*, pp. 32 f.

5. Ibid., pp. 44–47.

6. Ibid., p. 121.

7. Ibid., pp. 134, 166.

8. Ibid., pp. 178 f.

9. Ibid., pp. 194, 196, 225.

10. *Against Silence*, Vol. I, "Toward a Philosophy of Jewish Existence" (1968), p. 255; Vol. III, "Judaism" (1969), p. 301.

11. Wiesel, *A Beggar in Jerusalem*, p. 138.

12. Ibid., pp. 206–8.

13. Ibid., p. 210.

14. Wiesel, *One Generation After*, pp. 72, 70.

15. *Against Silence*, Vol. II, "The Storyteller's Prayer" (1970), p. 59; "To a Young Rebel" (1971), p.147; Vol. III, "Autobiographical" (1971), p. 275.

16. Wiesel, *Souls on Fire*, p. 166.

17. Ibid., pp. 168, 258.

18. *Against Silence*, Vol. II, "Hasidism and Man's Love of Man" (1972), p. 254; Vol. III, "The Holocaust" (1977), p. 313.

19. Wiesel, *The Oath*, pp. 7, 12, 14.

20. Ibid., pp. 68–70.

21. Ibid., pp. 73, 78, 80, 82, 93 f.

22. Ibid., pp. 123 f.

23. Ibid., p. 138.

24. Ibid., pp. 143 f.

25. Ibid., pp. 273, 279, 281.

26. Wiesel, *Ani Ma'amin*, pp. 13, 15.

27. Ibid., pp. 29, 69, 71, 95, 103, 105.

28. *Against Silence*, Vol. I, " 'And Thou Shalt Teach Your Children' " (1973), p. 289; Vol. III, "A Small Measure of Victory" (1973), p. 220; Vol. I, "Two Images, One Destiny" (1974), p. 303; Vol. III, "Question and Quest" (1974), p. 94; Vol. I, "There Must Be a Difference" (1975), p. 139.

29. Wiesel, *Zalmen*, p. 53; Wiesel, *Messengers of God*, p. 235.

30. Wiesel, *A Jew Today*, p. 106.

31. *Against Silence*, Vol. III, "Youth and His Students" (1976), p. 293; "Judaism" (1976, 1977), p. 303; Vol. I, "A Jew Today" (1978), p. 164; "Memory—And Building a Moral Society" (1978), p. 372.

32. Ibid., Vol. III, "The New Law" (1978), p. 47; "Questions and Answers: At Brandeis-Bardin, 1978," p. 251; "The Creative Act: Subject" (1980), p. 288; Vol. I, "Farewell Address at the Western Wall"

(World Gathering of Jewish Holocaust Survivors) (1981), p. 281; Vol. III, "Beyond the End of History—And After" (1981), pp. 267 f.

33. Wiesel, *The Testament*, pp. 72, 293.

34. Ibid., p. 316.

35. Fine, *Legacy of Night*, p. 26.

36. Ibid., pp. 144, 29.

37. Elie Wiesel, *Le Cinquième Fils* (Paris: Bernard Grasset, 1983), pp. 51, 58 f., 197. My translation. See Elie Wiesel, *The Fifth Son*, trans. by Marion Wiesel (New York: Summit Books, 1985).

38. Ibid., p. 203. My translation.

39. Ibid., p. 233. My translation.

40. Ibid., p. 224. My translation.

41. Ibid., p. 230. My translation.

42. Elie Wiesel in "Jewish Values in the Post-Holocaust Future: A Symposium," *Judaism*, Vol. XVI (1967), p. 299.

43. Berenbaum, *The Vision of the Void*, p. 148.

44. Brown, *Elie Wiesel*, p. 206.

45. Wiesel, *A Jew Today*, p. 167.

46. *Against Silence*, Vol. III, "*A Jew Today* and Its Author" (1978), p. 107; "The Victims of Injustice Must Be Cared For" (1979), p. 144; "Plea for the Boat People" (*Congressional Record–Senate*, June 27, 1979), p. 158; "For the Sake of History and Justice" (1979), p. 159.

47. Brown, *Elie Wiesel*, pp. 138, 129 f.

48. Wiesel, *Paroles d'étranger*, p. 30. My translation.

49. Ibid., p. 36. My translation.

50. *Against Silence*, Vol. I, "Yesterday's Victims Forgotten, Struggle Is on for Today's" (*Los Angeles Times*, September 19, 1980), p. 191; Vol. III, "Meeting Again" (1981), p. 181.

51. Ibid., Vol. I, "The Jewish Condition" (1982), p. 225; Vol. III, "Protest Against Iran" (1983), p. 191.

52. Ibid., Vol. III, "To Our Children" (1984), pp. 322–24.

53. Wiesel, *Paroles d'étranger*, pp. 60, 66, 72–74. My translation.

54. Ibid., p. 104. My translation.

55. Ibid., pp. 106 f. My translation.

56. Ibid., p. 148. My translation.

57. Ibid., pp. 144, 146, 151–53, my translation.

58. *The New York Times*, October 15, 1986, Vol. CXXXVI, No. 46, 928, pp. 1, 4.

59. Ibid.

CONCLUSION: "YOU ARE MY WITNESSES"

1. Arthur A. Cohen, *The Natural and the Supernatural Jew: An Historical and Theological Introduction* (New York: Pantheon Books, 1962). For a full-scale discussion of this book, which also deals with Hermann Cohen, Martin Buber, Leo Baeck, and Mordecai Kaplan, see Maurice Friedman, "The Natural and the Supernatural Jew," *Conservative Judaism*, Vol. XVIII, No. 3 (Spring 1964), pp. 48–54.

2. Eugene B. Borowitz, *A New Jewish Theology in the Making* (Philadelphia: The Westminster Press, 1968), p. 156.

3. Ibid., pp. 157 f.

4. Ibid., p. 158.

5. Maurice Friedman, *To Deny Our Nothingness: Contemporary Images of Man*, 3rd rev. ed. with appendix added (Chicago: University of Chicago Press, Phoenix Books, 1978), p. 83.

6. John C. Merkle, *The Genesis of Faith: The Depth Theology of Abraham Joshua Heschel* (New York: Macmillan, 1985).

7. Ibid., p. 267, n. 132.

8. Steven D. Kepnes, "A Narrative Jewish Theology," an unpublished paper presented in the "Modern Jewish Thought" section of the American Academy of Religion annual conference, December 21, 1983. For a copy, write Prof. Steven Kepnes, Department of Religion, Southern Methodist University, Dallas, TX 75275.

9. Berenbaum, *The Vision of the Void*, p. 11, n. 7.

10. Ibid., pp. 15 f., 79.

11. Ibid., pp. 127–29, 134 f., 148.

12. *Against Silence*, Vol. III, "God" (1977), p. 310.

13. Neher, "*Shaddai*," p. 155.

14. Ibid., pp. 156–58.

15. Sometime in the 1950s Heschel showed me a book on prophecy by a prominent English biblical scholar two-thirds of which was a direct plagiarism from Heschel's doctoral dissertation *Die Prophetie*. When the scholar begged Heschel to spare him exposure for the sake of his family,

Heschel, with his customary generosity, agreed to do so on the condition that the scholar translate *Die Prophetie* (which he did—in a translation so poor as to be of no value to Heschel). When I told Professor Arnold Bergstraesser (the chair of my dissertation committee at the University of Chicago) about this, Bergstraesser commented, "Since the book was published in Poland, he assumed that Heschel had been exterminated in the Holocaust."

16. Abraham Joshua Heschel, "No Religion Is an Island," *Union Seminary Quarterly Review*, Vol. XXI, No. 2, Part I (January 1966), p. 117.

17. From an interview with Heschel in 1963 by the Yiddish journalist Gershon Jacobson, on Heschel's recollections as a newcomer to America, *Day-Morning Journal* (June 13, 1963), quoted by Samuel Dresner in Heschel, *The Circle of the Baal Shem Tov*, p. xxv, n. 30.

18. Heschel, *Man's Quest for God*, pp. 147–51.

19. I fear that many of my professorial colleagues all over the world are in like case. If they have delivered their lectures to their satisfaction, they feel that now it is up to the students to show they have learned it. Everything is from the professor's point of view and the poor student has to guess as best she or he can what the professor means. That is exactly how it was in my courses as an undergraduate at Harvard College under some of the greatest professors of the time.

20. Buber, *Tales of the Hasidim*, "Hide-and-Seek," p. 97.